History of Computing:
Software Issues

T0242472

Springer
Berlin
Heidelberg
New York
Barcelona
Hong Kong
London
Milan
Paris
Tokyo

Ulf Hashagen
Reinhard Keil-Slawik
Arthur L. Norberg (Eds.)

History of Computing:
Software Issues

International Conference on the History of Computing,
ICHC 2000
April 5-7, 2000
Heinz Nixdorf MuseumsForum
Paderborn, Germany

Springer

Editors

Ulf Hashagen
Münchner Zentrum für Wissenschafts- und Technikgeschichte
Deutsches Museum
80306 München, Germany
u.hashagen@deutsches-museum.de

Reinhard Keil-Slawik
Heinz Nixdorf Institut
Universität Paderborn
Fürstenallee 11
33102 Paderborn, Germany
rks@upb.de

Arthur L. Norberg
Charles Babbage Institute
University of Minnesota
Department of Computer Science
200 Union Street, SE
Minneapolis, MN 55455, USA
norberg@cs.umn.edu

Library of Congress Cataloging-in-Publication applied for.

Die Deutsche Bibliothek - CIP-Einheitsaufnahme

History of computing: software issues / International Conference on the History of Computing (ICHC 2000),
April 5-7, 2000, Heinz-Nixdorf-MuseumsForum, Paderborn, Germany. Ulf Hashagen (ed.). -
Berlin; Heidelberg; New York; Barcelona; Hongkong; London; Mailand; Paris; Tokio: Springer, 2002

ISBN 978-3-642-07653-4 Springer-Verlag Berlin Heidelberg New York

Springer-Verlag is a member of BertelsmannSpringer Science+Business Media GmbH
http://www.springer.de
© Springer-Verlag Berlin Heidelberg 2010
Printed in Germany

Cover-Design: KünkelLopka Werbeagentur

Preface

The papers in this volume were presented at a conference that was designed to map out historical study needs in one area of the history of computing, namely, software. The Paderborn conference was sponsored by the Heinz Nixdorf MuseumsForum and co-sponsored by the Charles Babbage Institute and the Heinz Nixdorf Institute of the University of Paderborn. The idea for the conference emerged from the consideration of a larger concept that was to prepare a new handbook on the history of computing. Believing that preparation of the handbook would encounter obstacles in some areas of computing that have not received adequate attention from historians, the originators of the idea of the handbook decided on a series of mapping conferences to try to overcome the obstacles, of which the Paderborn conference is the first. The organizers of the conference invited a group of historians, sociologists, and computer scientists to present papers and comments about a selected set of issues in the history of software. The organizing committee consisted of William Aspray (Computing Research Association, Washington, D.C.), Martin Campbell-Kelly (University of Warwick, U.K.), Ulf Hashagen (Heinz Nixdorf MuseumsForum, Paderborn), Reinhard Keil-Slawik (Heinz Nixdorf Institute, University of Paderborn), Michael S. Mahoney (Princeton University) and Arthur L. Norberg (Charles Babbage Institute, University of Minnesota).

The ambitious overall objective of this conference was to review our present understanding of the history of software and to establish an agenda for further research. The program of the conference was an attempt to explore the topic of the history of software in a new way. We neither intended nor expected the product to be a finished history of any of the topics included in the conference, nor did we want a continuation of previous efforts to describe histories of individual software artifacts. The conference presenters were asked not to attempt to provide finished histories for any of the areas of software history. Instead, speakers and commentators were asked to comment on the fundamental elements that make software what it is, and offer an exploration of our current understanding of software and its history. The organizers decided to address two different perspectives in the conference: the perspective of the computer scientists and the perspective of the historians and sociologists interested in the larger context of a development. Hence, computer scientists, entrepreneurs, historians, and sociologists met to discuss the selected set of issues. Between speakers and commentators, we hoped to merge the two perspectives into one scheme for investigating the history of software.

We hope that the volume presented here is only the first step in a larger series of conferences and scholarly studies on the history of software. Many issues had to be left out, and the attempts to structure the field have to be regarded as immature. The dialogue started here, especially between historians and computer scientists, has to be continued. This dialogue will be by no means easy to conduct, because with software the object of historical study comes close to our personal life and experiences. It is, however, our dear hope that this dialogue will create for the reader as much of a challenging learning experience as it was for the historians and computer scientists attending this conference.

Acknowledgments

The way the book evolved also made great demands on everyone engaged in its production. We are especially indebted to Sandra Sewzyk (Heinz Nixdorf MuseumsForum), Andreas Brennecke (Heinz Nixdorf Institute, University of Paderborn) and Lars Klein (University of Paderborn), who coordinated the production of the book and eventually assumed responsibility for the layout of the text as a whole. Our gratitude also goes to Philip Bacon, who took care of correcting our non-native speakers' English. Finally, we would like to thank Ingeborg Mayer and Dr. Hans Wössner of Springer-Verlag. The extraordinary care and patience they all showed here have contributed to the overall quality of the book.

Ulf Hashagen
Reinhard Keil-Slawik
Arthur L. Norberg

Munich, Paderborn, and Minneapolis, January 2002

Table of Contents

Introduction

The stimulus for this conference came from a recognition that the historical software literature focuses too narrowly on a few technical developments and not enough on the wider range of issues in areas such as software development, application, processes, and people. In one perspective, the history of software is now about at the stage that hardware history was 15 years ago. Writers on computing history over the past two decades, both in and out of university settings, have focused primarily on hardware and firms. Entries about software topics seem to emulate articles on hardware, giving precedence to particular languages, or are set pieces about a particular application such as the United States Government's SAGE air defense project and the Bank of America's ERMA system, which stood for Electronic Recording Machine—Accounting, both projects of the 1950s. Within the expanding bibliography on the history of information processing, the history of software has the least number of entries. Virtually all the literature about the history of software presents reviews of the development of a particular software artifact. Articles on programming languages, operating systems, applications programming, and network protocols, to name only a few, make up the examples in this area, along with a group of essays on members of the software industry. While these articles and books are good and useful, we still have little appreciation for the overall history of software; certainly nothing similar to our history of hardware. While we focus on our way of interacting with one another through the Internet, people outside the field of computing as a profession often fail to appreciate the extent to which computers have become an integral part of our lives. Our ways of doing business have changed: we practice medicine in an entirely different, and more effective, manner, and many of us even play differently.

As a result, the scholarly literature about software history, good as it is for some topics, is inadequate for pursuing any complete analysis of the history of computing. In the view of the organizers, if we continue the trend of only preparing articles on separate topics in software history, such as another review of some operating system or a description of some ostensibly new application, we will only lengthen the time it will take to develop an overall picture of software's significance and history. We need to broaden our approach to the history of software, because the information processing activity marches on, relentlessly adding to our burden.

The group recognized that all matters of the history of software could not be addressed in a single conference, and focused on several new areas they thought scholars could address immediately. The ambitious overall objective of this conference was to review our present understanding of the history of software and to establish an agenda for further research. The program of the conference was designed to explore the topic of the history of software in a new way. We neither intended nor expected the product to be a finished history of any of the topics included in the conference, nor did we want a continuation of previous efforts to describe histories of individual software artifacts. The conference presenters were asked not to attempt to provide finished histories for any of the areas of software history. Instead, speakers and commentators were asked to comment on the fundamental elements that make software what it is, and offer an exploration of our current understanding of software and its history. The organizers decided to address two different perspectives in the conference: the perspective of the computer scientists and the perspective of the historians and sociologists interested in the larger context of a development. Hence, computer scientists, entrepreneurs, historians, and sociologists met to discuss the selected set of issues. Between speakers and commentators, we hoped to merge the two perspectives into one scheme for investigating the history of software. Speakers had the freedom to explore their assigned topics in whatever way they thought best. If this conference was successful in laying out a research agenda, then subsequent conferences and research projects could explore other software issues on a firm base of scholarship. The topics selected were:

- Software as Science,
- Software as Engineering,
- Software as Dependable Artifact,
- Software as Labor Process,
- Software as Economic Activity.

They were selected in order to provide the opportunity to define and refine a research agenda for each topic, and in other areas in software if the topics arose in discussion. In this sense, then, the conference is an opening gambit in achieving an overall history of software.

Presenters all received guidelines as to how to prepare their talks, in order to encourage similar treatments with the possibility to glean cross-cutting themes across issues. Presenters were asked to do three things, taking the opportunity to set the agenda for research in their area.

1. Map out the subject matter in the particular software domain, i.e., in one of the five topical areas. This mapping is to highlight only the significant issues needing historical treatment, but owing to the time allowed not to provide specific treatment.
2. Define the critical issues, directions, and research questions in the domain. Any presentation of the history of software should be incidental to your talk, used primarily for illustrative purposes.
3. Discuss the state of historical knowledge and/or research of other kinds useful in the domain by citing the relevant secondary literature and significant primary publications, as much as is within the knowledge of the presenter. For

those presenters with historical training, it would be helpful to connect your topic to histories of other subjects—such as the history of other technologies, the history of science, labor history, business and economic history, and cultural history. The goal here is to have future scholarship in the history of software informed by these other historical fields, so that contributions made in the history of software will be seen as contributions to them.

The impression one gets from reading the history of software literature is that many of our colleagues who write about software history tend to think of software products, that is, any program, as a technical development, with antecedents to be sure, but as basically an independent artifact. There are precedents for this type of history writing. This approach to history is common for nearly all scientists and engineers who write about historical episodes in their disciplines, and for politicians, too, I might add. At one level, examination of these artifacts gives us a great amount of information about the nature of software, but commentators from inside the field do not usually seek relationships among these artifacts—relationships that offer insights into the meaning of and behind an artifact.

To explain this further, we draw the reader's attention to a recent issue of the IEEE journal *Computing in Science and Engineering* devoted to descriptions of some important developments in computer science, namely algorithms. Ten algorithms are described in ten articles by different authors. The descriptions are very informative from a technical perspective, and occasionally an author will offer some information about historical lineage of the algorithm. This usually amounts to comments about the interest in the problems of earlier mathematicians, who offered help by providing solutions in ways similar to this algorithm. Needless to say, some authors in this issue on algorithms indicate applications for the algorithms without discussion, but there is little or no discussion about several aspects important to our understanding of the algorithms as software products. For example, the editors for this issue, Jack Dongarra and Francis Sullivan, illustrious computer scientists, "tried to assemble the 10 algorithms with the greatest influence on the development and practice of science and engineering in the 20th century."[1] Acknowledging that with whatever list they assembled there would be controversy, they still offer no reason why these ten made it into the issue. Maybe the choice is intuitive to computer scientists, but it is not to historians and others. This topic requires further analysis, but this issue of *Computing in Science and Engineering* is a grand beginning.

With a few exceptions, historians and writers interested in the history of software have also prepared tightly focused essays on a single development without trying to see the place of the development in the larger context of software's history.

The organizers of this conference decided to address two different perspectives in the conference: the perspective of the computer scientists illustrated by the example from Dongarra and Sullivan and the perspective of the historians and sociologists interested in the larger context of a development. Hence, we brought together computer scientists, entrepreneurs, historians, and sociologists. Between

---

[1] Jack Dongarra and Francis Sullivan, "Guest Editors' Introduction," *Computing in Science and Engineering* (January/February 2000): 22.

speakers and commentators, we hoped to merge the two perspectives into one scheme for investigating the history of software. Let us be even more specific about these two perspectives.

First, we have the perspective of the "insider," the participants in the development of computer science, such as the authors involved with this list of algorithms. We do not mean to belittle the exercise of identifying important developments such as those in the field of computer science. The computer scientist certainly appreciates these events as important to the development of his or her professional affiliation and historians should too. Computer scientists see these artifacts as one measure of their legacy. Historians need this type of analysis as well, because by it we are led to what the computer scientist believes are important developments for the field. However, historians need to be cautious in taking these analyses as defining the field for historians. The historical efforts of computer scientists are by and large concerned with intellectual developments internal to their field, with some concern for the consequences, for example, how many Internet users are there at some instant, what is the trend in overall Internet use, or what does C++ allow the user to accomplish that Fortran will not, and how has this changed (the computer scientist would say "advanced") the field of computing? These are important starting points for preparing a history of software.

Second, there is the view of the historian and of the sociologist, a complementary perspective. Historians and sociologists view technology often as a heavily intertwined fabric of people, technology, and institutions, and the principal task is to unravel the fabric to appreciate the contributions of each person and setting. It is important to understand the context of any development, in order to avoid the one-dimensionality characteristic of an intellectual technical approach.

Like the computer scientist, the historian, too, is interested in technological change, but in a different way. An example from the history of technology literature will illustrate this point for software. Starting with knowledge of significant artifacts, say the machine tools developed over the course of the 19th century, the historian traces the invention of and innovations in these tools, their use, the innovation in the process of production through the use of the new tools, and the responses of and changes in the institutions involved in this technological change. From this type of analysis, we obtain a deeper and richer understanding not just of the artifact, but also of its application and its effects on institutions and organizations. The historian does not prejudge any situation by focusing on firsts and only successes. The historian does not see change in the field as inevitable, in the way that many practitioners see their fields, and as portrayed in some of the historical writing by scientists and engineers.

We read in computer science texts about different philosophies behind, for example, operating systems. If we wanted to construct a history of operating systems along the lines of the historian's history of machine tools, we would need to examine many similar issues to the machine tool example. For example, what influenced these different philosophies? Is it architecture alone, or structure of programs? If either or both, what institutional, professional, economic, educational, and personal factors influence choices in each different system?[2]

---

[2] For this description of issues we have relied heavily on Michael S. Mahoney, "The History of Computing in the History of Technology," *Annals of the History of Computing*, 10 (1988):

Having pointed to the products of computer science and historical study needs, we can turn to practice. For the historian and sociologist, computer science and engineering is a discipline like any other, and, as such, might operate in similar ways. At the same time, the historian recognizes that differences exist or computer science and engineering would not be a separate discipline. The historian seeks for three categories of information and relationships among the categories. First, what is the nature of the discipline's content, that is, what are the nature of hardware and software and the uses of the artifacts in them? In this area there are many similarities to the perspective of the computer scientist interested in the history of the field. Second, the historian is interested in the borrowing from and the giving to other areas of technological endeavor. How is software science, and how does its practice employ established scientific principles, generate new ones, and offer the new ones to other disciplines? What is the nature of engineering practice in computer science and engineering, and how is this practice similar to and different from the practice in other engineering disciplines? We even have a phrase in computer science to capture this idea: "Software Engineering". The word "engineering" in software engineering is meant to convey the engineering aspects of software development, wherein "engineering principles and discipline are used to produce, in a timely and cost-effective manner, a workable product to solve a problem,"[3] as a recent computer science text published in the United States notes. We have one very cogent article on the use of the factory model to produce software, and a few on the similarities between the practices of software engineering and those of other engineering fields. We need more analysis of these two areas of science and engineering. Speakers addressed both of these themes in this conference.

As computer systems became more sophisticated making the systems more capable because of faster speeds and larger memories, programming emerged as a major activity of the computing enterprise. We know of the struggle to program the SAGE system in the 1950s, and the frustration of not being able to find enough programmers to do the work. People with a minimum of mathematical knowledge were added to the work force. Since then, there have been repeated warnings of a programmer shortage. Have there been other instances of programmer shortages? Can we identify the causes of such shortages? What new steps are taken to remove the shortages? Since this probably is accomplished by accepting people with less training, what effect does the acceptance of people without requisite training have on programming, on the nature of software? What new ways of doing things came into being, and how did these new ways shape programming as a profession? Underlying questions such as these are questions concerning the development and growth of programming, and of software as a product culture. There is also a series of labor questions involved in any series of technological developments. For some time, programming was viewed as a craft rather than a profession. What

113–25 and William Aspray, "Advantages and Problems of Bringing Together the Historical and Engineering Communities to Study Software Engineering History," in *The History of Software Engineering*, Dagstuhl Seminar Report 153, eds. William Aspray et al. (Dagstuhl, 1997).

[3] G. Michael Schneider and Judith L. Gersting, *An Invitation to Computer Science*, 2nd edition, (Pacific Grove, Calif., 1999), 371.

steps were taken in the discipline, both technical steps and the adoption of standards, which helped to raise the status of programmers? Concerns such as these lead to larger questions of discipline formation and professionalization.

The conference consisted of six sessions that focused on software as an entity, not on software examples as has been the case in the past, and those six sessions are reproduced in the six sections of the proceedings below. Each section begins with the principal paper of a session as given at the conference. This style is maintained in order to preserve the integrity of the comments made on the paper. Presenters were offered the opportunity to add an addendum to their paper as a form of rebuttal to the comments. The end of the volume contains an essay by Michael Mahoney, written after the conference, offering an analysis of the common themes across all the sessions.

The past emphasis on the history of software artifacts has obscured the scientific nature of software. In Part 1 of the text, the focus is on Software as Science. Michael Mahoney's paper elaborates the epistemological foundations of aspects of theoretical computer science to highlight this aspect of software. One of Mahoney's themes concentrates on "agendas." He offers as two example descriptions of the early "agendas" of computer science and of semantics. In computer science, he focused on the perspectives of electrical engineers, mathematical logicians, and neurophysiologists, noting the principal actors in these areas. For the "agendas" of semantics, he focuses on programming languages, mathematical logic, and artificial intelligence. In a tightly organized presentation to show the effects of the "agendas," he relates the "agendas" to activities in research and training and in mathematics and software engineering.

Software as engineering is a natural counterpoint to software as science, especially as it is in this topic that we can investigate software as a practical development. In designing programs, computer scientists operate within various constraints—economic, technical, regulatory, managerial, social. The design process is often more one of revising and maintaining programs, rather than simply creating new programs. James E. Tomayko of Carnegie-Mellon University took a different tack and discusses mainly the specific functional area in computer science known as software engineering. He begins with a consideration of the history of the art of engineering to prepare for his main argument about the art of software engineering and software as applied science. Given the lack of historical work in this area, he speculates on which thematic contexts, if explored, might yield a better understanding of the history of software. He offers examples such as development of visualization, individual design methods inspired by stepwise refinement and functional decomposition, and the concepts surrounding objects. He ends with a call for the collection of more primary documents to facilitate this work.

In the treatment of software as a dependable artifact, we need to pay special attention to the specific nature of software, and to the interplay of formal methods and cooperative processes, verification, testing, validation, and standards. In many parts of the software enterprise, reliability is a high priority, for example, in areas of safety-critical systems such as in medical systems and aircraft control systems. In other areas, such as in typical off-the-shelf packaged software, reliability is not a high priority. Practitioners in each of these domains seem to employ different tools and approach problems differently. An exploration of these differences could uncover the idiosyncrasies in software and its development and reveal the consequences of these differences. Donald MacKenzie, of the University of Edinburgh, using the concept of dependability sketches the historiography of this area, especially of safety of software systems. He traces the history of Hoare's paradox concerning the dangers inherent in software. This leads him into a discussion of the sociology of dependability, moral entrepreneurship, and the sociology of knowledge. He identifies some 34 instances of cases of possible computer-related accidental death due to various failures in computer systems.

In a wide-ranging analysis of labor and labor processes in software programs, Nathan Ensmenger, University of Pennsylvania, and William Aspray discuss the perception of an acute shortage of programmers over the decades since 1950, the changing professional status of programmers, the routinization of labor as managers tried to gain more control over the process, the management of programmers, and women in software. The structure of the presentation involves the identification of issues in software and labor, discussion of the historiography of the topic, and subjects needing further examination. Training and education of high-quality programmers reveals much about the nature of software. A view of programmers and their role in the computing enterprise can be obtained from analysis of professionalization and certification criteria. Recently, much attention has been paid to development of software in specific organizations. What are the common elements that are fundamental to software itself, and not subject to organizational idiosyncrasy? How are programmers managed in order to produce certain products? In other areas of the history of technology, an argument rages as to whether a gender bias is built into technology or is a by-product. A similar discussion is going on in computing. Is there a gender bias in software development? Do particular organizations influence software developments in certain directions, and how are these played out generally? Ensmenger and Aspray address all of these issues to some extent, paying special attention to the history literature in each area.

Martin Campbell-Kelly of the University of Warwick focuses on an examination of the size, location, and practices of software producers, as a way of gaining some insight into the economic activity surrounding software. Producers have included computer users and computer manufacturers, but software firms have increasingly taken center stage. Campbell-Kelly notes that we are getting a clearer picture of what the software industry is through a number of studies by historians and economists, but we still need a better appreciation of what role R&D played in software firms. In addition, he comments that we have no comprehensive picture of why the United States tends to dominate the software market. Moreover, we have yet to grasp the underlying principles behind software development. He briefly explores the evolution of the different sectors within the software industry, including programming services and packaged software firms. He relates the structure and strategies of firms to the ever changing technological and market environment as well as the broader economic and business context.

The organizers of the conference took the occasion to pay particular attention to the problem of exhibiting software in a session entitled "Software in Museum Exhibits". To aid discussion, Doron Swade (Science Museum, London), David Allison (Smithsonian Institution), Friedrich L. Bauer (consultant to the Deutsches Museum), and Ernst Denert (CEO of sd&m), and Klaus-Peter Löhr (Free University of Berlin), presented examples of how each of their museums approach the problem or what each is encountering in preparing a software exhibit. Some useful information emerged from the presentations for use in museum collecting and exhibiting of software.

There are many topics we could have chosen to emphasize in this conference and this volume. For example, we decided to address reliability specifically. An argument could have been made that we should have enlarged the topic to include a session on human factors, wherein we could have invited speakers to address such areas as the human-computer interface, interactive systems, software psychology, project and team organization, and reliability. We did not add these topics, not because we think these topics are less important, rather we chose the topics we did because of our emphasis on some basic issues concerning the nature of software. The basic issues on our minds were:

1. Isolation of epistemological connections between software and larger contexts of the development of science and technology as seen through the eyes of historians and sociologists.
2. Identification of fundamental starting points to address the history of software in the future.
3. Introduction of the approaches of historians to the study of software rather than the approaches of the computer scientist.
4. Development of a research agenda that the community can begin to engage in without the necessity for repeated questioning about where we begin with this history of software.

It is the hope of the organizing committee that what we learned from the areas we chose to emphasize will help us tremendously in exploring these other topics.

The results of the conference sessions are mixed, illustrative of the different available historical study in each area. They do provide some new questions needing exploration, but they do not offer a clear future research agenda. Rapporteurs' reports give a flavor of the discussion at the end of each session. Time limited the depth of discussion.

There is at least one larger reason for wanting to know more about the history of software. Among the general users of computer systems, people who are not technically trained, a remarkable ignorance exists about the nature and history of software. Recognition of the trends in software development and use should convince people that better knowledge of the nature of software would help them to understand the role of software in their lives, not simply its existence. Ray Kurzweil asserted in his new book *The Age of the Spiritual Machine: When Computers Exceed Human Intelligence* that "We will be software ..." and can inhabit any hardware we like. This reduces to a statement about the identity of artificial (i.e., robots) and human intelligence in the not too distant future. Such a merger requires us to know more about the nature of and implications for use of software. In future, we should not be just teaching people how to use software programs, but also educating them about the nature and implications of software. A new approach to the education of the general user about software will rely heavily on knowledge of the history of software, and we hope to influence this knowledge through the presentation of the results of this conference in this volume, which we hope will encourage more historical research and writing along the lines presented.

Prologue
A Computer Pioneer's Talk

A Computer Pioneer's Talk: Pioneering Work in Software During the 50s in Central Europe

Friedrich L. Bauer

Technische Universität München
Institut für Informatik
Arcisstraße 21
80209 München
Germany

Introduction

In the late 40s and early 50s, there were a few groups in the USA, in England, in Continental Europe and other countries that started to construct computers. To be precise they constructed the computer hardware. The computing machine in the modern sense had to replace desk calculators which were slow, had limited capabilities and lacked automatic performance of complex tasks.

In 1936, Alan Turing described the functioning of a computer in a theoretical way with the aim to create a sound basis for a definition of the concept of *computable numbers*. Turing's computer of 1936 would have been terribly slow if it had been constructed. However, Turing did not construct it at that time. Then Konrad Zuse, John Presper Eckert and John W. Mauchly and a few others constructed computer hardware with relays or even with vacuum tubes and they had to master immense difficulties of engineering nature. Their products were often clumsy since the main problem of the hardware designers was to make their machines function in the first place. Furthermore, they had to make compromises with respect to available technologies. Zuse's first outlines around 1934 (*"Vom Formular zur Programmsteuerung"*) showed for example a machine that used non-erasable storage and thus was much closer to functional programming than his later designs. However, he had to give up this approach and came to the solution of using erasable storage with appropriate writing and reading mechanisms.

Forerunners of Software

Long before the word *software* came into general use, it was necessary to describe longer, complicated sequences of calculation. For this purpose, it was customary to support the write-up of intermediate results on paper by means of forms indicating the course of calculation. For example, the well-known *Horner scheme* published[1] as early as 1819, was used by Rudolf Zurmühl[2] in 1962 for a polynomial of degree 4: $p(x) = a_4x^4 + a_3x^3 + a_2x^2 + a_1x + a_0$ in the following way:

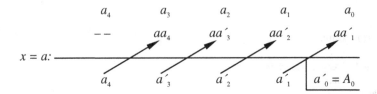

Its course of calculation can be described by a printed blank (Fig. 1a) with obvious meaning. In 1935, a blank of this kind used in calculating the superposition of two rectangular moment areas led Zuse to his first ideas of a formula-controlled computer. At the recommendation of Alwin Walther in Darmstadt, Paul Terebesi, in 1930, published[3] sets of 12 and 24 stencils for the calculation of Fourier coefficients as given by Carl Runge (Fig. 1b). In a certain sense, these blanks and stencils could be regarded as early forms of guidelines for *soft support* of a human calculator. In those days this sort of software was called derogatorily 'Anweisung an den menschlichen Geist' by the patent office and was not considered patentable.

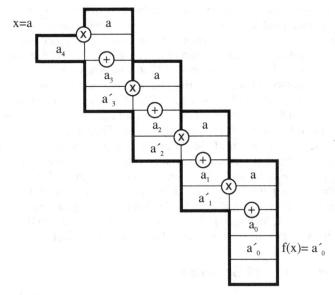

Fig. 1a. Horner course of calculation

[1] William G. Horner, "A New Method of Solving Numerical Equations of All Orders by Continuous Approximation," *Philosophical Transactions of the Royal Society* 109 (1819): 308-35.
[2] Rudolf Zurmühl, *Praktische Mathematik für Ingenieure und Physiker*, 4th ed. (Berlin, 1963), 36.
[3] Paul Terebesi, *Rechenschablonen für harmonische Analyse und Synthese* (Berlin, 1930).

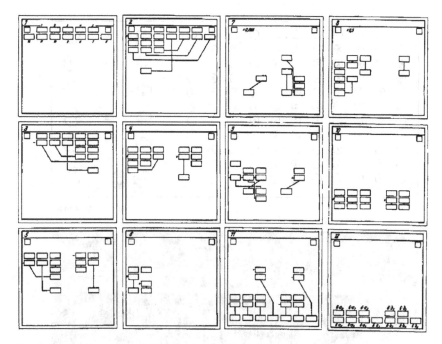

Fig. 1b. Terebesi stencils for calculation of Fourier coefficients

But *software*, as it developed in the late 40s and early 50s after the emergence of program-called machines offered even more possibilities.

How did a few people come to construct software? Roughly speaking, it was an attempt *to compensate for the inadequacies of the hardware* by using programmed features—in many cases features that hardware designers had forgotten or had not even thought to provide for. *Software necessarily became language-based.*

Heinz Zemanek has put it this way: "Software started with the translation of algebraic formulas into machine code." Thus, the *Plankalkül* of Konrad Zuse in 1945, the *Formelübersetzung* of Heinz Rutishauser and of Corrado Böhm in 1951, the *Algebraic interpreter* of Alick E. Glennie in 1953, the *Programming Program* of E. Z. Ljubimskii and Sergej Sergeevich Kamynin in 1954 and of Andrei Ershov in 1955 stood at the beginning of *software*, soon followed by Remington-Rand's Math-Matic (1955) and IBM's Fortran (1956). All these advances were made before the word '*software*' came into wider use in 1960, 1961 or 1962.

Now I will describe how we started to construct software in Munich and Zurich in the 50s, we being Klaus Samelson (1918-1980), Heinz Schecher (1922-1984) and myself in Munich and Heinz Rutishauser (1919-1970) in Zurich.

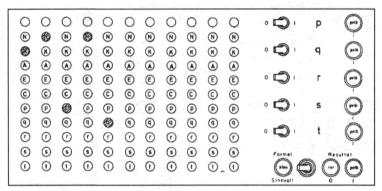

Prüfung – Auswertung

Fig. 2. STANISLAUS front view

Early Work in Munich and Zurich

In Munich, we were part of a group, under the supervision of the engineer Hans Piloty and the mathematician Robert Sauer, that constructed a computer. Our specific task was, to see to it that the computer under construction could perform the calculations it was intended for. Our group started in 1952, well-informed about the von Neumann report. Our first challenge was the EDSAC book of

Wilkes-Wheeler-Gill, published in 1951.[*] We learned from this book that we had to develop tools to make the programming job easier and more reliable. Only as a first step we decided to consider the subroutine technique advocated by Maurice V. Wilkes. We also were aware of Rutishauser's publication '*Über automatische Rechenplanfertigung bei programmgesteuerten Rechenanlagen*' in ZAMM 1951, where the idea to use the computer in order to write its own program was exemplified. For this reason first personal contact to Rutishauser was established in November 1952. Apart from our daily work of fabricating subroutines for Sauer and checking the engineers' design, we started modestly to think about such simple tools as a supervisory program, while Rutishauser wrote a program for his relay computer Z4 performing the automatic generation for his relay of a linear sequence of machine instructions from a loop.

In accordance with Rutishauser, we were convinced that 'automatic programming' was the direction we had to follow. Rutishauser knew that he could not use the Z4 for the realization of his 1951 ideas. Piloty's PERM in Munich was slightly ahead in time compared to Speiser's ERMETH in Zurich, so we aimed at constructing a practicable tool for 'automatic programming' as soon as our Munich machine was ready; in the meantime we followed closely the development in 'automatic programming' in the USA and in other countries, but we were not satisfied with the idea of constructing a 'compiler' that simply piled up prefabricated subroutines. Under the influence of Wilhelm Britzelmayr, our logic professor in Munich, we became more linguistically-oriented (when FORTRAN appeared in 1956, we were dissatisfied).

Nevertheless, we now knew that we had to look for a better solution. We had several ideas how to achieve this aim. The PERM machine was ready for tests in 1955 (it was completely usable in 1956), so we could actually proceed.

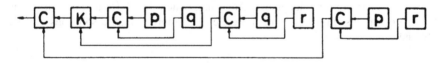

Fig. 3. Example of a mechanical evaluation of a propositional formula
[(p –> q) & (q –> r)] –> (p –> r).
C stands here for implication –>, K stands here for conjunction &

[*] Maurice V. Wilkes, David J. Wheeler, and Stanley Gill, *The Preparation of Programs for an Electronic Digital Computer. With Special Ref. to the EDSAC and the Use of a Library of Subroutines* (Cambridge, Mass., 1951).

Our decisive step was triggered by the occupation with STANISLAUS (Fig. 2), a relay calculator for the evaluation of propositional formulas in Polish notation; formulas had to be entered by keyboard. Following a proposal of Helmut Angstl, I designed it around New Year 1951. However, the actual completion was postponed several times, until I was put under pressure by Britzelmayr. Fig. 3 shows how it worked whereas Fig. 4 depicts the wiring diagram. In these diagrams, connections existed that might lead to lower and lower levels. They formed in fact a storage unit for intermediate results which we called 'Keller' (cellar). In fact, it was a hardware pushdown storage.

The Kellerprinzip

In 1955, when STANISLAUS was under construction, Samelson and I discussed how we would proceed with translating arithmetical formulas into machine code and suddenly we came to the conclusion that besides the 'Zahlkeller', that was used in Polish notation to postpone the intermediate results, we had to use an 'Operationskeller' in a similar way for postponing operations when dealing with parentheses or implicit precedence.

Soon, we found out that the functional principle we had discovered (we called it *Kellerprinzip*) "*postpone operations that you can not yet evaluate and evaluate them as soon as possible*" was not only suitable for the evaluation or translation of parenthesized formulas, but for any constructs that show a parenthesized, interlocked structure.[5]

Samelson in particular used the *Kellerprinzip* to make storage allocation efficient and when we designed step by step the programming language that we wanted to use for 'automatic programming,' we structured the language accordingly. It became known as Chomsky-2-language.

Rutishauser in particular showed how to use the *Kellerprinzip* in parameter transfer, bringing the spirit of the Lambda notation of formal logic into programming.

Our efforts finally led in 1958 to ALGOL and made ALGOL a well-structured, very safe programming language. As usual, when freed from the restrictions hardware implies, more elegant, more flexible, more versatile solutions can be obtained.

---

[5] The completely parenthesized structures we preferred also led (in a natural way) to the use of parallel evaluation. This was our introduction to concurrent programming and branched temporal logic. The *Kellerprinzip* showed how sequentialized programs could be derived.

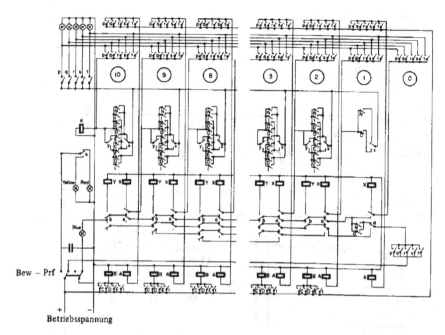

Fig. 4. Wiring diagram of STANISLAUS

Contacts:		Relays:	Switches
0	Empty	Relays for columns 0 to 10	Variable input (above)
N	negation	X, Y with contacts x, y	yellow lamps for 'true'
K	conjunction		dark lamps for 'false'
A	disjunction	Relays for connections:	
E	equivalence	A, B with contacts a, b	Result output (left):
C	implication		yellow lamps for 'true'
p	variable p		red lamps for 'false'
q	variable q		
r	variable r	Relays for checking	Switch Bew - Prf (below)
s	variable s.	Prf with contacts k	blue lamp for
t	variable t		'not wellformed'

A Hardware Patent

In 1956, we were instructed by the hardware engineer Hans Piloty to integrate our Kellerprinzip into the design of a PERM II computer, successor of PERM. Thus, we had to file a patent application, which showed the outline of a completely formula-controlled computer. Fig. 5 shows details of the control mechanism, the control matrix is found in Fig. 6. The machine could even work with numbers of variable length (Fig. 7), another natural side effect of the *Kellerprinzip*.

The German patent was filed in March 30, 1957, the U.S. Patent with a year. (The U.S. Patent was granted in July 1962.) Due to objections IBM raised, the German patent took much longer and was finally granted in 1971.

ZEICHNUNGEN BLATT I   AUSGABETAG: 1. DEZEMBER 1960   DAS 1094019

KL. 42 m 14

INTERNAT. KL. G 06 f

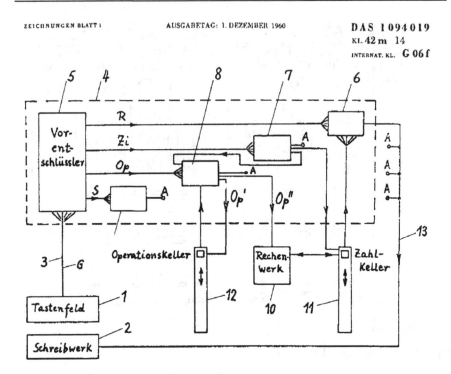

Fig. 5. A formula controlled computer (from German patent application, filed March 30, 1957)

Software Solution Replacing Machinery

Some time after we had started to prepare our patent application, Hans Piloty was informed by the National Research Council that they could not support his application for a grant to construct PERM II, since commercially constructed computers would be soon on the market. This was the moment when in 1957 Samelson, Schecher and myself definitely became software engineers: we knew how to *program* the device of the formula-controlled computer, described in the patent, for the PERM computer. Thus, in close cooperation with Rutishauser in Zurich, we followed his former idea to use the computer to program its own programs, and the program that did it (Rutishauser had called it 'Superplan,' elsewhere it was still called *compiler*) was our first software product. In fall 1957, our *formula translator* program ('Formelübersetzer') was outlined. In May 1958, ALGOL was at hand. By the end of 1958, after I had moved to Mainz, the software which had been constructed with the help of Manfred Paul in Mainz for the Zuse Z22, Gerhard Seegmüller in Munich for the PERM and Peter Läuchly in Zurich for the ERMETH, was working. After all this, we were glad that we did not have to follow up the troublesome construction of the PERM II and that we were free to develop software.

In fact, the software solution of our idea of a *formula-controlled computer* turned out to have more features than we could ever have expected from a hardware solution, and this at practically no extra costs. An additional function needed no more effort than to be programmed once since it could be copied so easily.

In the meantime, the word *software* had gained acceptance. In the first instance it was regarded as a funny analogon to *hardware* and had a derogatory touch. However, step by step things changed. More and more the use of computers surpassed the original realm of numerical computation. Program systems of all kinds originated in the late 50s.

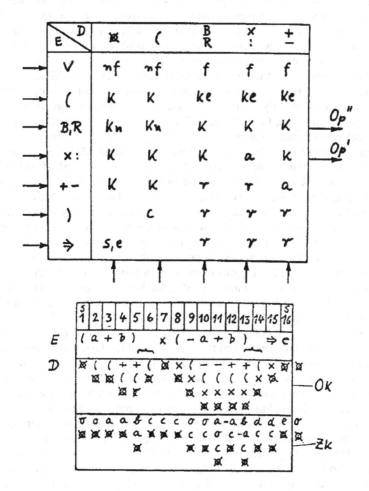

Fig. 6. The control matrix of the formula-controlled computer and an example of its operation (from the German patent application, filed on March 30, 1957)

Other Early Examples of Software

Early examples of software solutions which replaced in the 50s hardware machines emerged in logic, algebraic manipulation, chess-playing, and many other fields.

In 1951, R. Abbot reported on 'Computing Logical Truth with the California Digital Computer.' His program had 115 instructions and the length of the logical formula was in contrast to the STANISLAUS machine only restricted by the computing time. However, the *Kellerprinzip* was not applied; calculations were done, in analogy to Rutishauser's parsing method from inside to outside. In 1954, Robert S. Ledley used a map of the logical formula into a binary word which was further processed by computer. A related method was published in 1956 by A. I. Kitov.

Other examples of software solutions for problems which were too difficult to be solved by hardware machines occurred frequently. In 1956, Allan Newell and Herbert A. Simon wrote complex programs for proving theorems in propositional logic. In order to simplify operational work, they designed before 1959 a special programming language, GPS ('General Problem Solver'), the first definitely non-numerical programming language. John McCarthy developed in 1959 'A Programming System for Symbolic Manipulations,' called LISP ('List Processing Language'). A certain peak was reached by Hao Wang in 1960 ('Proving Theorems by Pattern Recognition'). Heuristic proofs for theorems in plane geometry were programmed by Herbert Gelernter and Nathaniel Rochester (1958).

Primitive games like Nim, the complete theory of which was already given by Charles Leonard Bouton in 1901, were favorable topics of recreation for computer scientists in the 50s. 'Making a Computer Play Draughts' (Arthur L. Samuel, 1956) represented the more serious approach, with Christopher Strachey (1952) as a forerunner. In 1958, P. Huggins even wrote a program for 'Bridge-Playing by computer.' Chess, of course, ranks top: after the Kempelen machine (1769), which was a hoax, it took a long time until Torres y Quevedo, in 1912, constructed a machine for the end game *King and Rook against King*. In 1952, D. G. Prinz ('Robot Chess') programmed the Manchester machine for end games. Progress of the full game was slow, since even the processing of the fastest available machines was not fast enough. In 1958, with an IBM 704 running at 42,000 operations per second, one move took 8 minutes; the program had 7,000 instructions and even lost against a good amateur chess player. Meanwhile, computer chess is an area of its own and even Grand Masters can lose against a computer program.

In this context very ambitious notions came up: 'Intelligence-Amplifier' (W. Ross Ashby, 1956), 'Learning Machine' (R. M. Friedberg, 1958, and A. M. Andrew, 1958), 'Self-Organizing System' (J. K. Hawkins, 1961), and finally 'Steps Towards Artificial Intelligence' (Marvin Minsky, 1961). However, in 1949, Berkeley had already spoken of 'Giant Brains—Machines that Think,' in 1950, Turing talked about 'Computing machinery and Intelligence,' John von Neumann (published in 1958) wrote a paper entitled 'The computer and the brain.' Such notions have frequently been misunderstood by non-professional people.

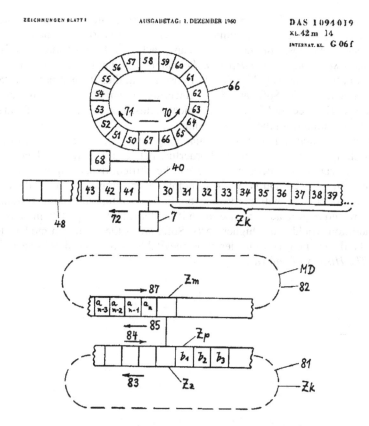

ZEICHNUNGEN BLATT 1   AUSGABETAG: 1. DEZEMBER 1960   DAS 1094019
KL. 42 m 14
INTERNAT. KL. G 06 f

Fig. 7. The device for working with numbers of variable length (from the German patent application, filed March 30, 1957)

In 1965, Joseph Weizenbaum published 'A Computer Program for the Study of Natural Communication Between Man and Computer,' better known by the name ELIZA. The dialog between a computer-simulated psychiatrist and a patient sitting at the keyboard became famous and some psychiatrists even thought, psychoanalysis could be left to the computer. Maybe, the imagination of people that the brain is soft meant a lot of support for the expression *software* that came into wide use in these years.

In the 60s and later on, the number of software solutions became widespread and immense. Today's users of the word *software* may have never heard of the word *hardware*, and the users who know it do know that software is the big business at the expense of hardware. Now software is everywhere: operating systems, typesetting systems, table handling systems, graphic systems, and many other systems are software products. With storage becoming continuously cheaper *and* faster, programmed functions are the essence of today's computers. Nowadays software can easily be modified and improvements can be made even after years without touching the hardware.

'Software as Science' and 'Software as Engineering' are two (main) topics of the Conference. Software is an immaterial product, if it is sold, the mere idea will be sold, since the costs of duplication can practically be neglected: "*Software represents a set of ideas encoded in a language*" (Gerhard Goos). Dealing with software implies a relatively high level of abstraction, thus the gap between 'Software as Science' and 'Software as Engineering' is smaller than it is between 'Science and Engineering' in other technical fields. For this reason software attracted my attention from the very beginning.

Computer Science and *Software Engineering* represent two aspects of one and the same thing. To some extent, the borderline between hardware realization and software realization of a certain feature can be shifted, depending on considerations concerning speed and costs. In principle, everything that can be done with software could be done with hardware, too, but a desk-top publishing system, for example, would require an immense room if implemented completely in hardware, and in addition would cause higher costs. Software is the winner in modern technology, hardware may be considered as inevitable evil. Now it is time to start writing *The History of Software*.

Part 1
Software as Science

Software as Science—Science as Software.

Michael S. Mahoney

Princeton University
303 Dickinson Hall
Princeton, NJ 08544
USA

E-mail: mike@princeton.edu

> I don't really understand the title, Computer Science. I guess I don't understand science
> very well; I'm an engineer. ... Computers are worth thinking about and talking about and
> doing about only because they are useful devices, which do something for somebody. If
> you are just interested in contemplating the abstract, I would strongly recommend the
> belly button, which would survive any war that man survives.
>
> John R. Pierce[1]

Defining the Subject Historically

Software should be of great interest to historians of science. That may seem
strange, given that it is of such recent origin. Software is no older than the modern
electronic computer and the activity of writing programs for it. It is still experiencing growing pains. Yet, over the past fifty years, it has become the subject of its
own thriving science and a ubiquitous medium for pursuing other sciences. In both
instances software represents a new kind of science. It is what Herbert Simon calls
a "science of the artificial."[2] There is nothing natural about software or any science
of software. Programs exist only because we write them, we write them only because we have built computers on which to run them, and the programs we write
ultimately reflect the structures of those computers. Computers are artifacts, programs are artifacts, and models of the world created by programs are artifacts.
Hence, any science about any of these must be a science of a world of our own
making rather than of a world presented to us by nature.[3] What makes it both challenging and intriguing is that those two worlds meet in the physical computer,
which enacts a program in the world. Their encounter has posed new and difficult
epistemological questions concerning what we can know both about the workings

---

[1] Keynote Address, Conference on Academic and Related Research Programs in Computing
Science, 5-8 June 1967; publ. in *University Education in Computing Science*, ed. Aaron Finerman (New York, 1968), 7. Renowned for his work in information theory, Pierce at the time
was Executive Director of Research, Communications Sciences Division, Bell Telephone
Laboratories.
[2] Herbert Simon, *The Sciences of the Artificial* (Cambridge, Mass., 1969; 2nd ed. 1981, 3rd ed.
1996).
[3] Let me leave aside for the moment questions about how much "nature" ever presents itself to
us directly.

of the models and about the relation of the models to the phenomena they purport to represent or simulate. Answers to those questions would seem to depend, at least in part, on understanding programs as dynamic systems.

Because software as science is both new and artificial, it brings to the fore questions of when and how and who. It took some time before programs and programming became subjects of inquiry in themselves. Once they did, it was not clear what one wanted to know about the programs or the activity of writing them, or indeed could know about these subjects. Debate seems to have been particularly lively in the late 1960s. Most practitioners viewed the subject as inherently mathematical. Yet, Marvin Minsky decried excessive formalism, pointing to the "defeatism" of theorems about the limits of computability and to the inadequacy of formal systems to provide an explanatory account of what computers could actually do.[4] Allan Newell and Herbert Simon insisted even more strongly on treating computer science as an empirical discipline. It is the study of the computer as a dynamic physical device and of what programmers are capable, intentionally or not, of making it do.[5] Donald Knuth insisted on the craft nature of programming, characterizing it as an "art." In what began as a "light-hearted attempt to stir up some controversy regarding the nature of computer science," Peter Wegner tried in "Three Computer Cultures" to differentiate the concerns of the computer science from those of both the mathematician and the engineer.[6] While George Forsythe offered counsel on "What to Do until the Computer Scientist Comes," John Pierce ended the keynote address cited above with the hope that "computer scientists, whatever they are, get organized effectively, and I wish them good luck."[7]

So the history with which we are concerned begins with the question of who created the science(s) of software, when, where, why, and how? That is, who thought it necessary or desirable to place programs and programming on some sort of scientific foundation? What was such a foundation meant to accomplish? To what questions would it provide answers? What theoretical and practical benefits did it promise? What sort of science did its creators envision? That is, what established scientific disciplines did they take as models and resources for their new enterprise? How did these aspirations shape the science(s) that emerged, and how did the development of the science(s) reshape the aspirations? As the science(s) developed, how did it (or they) interact with other sciences, especially those that looked to the computer as a tool and then as a medium of investigation? What did those sciences contribute to the science of software and what in turn did they take from it? What about other disciplines not generally considered scientific?

These questions clearly intersect with those of the other areas on our program. The mathematical verification of programs as a warrant of reliability lies at the

[4] Marvin Minsky, "Form and Content in Computer Science" (1969 Turing Award), *ACM Turing Award Lectures: The First Twenty Years, 1966-1985* (New York, 1987), 219-42.

[5] Allan Newell and Herbert Simon, "Computer Science as Empirical Inquiry: Symbols and Search" (1975 Turing Award), *ACM Turing Award Lectures*, 287-313. Newell and Simon had earlier joined with Alan Perlis in taking a similar position in "What is Computer Science?" a Letter to the Editor of *Science* 157 (22 September 1967): 1373-4.

[6] Peter Wegner, "Three Computer Cultures: Computer Technology, Computer Mathematics, and Computer Science," *Advances in Computers* 10 (1970): 7-78.

[7] Forsythe, in *American Mathematical Monthly* 75/5 (1968): 454-62; Pierce, in Finerman, 24.

root of formal semantics. Moreover, if one views engineering as applied science, then one faces the question of what science it is that software engineering applies. Conversely, one may ask what role the theory that has emerged has played in the practice of programming, especially programming in the large, and how that role fits with the status accorded to theory (and to those who pursue it) in the profession at large. The answers to those questions impinge in evident ways on the nature and organization of software as a labor process.

The science mainly in question here is mathematics, the relation of which to computing has evolved dynamically over the past half-century. As a physical device, the modern computer was built for mathematicians to carry out numerical calculations, especially for problems which could not be solved analytically. As a theoretical concept, the modern computer was designed by mathematical logicians to understand the nature of computability and the limits of what can be known by it. As a dynamic computational system, the modern computer has posed new mathematical problems and opened new fields of mathematical research. At the same time, the computer has proved elusive, as central concerns of programming remain beyond the effective reach of mathematics and thus again raise the question of what software as science has to do with software as engineering or as reliable artifact.

No differently from any other science, software as science involves more than a body of knowledge and practice. It means communities of practitioners recognized as possessing that knowledge and charged with extending and disseminating it. The science in question is what they know and do in common. Taking this approach allows for the science(s) of programs and programming to take different forms among different groups of practitioners. That is, it allows for different answers at different times in different places to the question "what is software and what may be said scientifically about it?" or indeed, "what needs to be said scientifically at all about software?" To the extent that a consensus has emerged, it requires an explanation, and historians of science have found that the explanation is likely to be as much social as intellectual.

Over the past fifty years, computer scientists have grown from a handful of people to an extensive network of practitioners in industry, academia, and private practice. They occupy positions of prominence in colleges and universities; indeed, together with molecular biology (with which they have intellectual ties), they constitute the fastest growing sector of academia. Generously funded by industry and government, they have professional associations (ACM, IEEE Computer Society, BCS, etc.), journals, monographs, textbooks, and an elaborate reward structure.[8] Much of this growth rests on a claim to be pursuing a scientific enterprise, even as practitioners have debated among themselves just how scientific it is or should be. How practitioners achieved recognition of that claim is an integral part of the history of software as science.

---

[8] The Turing Award is considered the ACM's highest honor. "It is given to an individual selected for contributions of a technical nature made to the computing community. The contributions should be of lasting and major technical importance to the computer field." (http://www.acm.org/awards/taward.html). A look at the list shows that "technical" has usually (but not always) been construed as "theoretical," indeed "mathematical."

Agendas

Elsewhere I have suggested that the practice of a discipline can be fruitfully approached through the notion of "agenda."[9] At the risk of repeating myself, it might be worth recapitulating what I mean by that. The *agenda* of a field consists of what its practitioners agree ought to be done, a consensus concerning the problems of the field, their order of importance or priority, the means of solving them, and perhaps most importantly, what constitutes a solution. Becoming a recognized practitioner means learning the agenda and then helping to carry it out. Knowing what questions to ask is the mark of a full-fledged practitioner, as is the capacity to distinguish between trivial and profound problems; "profound" means moving the agenda forward. One acquires standing in the field by solving the problems with high priority, and especially by doing so in a way that extends or reshapes the agenda, or by posing profound problems. The standing of the field may be measured by its capacity to set its own agenda. New disciplines emerge by acquiring that autonomy. Conflicts within a discipline often come down to disagreements over the agenda: what are the really important problems?

As the shared Latin root indicates, agendas are about action: what is to be *done*? By emphasizing action, the notion of agendas refocuses attention from a body of knowledge to a complex of practices. Since what practitioners do is all but indistinguishable from the way they go about doing it, it follows that the tools and techniques of a field embody its agenda. When those tools are employed outside the field, either by a practitioner or by an outsider borrowing them, they bring the agenda of the field with them. Using those tools to address another agenda means reshaping the latter to fit the tools, even if it may also lead to a redesign of the tools, with resulting feedback when the tool is brought home. What gets reshaped and to what extent depends on the relative strengths of the agendas of borrower and borrowed.

Theoretical Computer Science

That tools embody agendas has particular importance for new sciences. For, a new science means a new agenda, and tracing the emergence of a new science means showing how a group of practitioners coalesced around a common agenda different from other agendas in which they had been engaged. In the case at hand, what questions or problems drew people to the computer? What tools did they bring with them and how did they apply those tools? How did their involvement shape the emerging agenda of the new field?

That brings me to what is generally considered the scientific basis of software, namely, theoretical computer science.[10] It took shape between 1955 and 1975 as practitioners from a variety of fields converged on a small set of related agendas

---

[9] Michael S. Mahoney, "Computer Science: The Search for a Mathematical Theory," in *Science in the 20th Century*, ed. John Krige and Dominique Pestre (Amsterdam, 1997), Chap. 31.

[10] It is curious that to this day the community distinguishes between computer science and *theoretical* computer science, as if the former involves some kind of science other than theoretical science. It is not clear what that other kind of science might be nor what is scientific about it.

that came to constitute the core of the field: automata and formal languages, computational complexity, and formal semantics. None of those agendas had existed before 1955. By the early 1970s their status as constituents of an autonomous discipline was marked by a main heading in *Mathematical Reviews*, by a growing number of dedicated textbooks, and by the establishment of curricula at both the undergraduate and graduate levels. Perhaps even more strikingly, by the mid-70s theoretical computer science had begun to gain recognition as a field of mathematics in its own right and to serve as resource for other sciences, most notably theoretical biology.

My charge is not to provide a history of that development but to suggest what such a history might look like and how it might be most productively pursued, in short, to offer an agenda for history of software viewed as science. So let me restrict my account to the following diagrams (Figs. 1 and 2), which encapsulate my own efforts to trace the emergence of some of the agendas of theoretical computer sciences from the intersection and interaction of a variety of agendas in fields ranging from electrical engineering to linguistics.[11] The schemes suggest a number of lines of fruitful inquiry.

To begin with, it seems clear that theoretical computer science can be viewed from a number of disciplinary perspectives. Indeed, its formation can be understood only from those perspectives. Computing had no science of its own at the start. Mathematical logic had established what computers could not do, even with endless resources of time and space. Switching theory showed how to analyze and synthesize circuits for basic operations. But no science accounted for what finite machines with finite, random access memories could do or how they did it. That science had to be created, and its creation depended heavily on what was going on in other fields at the time, most notably linguistics. Before the science of computing began to accumulate a history of its own, it was heir to several different histories. Understanding its subsequent development may well involve keeping those histories in mind and looking for their continuing influence.

At each point of convergence the nascent field acquired a set of tools from an antecedent discipline. One may ask what those tools were originally developed to accomplish, how their application to computing contributed to shaping the new subject, to what extent the application in turn reshaped the tools or redefined their status in the parent discipline. An example is the new mathematical interest acquired by finite Boolean algebras as a result of their application to questions of the minimization and optimization of sequential circuits.[12]

---

[11] Michael S. Mahoney, "Computer Science," see also "The Structures of Computation," in *The First Computers—Histories and Architectures*, ed. Raul Rojas and Ulf Hashagen (Cambridge, Mass., 2000), 17-31.

[12] For this and other examples of feedback from computer science to mathematics, see Garrett Birkhoff, "The Role of Modern Algebra in Computing," *Computers in Algebra in Number Theory* (Providence, R. I., 1971), 1-47. For a discussion of the changes in the mathematics curriculum prompted by computer science, see Anthony Ralston, "Computer Science, Mathematics, and the Undergraduate Curriculum in Both," *American Mathematical Monthly* 81/7 (1981): 472-85.

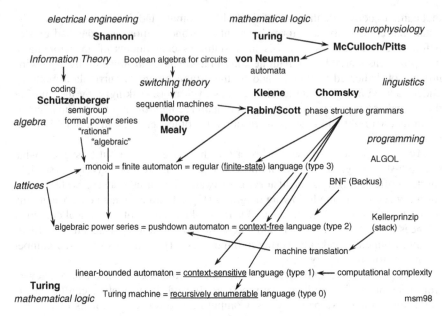

Fig. 1. The agendas of automata and formal languages

Indeed, one of the uncanny aspects of the development of theoretical computer science has been the way it has given practical meaning to the most abstract mathematical structures: semigroups, lattices, categories. None of these was created with computers in mind, and in each case it is not hard to find statements by mathematicians of the time insisting on their uselessness even to mathematics. Each is fundamental to modern computer science, which has arguably created the notion of "applied algebra," even to the point that one recent book offers "category theory for the working computer scientist."[13] Though not originally a mathematical construct, the lambda calculus has similarly moved from theoretical structure to practical tool (especially once Scott provided a mathematical model in continuous lattices) and indeed recently has begun to move out from computing per se into the area of theoretical biology.[14]

[13] See, for example, Garrett Birkhoff and Thomas C. Bartee, *Modern Applied Algebra* (New York, 1970); Rudolf Lidl and Gunter Pilz, *Applied Abstract Algebra* (New York, 1984); Andrea Asperti, *Categories, Types, and Structures: An Introduction to Category Theory for the Working Computer Scientist* (Cambridge, Mass., 1991).

[14] See W. Fontana and Leo W. Buss, "The Barrier of Objects: From Dynamical Systems to Bounded Organizations," in *Boundaries and Barriers*, ed. J. Casti and A. Karlqvist (Reading, Mass., 1996), 56-116.

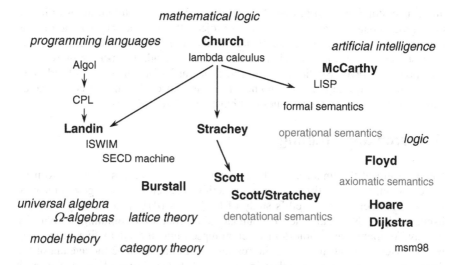

Fig. 2. The agendas of semantics

The diagrams indicate, however sketchily, that various parts of the agenda took shape initially in different places. For example, the identification of formal power series, pushdown automata, and context-free languages brought together at MIT agendas ranging from the algebraic coding theory of Marcel Schützenberger in Paris to the work on sequential formula translation of Fritz Bauer and Klaus Samelson in Munich, which in turn drew on Heinz Rutishauser's early efforts at automatic programming. To take another example, the notion of using the lambda calculus as the basis for formal semantics seems clearly to have originated with John McCarthy, who needed it as a means of abstracting functions for his work on mechanical theorem-proving and on commonsense reasoning by computers. Yet, it seems equally clear from activities surrounding the Algol meetings that others besides McCarthy were familiar with the lambda calculus and were exploring its use as a vehicle for defining the semantics of the new language. Indeed, the lambda calculus and formal semantics quite quickly crossed the Atlantic in the early 60s, settling in primarily with Peter Landin and Christopher Strachey at Cambridge but then spreading to Vienna and Amsterdam, where Dana Scott's seminal collaboration with Jaco de Bakker took place. While McCarthy's work spoke to an agenda already underway elsewhere, transcripts of a Working Conference on Mechanical Language Structures held in Princeton in 1963 suggest that it received a cooler reception closer to home, where more pragmatic concerns dominated.[15]

These are just two examples, I suspect, of how agendas at first reflect local interests and ways of doing things. Different groups of people constitute different mixes of scientific training, taste, and aspirations, reflecting in many cases their

---

[15] The proceedings of the Conference were published in *CACM* 7/2 (1964): 51-136; see in particular the "Summary Remarks" by Saul Gorn and the "General Discussion" that followed, pp. 133-6.

differing cultural and institutional backgrounds.[16] In addition to questions of how a local group coalesces around a common project, there is the larger issue of how that project then moves onto the agenda of the profession as a whole.[17] Of great interest among historians of science over the past decade has been a question of how practices travel. Studies have revealed the particular importance of individuals moving from one place to another, learning and conveying by collaboration and example results and techniques that have not yet reached print.

Research and Training

One measure of the importance of an agenda are the resources allocated to it by the community of practitioners, usually acting as agents for the government or industry. Norberg and O'Neill's study of DARPA's IPTO and the as yet unpublished study of National Science Foundation's Office of Computing Activity by Aspray, Williams, and Goldstein offer glimpses into the interactive process by which government agencies and the research community shape the agenda of the discipline.[18] As in so many other instances, Dick Hamming offers historians a valuable perspective on what was at stake. In his Turing Lecture of 1968, at a time when the nature of the field seemed uncertain, he warned his audience:

> In the face of this difficulty [of defining "computer science"] many people, including myself at times, feel that we should ignore the discussion and get on with *doing* it. But as George Forsythe points out so well[19] in a recent article, it *does* matter what people in Washington D.C. think computer science is. According to him, they tend to feel that it is a part of applied mathematics and therefore turn to the mathematicians for advice in the granting of funds. And it is not greatly different elsewhere; in both industry and the universities you can often still see traces of where computing first started, whether in electrical engineering, physics, mathematics, or even business. Evidently the picture which

---

[16] Such differences shine through the protocols of the Software Engineering Conferences at Garmisch and Rome. People differed about what it would mean to make the subject scientific, about the extent to which one can do so, about the importance of trying to make it so, about the means for achieving that goal. They had different agendas.

[17] Not all agendas have converged on the current configuration. For example, Ershov and other Russian computer scientists took their own approach to a science of software but did so in relative isolation from research in the West. To the historian, this independent line of development offers an opportunity for comparisons and contrasts, and holds out the possibility of linking agendas to the political, social, and economic context within which they take shape. See, for example, Andrei P. Ershov, *Origins of Programming: Discourses on Methodology* (New York, 1990); Ershov and M. R. Shura-Bura, "The Early Development of Programming in the USSR," in *A History of Computing in the Twentieth Century*, ed. N. Metropolis et al. (New York, 1978), 137-96; R. A. Di Paola, "A Survey of Soviet Work in the Theory of Computer Programming," Rand Memorandum RM-5424-PR (Santa Monica, 1967).

[18] Arthur L. Norberg and Judy E. O'Neill, *Transforming Computer Technology: Information Processing for the Pentagon, 1962-1986* (Baltimore, 1996). William Aspray, Bernard O. Williams, and Andrew H. Goldstein, *Computing as Servant and Science: The Impact of the National Science Foundation*, unpub. draft, 1992; cf. Aspray and Williams, "Arming American Scientists: NSF and the Provision of Scientific Computing Facilities for Universities, 1950-1973," *Annals of the History of Computing* 16/4 (1994): 60-74.

[19] [Hamming's note]: G. E. Forsythe, "What to do Until the Computer Scientist Comes," *American Mathematical Monthly* 75/5 (May 1968): 454-61.

people have of a subject can significantly affect its subsequent development. Therefore, although we cannot hope to settle the question definitively, we need frequently to examine and to air our views on what our subject is and should become.[20]

Research funding is a matter of more than just money. Until a field gains autonomy over its own agenda, its development depends on what other disciplines think its practitioners should be doing.

Proposals and requests for proposals (RFPs) provide valuable insight into the articulation of agendas. They aim at enlisting support and hence must tie the proposers' aims to those of their reviewers and their reviewers' institutions. Moreover, they capture the proposers' thinking before the work has been carried out and thus offer a chance of comparing shifts in direction as questions are answered, sometimes in unanticipated ways. It is revealing, for example, to see how Minsky, McCarthy, Shannon, and Rochester viewed the agenda they called "artificial intelligence" in proposing their famous summer workshop in 1956.[21] McCarthy has subsequently insisted on the value of such documents in establishing the aims and methods of scientific research.

Viewing a science in terms of its evolving agenda means, among other things, seeing how the agenda is communicated to the next generation of practitioners. In explaining what I mean by "agenda," I said that one becomes a practitioner by learning what is to be done, i.e. by learning what the questions or problems of the field are, how they are tackled and resolved, and what constitutes a solution. Kuhn's notion of "paradigm" fits well here, especially as he subsequently clarified it through the concept of a "disciplinary matrix."[22] Science is conveyed by exemplars, by models of problem-solving. Students start with what is best established and most familiar to practitioners, and then move from there onto rougher terrain until they come to the edges of known territory. In the sciences in particular, that does not mean that students must recapitulate the entire history of the discipline. On the contrary, what makes certain solutions paradigmatic is precisely the way in which they encompass and give structure to a range of problems, transforming their hard-won solutions into corollaries.

That is what makes textbooks and curricula an important resource for tracing the emergence and development of a discipline. They reflect its agenda not at the frontiers of research but at the starting point for reaching those frontiers. They are statements about what current practitioners at a particular time think students must know to become the next generation of practitioners. Hammering out a curriculum can be a harrowing experience for participants precisely because it means reaching agreement on what the subject is about: what is central and what peripheral, what must everyone know and what can be an elective, in what order are these things to be learned? To the historian, the process of hammering out is as important as, or perhaps even more important than the end result. We have the published versions of a succession of ACM curricula in computer science and responses to them.[23] I

[20] Richard W. Hamming, "One Man's View of Computer Science," *ACM Turing Award Lectures* (n. 4 above), 207-18 at 208.

[21] Available at http://www-formal.stanford.edu/jmc/history/dartmouth.html.

[22] Thomas S. Kuhn, *The Structure of Scientific Revolutions* (Chicago, 1962; 2nd ed. 1970).

[23] For example, ACM Curriculum Committee on Computer Science, "An Undergraduate Program in Computer Science—Preliminary Recommendations," *CACM* 8 (1965): 543-8; "Cur-

hope we also have the minutes of the meetings of the committees that wrote them, not to say copies of the exchanges that went on between meetings.

What the profession as a whole was trying to accomplish was happening in colleges and universities, as computer scientists sought to define a place for themselves in their institutions and to justify their recognition as distinct academic units on a par with those already established. The volume on *University Education in Computing Science* edited by Aaron Finerman in 1968 provides a good survey of the range of thinking on the matter at that crucial time. The local strategies of practitioners, in particular the alliances they forged with other disciplines, should also prove revealing. Anniversaries and retirements of founders have provided largely celebratory accounts for departments at Purdue, Cornell, MIT, and elsewhere, but no one has yet undertaken a critical, documented analysis of how the new science of computing established itself at a university.[24]

Mathematics and Software Engineering

In addition to being new and artificial, software as science should hold interest for historians of science in the perspective it affords on the question of the relation of theory to practice. In *Science, the Endless Frontier*, the document that determined American post-war science policy, Vannevar Bush took as axiomatic the proposition that technology emerges from basic science.[25] It was a widely held view, which we see reflected in John McCarthy's vision of a mathematical theory of computation, expressed at IFIP 1962:

> In a mathematical science, it is possible to deduce from the basic assumptions, the important properties of the entities treated by the science. Thus, from Newton's law of gravitation and his laws of motion, one can deduce that the planetary orbits obey Kepler's laws.[26]

As McCarthy and his audience well knew, one can also deduce the laws of the motion of terrestrial bodies and all the mechanics that derives from them. He extended the analogy at the conclusion of his 1963 article, "A Basis for a Mathematical Theory of Computation," by reference to later successes in mathematical physics:

---

riculum 68—Recommendations for Academic Programs in Computer Science," *CACM* 11 (1968): 151-97; "Curriculum 78—Recommendations for the Undergraduate Program in Computer Science," *CACM* 22 (1979): 147-66; A. Ralston and M. Shaw, "Curriculum 78—Is Computer Science Really That Unmathematical?" *CACM* 23 (1980): 67-70.

[24] For Purdue, see John Rice and Richard A. DeMillo, eds., *Studies in Computer Science in Honor of Samuel D. Conte* (New York and London, 1994); for Cornell, David Gries, "Twenty Years of Computer Science at Cornell," *Engineering: Cornell Quarterly* 20/2 (1985): 2-11.

[25] Vannevar Bush, *Science, the Endless Frontier: A Report to the President on a Program for Postwar Scientific Research* (Washington, D.C., 1945; reprint, 1960, 1990). For a thoughtful critique of Bush's basic premise, see Donald E. Stokes, *Pasteur's Quadrant: Basic Science and Technological Innovation* (Washington, DC, 1997).

[26] "Towards a Mathematical Science of Computation," *Proc. IFIP Congress* 62 (Amsterdam, 1963), 21-28 at 21.

It is reasonable to hope that the relationship between computation and mathematical logic will be as fruitful in the next century as that between analysis and physics in the last. The development of this relationship demands a concern for both applications and mathematical elegance.[27]

The applications of mathematics to physics had produced more than new theories. The mathematical theories of thermodynamics and electricity and magnetism had informed the development of heat engines, of dynamos and motors, of telegraphy and radio. Those theories formed the scientific basis of engineering in those fields. McCarthy expected that the theory of computation would do the same for programming, to the point that "no one would pay money for a computer program until it had been proved to meet its specifications."[28]

In light of that original program, it is all the more striking to hear the lament of Christopher Strachey shortly before he and Dana Scott realized McCarthy's theoretical goal of a mathematical semantics. In a discussion on the last day of the second NATO Conference on Software Engineering held in Rome in October 1969, Strachey observed that "one of the difficulties about computing science at the moment is that it can't demonstrate any of the things that it has in mind; it can't demonstrate to the software engineering people on a sufficiently large scale that what it is doing is of interest or importance to them."[29] Ten years later, the Computer Science and Engineering Research Study (COSERS) took stock of the field and its current directions of research and published the results under the title *What Can Be Automated?* The committee on theoretical computer science argued forcefully that a process of abstraction was necessary to understand the complex systems constructed on computers and that the abstraction "must rest on a mathematical basis."[30] Defining theoretical computer science as "the field concerned with fundamental mathematical questions about computers, programs, algorithms, and information processing systems in general," the committee acknowledged that those questions tended to follow developments in technology and its application, and hence to aim at a moving target—strange behavior for mathematical objects.

---

[27] "A Basis for a Mathematical Theory of Computation," in *Computer Programming and Formal Systems*, ed. P. Braffort and D. Hirschberg (Amsterdam, 1963), 33-69 at 69.

[28] Interview with M. S. Mahoney, 3 December 1990.

[29] Peter Naur, Brian Randell, and J. N. Buxton, eds., *Software Engineering: Concepts and Techniques. Proceedings of the NATO Conferences* (New York, 1976), 147.

[30] They offered for three main reasons: "(1) Computers and programs are inherently mathematical objects. They manipulate formal symbols, and their input-output behavior can be described by mathematical functions. The notations we use to represent them strongly resemble the formal notations which are used throughout mathematics and systematically studied in mathematical logic. (2) Programs often accept arbitrarily large amounts of input data; hence, they have a potentially unbounded number of possible inputs. Thus a program embraces, in finite terms, an infinite number of possible computations; and mathematics provides powerful tools for reasoning about infinite numbers of cases. (3) Solving complex information-processing problems requires mathematical analysis. While some of this analysis is highly problem-dependent and belongs to specific application areas, some constructions and proof methods are broadly applicable, and thus become the subject of theoretical computer science. *What Can Be Automated?* [hereafter COSERS], ed. Bruce W. Arden (Cambridge, Mass., 1980), 139. The committee consisted of Richard M. Karp (Chair; Berkeley), Zohar Manna (Stanford), Albert R. Meyer (MIT), John C. Reynolds (Syracuse), Robert W. Ritchie (Washington), Jeffrey D. Ullman (Stanford), and Shmuel Winograd (IBM Research).

Nonetheless, the committee could identify several broad issues of continuing concern, which were being addressed in the areas of computational complexity, data structures and search algorithms, language and automata theory, the logic of computer programming, and mathematical semantics. In each of these areas, it could point to substantial achievements in bringing some form of mathematics to bear on the central questions of computing. Yet, in the summaries at the end of each section, they repeatedly echoed Christopher Strachey's lament. For all the depth of results in computational complexity, "the complexity of most computational tasks we are familiar with—such as sorting, multiplying integers or matrices, or finding shortest paths—is still unknown." (COSERS, 215) Despite the close ties between mathematics and language theory, "by and large, the more mathematical aspects of language theory have not been applied in practice. Their greatest potential service is probably pedagogic, in codifying and given clear economical form to key ideas for handling formal languages." (COSERS, 234) Efforts to bring mathematical rigor to programming quickly reach a level of complexity that makes the techniques of verification subject to the very concerns that prompted their development. Mathematical semantics could show "precisely why [a] nasty surprise can arise from a seemingly well-designed programming language," but not how to eliminate the problems from the outset. As a design tool, mathematical semantics was still far from the goal of correcting the anomalies that gave rise to errors in real programming languages. If computers and programs were "inherently mathematical objects," the mathematics of the computers and programs of real practical concern had so far proved elusive.

Five years later, C. A. R. Hoare echoed the committee's expression of belief and admission of fact. In a postponed Inaugural Lecture as Professor of Computation at Oxford in 1985 (he had been appointed in 1976), Hoare declared,

> Our principles may be summarized under four headings.
>
> (1) *Computers are mathematical machines.* Every aspect of their behavior can be defined with mathematical precision, and every detail can be deduced from this definition with mathematical certainty by the laws of pure logic.
>
> (2) *Computer programs are mathematical expressions.* They describe with unprecedented precision and in every minutest detail the behaviour, intended or unintended, of the computer on which they are executed.
>
> (3) *A programming language is a mathematical theory.* It includes concepts, notations, definitions, axioms and theorems, which help a programmer to develop a program which meets its specification, and to prove that it does so.
>
> (4) *Programming is a mathematical activity.* Like other branches of applied mathematics and engineering, its successful practice requires determined and meticulous application of traditional methods of mathematical understanding, calculation and proof.
>
> These are general philosophical and moral principles, and I hold them to be self-evident •which is just as well, because all the actual evidence is against them. Nothing is really as I have described it, neither computers nor programs nor programming languages nor even programmers.

In the first three cases, sheer size and complexity stood in the way of mathematical understanding. In the case of programmers, "ignorance or even fear of mathematics" blocked many, while those trained in mathematics did not apply it.[31]

What should interest the historian of science here is a continuing dissonance between the premises of theoretical computer science and the experience of programming. It constitutes a prime example of how modern technoscience confounds traditional categories of theory and practice.[32] In principle, the computer should be accessible to mathematics. In practice, it is not.

There are two features of the situation which have implications for how we might approach the history of software. First, as COSERS itself observed, "[E]ven though all the levels of the hierarchy which comprise computer systems can be interpreted as algorithms, the *study of algorithms* and the *phenomena related to computers* are not coextensive, since there are important organizational, policy, and nondeterministic aspects of computing that do not fit the algorithmic mold."[33] The observation raises the questions of what mold those aspects do fit, that is to say, what science, if any, encompasses the phenomena not covered by algorithms. The second feature is the complexity of computer systems that seems to place even their algorithmic aspects beyond the reach of mathematics. The first feature has implications for software as engineering, the second for science as software.

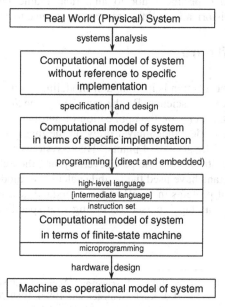

Fig. 3. Software development: levels of abstraction

[31] C. A. R. Hoare, "The Mathematics of Programming," in his *Essays in Computing Science* (Hemel Hempstead, 1989), 352.

[32] For a discussion of some of the issues, together with case studies, see Andrew Pickering, *The Mangle of Practice: Time, Agency, & Science* (Chicago, 1995).

[33] COSERS, 9.

Viewing Hoare's principles as ideals to be pursued by ever more rigorous methods risks misleading both the historian and the software engineer. To see why, consider the following variation on the traditional "waterfall" model of software development (Fig. 3). Relatively few errors now occur in the stages in the bottom half of the scheme. That is not surprising, given that they are the aspects of computing best understood mathematically, and that understanding has been translated into such practical tools as diagnostic compilers for high-level programming languages.

However, as Fred Brooks pointed out in "No Silver Bullet," the problems thus addressed were accidental, rather than essential, to the task of designing large, complex computer systems.[34] At the top of the scheme, the situation is different. That is where the bulk of the crucial errors have been made, and that is where software engineering has focused its attention since the 1970s. But that is also where the science of software moves away from the computer into the wider world and interacts with the sciences (if they exist) pertinent to the systems to be modeled computationally. There it becomes a question of how to express those sciences computationally and of how to evaluate the fit between the target system and the computational model.[35] But that is a question that software engineers share with scientists who have turned to the computer to take them into realms that are accessible neither to experiment nor to analytical mathematics. Intellectually, professionally, and historically, it links software as science to science as software.

Science as Software

Recent (and not so recent) trends in computer modeling reverse the perspective of the question of software as science. By the mid-1960s, the *Journal of Theoretical Biology* was carrying articles on the application of automata to development, and in the early 1970s Aristide Lindenmayer drew on the theory of formal languages to construct models of the growth of plants.[36] His L-systems soon became the topic of a considerable literature. Over the past several years, theoretical biologists Leo Buss and Walter Fontana have used the lambda calculus to model the development through interaction of proteins in an effort to understand how evolution began. In general, the model of a "tape" parsed according to a specified (and specifiable)

---

[34] Frederick P. Brooks, "No Silver Bullet—Essence and Accidents of Software Engineering," *Information Processing* 86, ed. H. J. Kugler (Amsterdam, 1986), 1069-76; reprint in *Computer* 20/4 (1987): 10-19; and in the Anniversary Edition of Frederick P. Brooks, *The Mythical Man-Month: Essays on Software Engineering* (Reading, Mass., 1995), Chap. 16. Chap. 17, "'No Silver Bullet' Refired" is a response to critics of the original article and a review of the silver bullets that have missed the mark over the intervening decade.

[35] Since the late 1980s, this interaction has been moved to a meta-level, as researchers have sought to model the process by which the computational model is designed. See, for example, Leon Osterweil, "Software Processes are Software Too," *Proceedings: 9th International Conference on Software Engineering* (Los Angeles, Calif., 1987), 2-13.

[36] Aristide Lindenmayer, "Mathematical Models for Cellular Interactions in Development," *Journal of Theoretical Biology* 18 (1968): 280-99, 300-15.

syntax is fundamental to current thinking in biology, which in a very real sense considers life in terms of software.[37]

Computer modeling in general poses substantive issues for a science of software. Traditionally, models have served the purpose of capturing the workings of phenomena in terms of mechanisms or mathematical relations that are better understood or at least more immediately accessible to manipulation. The empirical fit of the model with the observed behavior of the phenomenon attests to the model's goodness. Understanding how the model has produced that behavior supposedly gives insight into how that behavior was produced in the physical system. Since the 17th century (and even earlier in astronomy), scientists have sought to reduce nature to physical models and the physical models to mathematical relations. They have proceeded on the premiss that the structures of those relations mirrored the structures of the physical models, which in turn mirrored the structures of nature.

John von Neumann changed that traditional view by arguing against the need for a physical model to mediate between nature and mathematics. Mathematical structures themselves sufficed to give insight into the world, both physical and social. The job of the scientist was to build models that matched the phenomena, without concern for whether the model was "true" in any other sense.

> To begin with, we must emphasize a statement which I am sure you have heard before, but which must be repeated again and again. It is that the sciences do not try to explain, they hardly even try to interpret, they mainly make models. By a model is meant a mathematical construct which, with the addition of certain verbal interpretations, describes observed phenomena. The justification of such a mathematical construct is solely and precisely that it is expected to work—that is, correctly to describe phenomena from a reasonably wide area. Furthermore, it must satisfy certain esthetic criteria—that is, in relation to how much it describes, it must be rather simple. I think it is worth while insisting on these vague terms—for instance, on the use of the word rather. One cannot tell exactly how "simple" simple is. Some of the theories that we have adopted, some of the models with which we are very happy and of which we are very proud would probably not impress someone exposed to them for the first time as being particularly simple.[38]

But even then von Neumann assumed that the mathematical structure of the model would be accessible to analysis and the researcher would understand how the model worked.

But here the state of mathematics placed him in a quandary. Current methods offered little insight into the problems of interest at the time, the class of problems exemplified by hydrodynamics which, he noted in 1945, was "the prototype for anything involving non-linear partial differential equations, particularly those of the hyperbolic or the mixed type, hydrodynamics being a major physical guide in this important field, which is clearly too difficult at present from the purely

---

[37] For a richly detailed and critical account of this development, see Lily Kay, *Who Wrote the Book of Life? A History of the Genetic Code* (Stanford, 2000). Evelyn Fox Keller also explores the metaphor critically in "The Body of a New Machine: Situating the Organism Between the Telegraph and the Computer," in *Refiguring Life: Metaphors of Twentieth-Century Biology* (New York, 1995).

[38] John von Neumann, "Method in the Physical Sciences," in *The Unity of Knowledge*, ed. L. Leary (Garden City, N.J., 1955); reprint in John von Neumann, *Works*, VI, 492.

mathematical point of view."[39] A year later he and Herman Goldstine echoed that theme in their draft paper "On the Principles of Large-Scale Computing Machines:"

> Our present analytical methods seem unsuitable for the solution of the important problems arising in connection with non-linear partial differential equations and, in fact, with virtually all types of non-linear problems in pure mathematics. The truth of this statement is particularly striking in the field of fluid dynamics. Only the most elementary problems have been solved analytically in this field. Furthermore, it seems that in almost all cases where limited successes were obtained with analytical methods, these were purely fortuitous, and not due to any intrinsic suitability of the method to the milieu.
>
> ... A brief survey of almost any of the really elegant or widely applicable work, and indeed of most of the successful work in both pure and applied mathematics suffices to show that it deals in the main with linear problems. In pure mathematics we need only look at the theories of partial differential and integral equations, while in applied mathematics we may refer to acoustics, electro-dynamics, and quantum mechanics. The advance of analysis is, at this moment, stagnant along the entire front of non-linear problems.[40]

That is what made the computer so attractive. In the absence of analytic solutions, it could at least provide numerical results and, more importantly, produce them quickly enough to make the mathematics useful as a model.

However, the model would only bring insight if one understood how the mathematics worked, if not analytically, at least computationally. But here again, the state of knowledge posed a barrier to understanding, as that approach encountered difficulties. Numerical solutions did not offer the structural insights of the analytical models, making it difficult to determine where the problem lay when the numerical results did not meet expectations. Moreover, it gradually became clear that the numerical techniques developed for the purpose were generating their own problematic behavior, as the truncation and rounding required by finite representation in the machine took calculations in unanticipated directions. To understand that behavior would require a theory of computation that did not yet exist.

As von Neumann pointed out in his 1948 Hixon lecture on the theory of automata,

> There exists today a very elaborate system of formal logic, and, specifically, of logic as applied to mathematics. This is a discipline with many good sides, but also with certain serious weaknesses. This is not the occasion to enlarge upon the good sides, which I certainly have no intention to belittle. About the inadequacies, however, this may be said: Everybody who has worked in formal logic will confirm that it is one of the technically most refractory parts of mathematics. The reason for this is that it deals with rigid, all-or-none concepts, and has very little contact with the continuous concept of the real or of the complex number, that is, with mathematical analysis. Yet analysis is the technically most successful and best-elaborated part of mathematics. Thus formal logic is, by the nature of its approach, cut off from the best cultivated portions of mathematics, and forced onto the most difficult part of the mathematical terrain, into combinatorics.

---

[39] John von Neumann to Oswald Veblen, 26 March 1945, in John von Neumann, *Works*, VI, 357.

[40] H. Goldstine and John von Neumann, "On the Principles of Large-Scale Computing Machines," ca. 1946, in John von Neumann, *Works*, V, 2.

> The theory of automata, of the digital, all-or-none type, as discussed up to now, is certainly a chapter in formal logic. It will have to be, from the mathematical point of view, combinatory rather than analytical.[41]

It is important to recall that von Neumann's call for a theory of automata arose not out of concern for programming computers but for using them to model physical systems. The theory was meant to compensate for the failures of analytical mathematics. Although he would not have phrased it so at the time, the science of software was not only about computers; it was about the world.

The agenda that von Neumann laid out in his "General Theory" has not received much attention from historians of computing or historians of science. This is not the occasion to try to trace the story in any detail. It leads from von Neumann to Arthur Burks's Logic of Computing Group at the University of Michigan and from there to the Santa Fe Institute. It involves research in cellular automata, complex adaptive systems, genetic algorithms, and similar expressions of what von Neumann characterized as "growing automata." Given new life in the 1980s by the development of computer graphics, the emergence of chaos theory, and the leadership of Stephen Wolfram, it has attracted practitioners from a broad range of sciences.

Yet, even here the relation between what can be done with the computer and what can be accounted for mathematically remains problematic. Almost fifty years after von Neumann wrote of the need for a theory of computation, John Holland, an early member of the Burks group and the creator of genetic algorithms, expressed a similar concern. In the concluding chapter of *Hidden Order: How Adaptation Builds Complexity*, Holland looks "Toward Theory" and "the general principles that will deepen our understanding of *all* complex adaptive systems [*cas*]." As a point of departure he insists that:

> Mathematics is our sine qua non on this part of the journey. Fortunately, we need not delve into the details to describe the form of the mathematics and what it can contribute; the details will probably change anyhow, as we close in on our destination. Mathematics has a critical role because it alone enables us to formulate *rigorous* generalizations, or principles. Neither physical experiments nor computer-based experiments, on their own, can provide such generalizations. Physical experiments usually are limited to supplying input and constraints for rigorous models, because the experiments themselves are rarely described in a language that permits deductive exploration. Computer-based experiments have rigorous descriptions, but they deal only in specifics. A well-designed mathematical model, on the other hand, generalizes the particulars revealed by physical experiments, computer-based models, and interdisciplinary comparisons. Furthermore, the tools of mathematics provide rigorous derivations and predictions applicable to all *cas*. Only mathematics can take us the full distance.[42]

---

[41] John von Neumann, "On a Logical and General Theory of Automata," in *Cerebral Mechanisms in Behavior—The Hixon Symposium*, ed. L. A. Jeffries (New York, 1951), 1-31; reprint in *Papers of John von Neumann on Computing and Computer Theory*, ed. William Aspray and Arthur Burks (Cambridge, Mass./London/Los Angeles/San Francisco, 1987), 391-431 at 406.

[42] John H. Holland, *Hidden Order: How Adaptation Builds Complexity* (Reading, Mass., 1995), 161-2.

Details aside, Holland's goal, with which he associates his colleagues at the Santa Fe Institute, reflects a vision of mathematics that he and they share with mathematicians from Descartes to von Neumann.

As von Neumann insisted in 1948, the mathematics will be different. To meet Holland's needs it "[will have to] depart from traditional approaches to emphasize persistent features of the far-from-equilibrium evolutionary trajectories generated by recombination."[43] Moreover, that mathematics will be about software. Wolfram's now seminal papers on cellular automata and their application to the "engineering of complexity" rest on the theory of automata and formal languages created during the 1960s through a convergence of agendas in electrical engineering, neurophysiology, mathematical logic, linguistics, computer programming, and abstract algebra. Other contributing branches to the agenda of Artificial Life, in particular from mathematical biology, draw on the same resources in theoretical computer science.

As I said at the outset, software should be of great interest to historians of science. But not only because it is new, or even because it represents a new, artifactual form of science. In that case, writing its history would be simply a matter of extending the coverage of the field to include developments over the past fifty years, to be achieved by tacking another chapter onto the story. Much more importantly, as the computer has changed its role in science from tool to instrument to medium (and indeed to surrogate for reality), understanding of the world has come to depend on understanding of computation as itself a complex dynamic process. Scientists and software engineers face many of the same problems of building computational models that reliably simulate portions of the world of interest to them and that do so in ways that allow analysis and understanding of the process. As we make the turn into a new century, software verges on becoming emblematic of science itself. How that happened over the second half of the twentieth century should soon be a big question in the history of science. Having a historically sensitive history of software will help to answer it.

Addendum

Aimed at defining an agenda for historical research, my paper instead provoked considerable discussion about the nature of software and about whether it is or could be a science. The discussion included various assertions, both historical and philosophical, concerning the nature of science and of its relation to mathematics. As lively and provocative as the debate was, I think it led us away from our goal of defining an agenda for the history of software, or at least one aspect of it, and even revealed some misunderstanding of how historians work. The detour may have derived in part from people's not having had a chance to read the paper beforehand and from my having assumed agreement on the meaning of "software" for the purposes of the workshop. Before responding to some of the issues raised in the discussion, let me clarify how I was using "software" and hence what I understood by the phrase "software as science."

---

[43] Ibid., 171-2.

Software as Science

In common English usage, "software" is a mass term for programs, for what computers process, as opposed to the machines themselves. When the term first arose in the late 1950s, it was used as the antonym of "hardware."[44] As the *Oxford English Dictionary* defines it, noting its formation on the model of "hardware," software is "[t]he programs and procedures required to enable a computer to perform a specific task, as opposed to the physical components of the system." By the mid-60s, the term had taken on a more specific sense of systems software, what people use to construct and run programs. That is what John Tukey had in mind when he introduced the term in 1958.[45] But the term retained its broader meaning; the "software houses" that sprang up in the mid-60s were producing applications along with systems.

In my essay "software" means simply programs and, by extension, the activity of writing them, programming. In speaking then of "software as science" I do not mean to assert that programs in and of themselves constitute a science, or that the writing of them is an inherently scientific activity. Clearly, neither is the case. As I pointed out at the start, programs are artifacts—literally, things crafted—and they are no more inherently scientific than any other made object in the world. However, just as other sciences have arisen from the investigation of artifacts, e.g. thermodynamics from the steam engine, so one may ask about a science of programs and programming. Or rather, one may look for efforts by practitioners of computing to make programs and programming the subjects of a scientific inquiry, to place them on a scientific foundation. That is how I construe "software as science" for the purposes of historical inquiry.

To judge from the discussion, people in computing evidently disagree about whether such a science is possible, desirable, or relevant. That is not a matter for historians to decide, nor do historians require consensus on the matter among computer people; indeed, the continuing disagreement is of greater interest than consensus. For historians it is enough that from the mid-1950s people of reputation in computing have believed that a science of software is desirable and feasible and have set forth what they take that science to be. Most have them have looked to mathematics as the foundation. Tony Hoare represents perhaps the extreme in his insistence on the inherently mathematical nature of programs and programming, but he hardly stands alone out there. Others have taken a more empirical approach, believing that mathematics is not adequate to explain what computers can do, especially when we have not told them (or do not believe we have told

---

[44] In introducing the ACM to readers of the first issue of its Journal in January, 1954, S. B. Williams anticipated the coinage: "Until the engineering societies, AIEE and IRE, became sufficiently interested to struggle with 'hardware,' the Association provided a forum for all phases of the field. Now the Association can direct its efforts to the other phases of computing systems, such as numerical analysis, logical design, application and use, and, last but not least, to programming," *Journal of the ACM* 1/1 (1954): 3.

[45] John Tukey, "The Teaching of Concrete Mathematics," *American Mathematical Monthly* 65/1(1958): 1-9 at 2: "Today the 'software' comprising the carefully planned interpretive routines, compilers, and other aspects of automative [sic] programming are at least as important to the modern electronic calculator as its 'hardware' of tubes, transistors, wires, tapes and the like."

them) to do it. But, as envisioned by Herbert Simon, the empirical science of computational processes would be no less scientific for being empirical and, indeed, a science of the artificial.

To justify a history of the science of software, it would seem enough to point to the two-volume *Handbook of Theoretical Computer Science*, of which neither the contents nor even the constituent subjects existed in 1950.[46] The extensive bibliographies accompanying each of the 37 chapters testify to the immense intellectual effort and hence social investment that the *Handbook* is meant to codify. My sketch of the development of just two of those constituents, formal languages and formal semantics, aimed at suggesting how historians might go about tracing the origins and growth of the field and determining how it attracted the investment. I am fairly confident that the notion of agendas and their convergence on the computer will go a long way in explaining the emergence of such subjects as computational complexity, databases, computational geometry, and parallel computing. Whether or not it does, the *Handbook* evidently purports to constitute a science of software and to base that science for the most part on mathematics. The job of the historian is not to question whether the *Handbook* should exist but to explain how it came about.

The *Handbook* speaks to another point raised in the discussion. Several in the audience suggested that in speaking of "software as science" I was laboring under a misapprehension rooted in the English use of "computer science" to denote a subject other languages refer to as "informatics." Perhaps the name was leading me to look for science where there was none. Considering that slightly more than half the authors of the *Handbook* are Europeans engaged in informatics, the objection is puzzling. It is all the more so, since I need only turn to my bookshelf to find a volume, *Theoretische Informatik—kurzgefaßt* by Uwe Schöning, the contents of which cover roughly the same ground as, say, *Computability, Complexity, and Languages: Fundamentals of Theoretical Computer Science* by Martin Davis, Ron Sigal, and Elaine J. Weyuker. Turning to Schöning's institutional homepage, the Fakultät für Informatik at the University of Ulm, I see *Theoretische Informatik I/II* as part of the *Grundstudium*, side-by-side with *Technische Informatik I/II*, laying the foundation for further study. The rest of the curriculum does not look substantially different from what is taught in any American department of computer science. So I must wonder, as Shakespeare's Juliet once did, "What's in a name?" Here too the rose smells the same.[47]

[46] Jan van Leeuwen, ed., *Handbook of Theoretical Computer Science* (Amsterdam, Cambridge, Mass., 1990), vol. A, *Algorithms and Complexity*; vol. B, *Formal Models and Semantics*.

[47] Only after writing these words did I discover that Wolfgang Coy had asked the same question, "'Informatique': What's in a Name?" and had reached the same conclusion in his essay "Defining Discipline", in Ch. Freksa, M. Jantzen, R. Valk (eds.), *Foundations of Computer Science: Potential – Theory – Cognition* (Springer: Berlin, Heidelberg, New York 1997): "But the German 'Informatik' made a strange twist: While it uses the French word, it sticks firmly to the American usage of computer science (with elements from computer engineering)." Together with many colleagues, Coy would like *Informatik* to be something quite different; but it is not yet, and it has not been so historically. See, *inter alia*, his "Für eine Theorie der Informatik!" in Wolfgang Coy *et al.* (eds.) *Sichtweisen der Informatik* (Braunschweig, Wiesbaden: Vieweg, 1992), 17-32.

Science as Software

A major theme of my essay is the inversion suggested in the title. In some instances, the science of computation has laid the groundwork for computational science. What began as an effort to establish the scientific foundations of programs and programming has led to the application of the resulting theory back onto the sciences; the field of cellular automata is a good example. Some members of the workshop felt that in so moving from theoretical computer science to computational science, I was skipping over the sciences on which developers draw in designing software. Critics pointed for example to the various fields of psychology applied to computer-human interfaces, but one might equally well have included the perceptual, optical, and mathematical issues involved in the development of computer graphics. Indeed, the whole field of artificial intelligence would then fall under the scope of software as science. Given that AI was the context for seminal work in theoretical computer science, most notably McCarthy's formal semantics, there is certainly an argument for including it.

However, once one becomes that inclusive, it is hard to see how to distinguish the science of programs and programming from programming itself. As maligned as the dichotomy between "pure" and "applied" has recently become, it perhaps retains some value here. It is a question of focus and motivation. Does one want to understand the nature of programs and programming, or does one write programs for the purpose of achieving or understanding something else? In the latter case, the science applied offers no insight into the nature of software. Indeed, as I argue in conclusion, the software more often becomes a means of investigating the science, even to the point of replacing the science's real-world objects.

Where one might be able to argue for the incorporation of science into software for the sake of the software is the recent use of biological models for "growing" software. Albert Endres alluded to it in his comment on James Tomayko's paper.[48] However, here it is worth noting that the biological models themselves are the product of the science of software. Genetic algorithms are the outgrowth of research into complex adaptive systems, which themselves grow out of the study of cellular automata, which in turn stem from John von Neumann's "General and Logical Theory of Automata." If I may introduce yet another scheme of agendas, Fig. 4 shows a sketch of the path that leads from von Neumann to Santa Fe. Note the fork that links theoretical computer science to cellular automata. Clearly, the scheme defines an agenda for the history of software, but it seems to me to be included in the complex of issues to which I was pointing in speaking of science as software.

---

[48] "We certainly cannot expect that the scientific basis of software can come from physics as in the older engineering branches. It may come from mathematics or from biology. Mathematics has clearly brought some help already, be it in cryptology or in program proof automation. Biology is largely untapped."

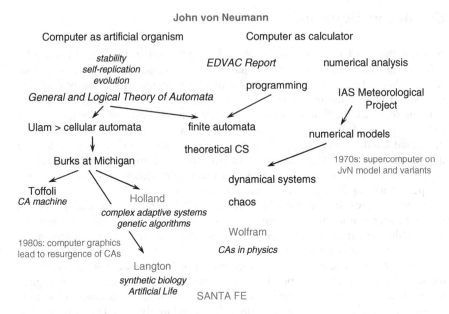

Fig. 4. Von Neumann's agendas for computer science

Nature, Science, and Mathematics

In the course of the discussion, participants asserted several principles as indisputable, in particular that science is about nature, not about things of our own creation, and that mathematics is not a science, but a tool for doing science. From the first, some people concluded that, as an artifact, software could not be the subject of a science; from the second, that grounding software in mathematics did not make a science of it. Despite my own insistence on computers and programs as artifacts, neither of these principles is quite as firm as it seems. Much of the work in history of science over the past half-century speaks against them.

The radical change in natural philosophy that we refer to as the Scientific Revolution of the 17th century rested in large part on the rejection of the classical distinction between nature and artifact. The metaphor of the "clockwork universe," which the mechanical philosophy transformed into a metaphysics of matter in motion, placed nature (or rather, nature's God) and human on a par as artisans. "Nature, to be commanded, must be obeyed," decreed Francis Bacon. While he meant thereby to deny supernatural powers to the magician, he also placed the laws of nature at the disposal of humans. Discovering those laws and then obeying them put the world at our command. Insisting that "truth and utility are one and the same thing," he demanded that scientists be able to translate their knowledge into action. That is what enfranchised experiment as a method both of investigation and demonstration. It made the laboratory a surrogate for nature, and it brought nature within the grasp of the instruments employed there. In the laboratory, scientists took nature apart to see how it works and then put a small part of nature back together to testify to their understanding. Is a nuclear explosion a natural phenomenon or a human creation? How about vaccines? How about synthetic drugs? How about gene therapy, or genetic engineering?

A second feature of the mechanical philosophy is pertinent here. It was closely tied to mathematics and thus shared in its certainty. As the new science of machines was transformed into the more universal science of mechanics, couched in the language of analysis (algebra and the calculus), it made Newton's *Principia* the touchstone for all the sciences, establishing a mathematically structured hierarchy that persists to this day.[49] By the early twentieth century, theoretical physics had all but disappeared into mathematics, leading Eugene Wigner to wonder about "The Unreasonable Effectiveness of Mathematics in the Natural Sciences," and recent philosophy of mathematics has revived the question of the subject's empirical origins.[50]

These two features come together in thermodynamics, the mathematical laws of which originated in the steam engine, abstracted by Carnot to the concept of a heat engine. The first and second laws in effect say that we can't build a perpetual-motion machine of the first or second kind. They are negative laws that set limits, without saying much about what can be achieved within those limits. Shannon's mathematical theory of communication similarly built a science out of artifacts, in this case various communications technologies. The theory sets a limit on channel capacity and specifies the tradeoff between redundancy and accuracy. The fruitful interaction between thermodynamics and information theory in explaining physical phenomena, as in the work of Stephen Hawking, seems to work against any effort at distinguishing the natural from the artificial or the mathematical from the physical.

So too with the theory of computation. Does it have laws? Surely Turing's halting theorem sets a limit on what can be computed by demonstrating what cannot be. Showing that a problem is equivalent to the halting problem relegates it to the realm of the incomputable. Similarly, the theory of computational complexity dictates through a variety of models of limited Turing machines the resources that are required to compute classes of problems and the tradeoffs between time and space that are involved in doing so. Are these scientific results about nature? Well, there's a body of literature that says yes. It is a tenet of the new computational sciences that nature can't compute any better than a Turing machine.[51] Or rather, anything nature can do, a computer can do too, given enough time and memory.

---

[49] See Michael Mahoney, "The Mathematical Realm of Nature," in *The Cambridge History of Seventeenth-Century Philosophy*, vol. 1, ed. Daniel Garber and Michael Ayers (Cambridge, 1997), 702-55.

[50] Wigner's article, based on the Richard Courant Lecture at New York University in 1959, appeared in *Communications on Pure and Applied Mathematics* 13 (1960): 1-14; cf. Mark Steiner's recent book, *The Applicability of Mathematics as a Philosophical Problem* (Cambridge, Mass., 1998).

[51] See Robert Rosen, "Effective Processes and Natural Law," in *The Universal Turing Machine: A Half-Century Survey*, ed. Rolf Herken (Wien/New York, 1994/5), 485-98; cf. his earlier article, "Church's Thesis and its Relation to the Concept of Realizability in Biology and Physics," *Bulletin of Mathematical Biophysics* 24 (1962): 375-93.

Are these laws of software? In discussing the implications of software as science for software as engineering, I addressed the limits of theoretical computer science in addressing the software development process. That process begins with the translation of a portion of the real world into the first of a series of computational models which culminate in a program running on a specific machine. Verification of the result involves two different issues: the goodness of the computational model with respect to the world it is supposed to model and the accuracy of the translation of that model into the instruction set of the computer on which it is running. Whether the model itself is adequate is ultimately not a question of software but of the developer's understanding of the world. It may be a scientific question, but the science involved is not about software or computers. The science of software as I have construed it pertains to the second issue. It begins where the model becomes a program: how, and to what extent, can we assure ourselves that the program is doing what we have written it to do? How that question has been formulated and addressed is the subject of the history of software as science, or at least that is how I construed my charge.

Commentary on Michael S. Mahoney, "Software as Science"

David Edge

Editor, *Social Studies of Science*
25 Gilmour Road
Edinburgh EH16 5NS
Scotland, UK

E-mail: d.edge@ed.ac.uk

Introduction

As its brochure announces, this conference is designed "to provide the opportunity to define and refine a research agenda" for the field of the history of software and, in this particular Workshop, to (in Michael Mahoney's words) "offer an agenda for history of software viewed as science." This Mahoney has done admirably. He lays out clear and stimulating guidelines, and suggests topics for further research which are likely to be fruitful. I will group my comments under two headings: first, some reflections on the problems of *boundary-work*; second, some suggestions for possible comparative studies.

Boundary-Work

In looking back on the development of theoretical computer science (TCS), and thus of software, it is tempting to think that two distinct kinds of *boundary drawing* are at work.[1] First, boundaries must be drawn around the *technical content* of TCS—to make it a recognisable, definable 'it'. And second, boundaries are required to distinguish 'it', as science (mathematical, empirical, etc.), from *non-science* (art, engineering, and so on). But, as Mahoney demonstrates, no such clear distinction can be made between these two aspects of TCS boundary-work. In defining what 'it' is, claims to its 'scientific' status form just one part of the whole negotiation: practitioners want to place programming "on some kind of *scientific* foundation," to be seen to be "pursuing a *scientific* enterprise." The demands and expectations of funding agencies (etc.) led TCS pioneers to make such claims, to establish credibility; and the technical content of TCS, what its practitioners actually DO, is shaped by that context.[2]

---

[1] For an extensive discussion of boundary-work, see Thomas F. Gieryn, *Cultural Boundaries of Science: Credibility on the Line* (Chicago, 1999).

[2] In discussing the controversy in AI over neural nets, Jon Guice points to the influence of military funding on the course of the controversy: Jon Guice, "Controversy and the State: Lord

When consensus finally emerges, the explanation of that consensus, Mahoney claims, "is likely to be as much social as intellectual." Being an SSK pedant of the Edinburgh School, I question whether 'social' and 'intellectual' can be thought of as independent explanatory categories, engaging in some kind of 'zero-sum' game; to my mind, it is more fruitful to think, not of *either/or*, but of *both/and*— the *social* including the *cognitive* ('intellectual'), inseparably. But I greatly welcome Mahoney's formulation: its insight is at the heart of the matter.

As Mahoney points out, this intimate relationship between the *social* and the *cognitive* implies a research emphasis on particular groups and their local circumstances—to the questions of "who, where, when, why and how?" This is a vital preliminary to any satisfactory history of this diffuse and complex topic. As Mahoney rightly suggests, such research will not only need to catalogue the names and disciplinary academic records of the pioneers and their associates, but also of the key funding committees to which they appealed for finance, and of those groups on their campuses whose support was necessary for their institutional survival. The focus here has to be very specific and *local*: the political subtleties may be surprisingly contingent. Only when such a *local* basis can be established are there any 'practices' to 'travel' (any *immutable mobiles*, to use Latour's phrase): a global profession must have such roots if it is just to (in Hamming's words) "get on with *doing* it". Mahoney argues convincingly that archival records of committees, proposals and RFPs, minutes of meetings, correspondence between members, and so on, will all illuminate the confluence of *social* and *intellectual* (and *rhetorical*) factors in the emergence of a consensual community. And I winced at Mahoney's comment that "hammering out a curriculum can be a harrowing experience," knowing how difficult that task was in refining the agenda of 'science studies'! Again, archival records of teaching in TCS are likely to reveal much of the early uncertainties.

One common boundary encountered by emerging professions with scientific aspirations is between images of *practice as art* and *practice as technique*. One thinks of the claims within clinical medicine that, despite the increase of scientific understanding, the clinician is essentially practising an 'art', exercising *clinical judgement*. Similar claims are made by econometricians,[3] and I sense, from Mahoney's comments on the increasingly perceived impotence of purely *logical*, strictly *mathematical* approaches within TCS (e.g. in Hoare's inaugural lecture), of the problematic relationship between theory and practice, and "the continuing dissonance between the premises of TCS and the experience of programming," that similar tensions and rhetoric will be visible in TCS. Many of us worry about the relation between formal models and 'reality'!

Another aspect of the elusive boundary between the *social* and the *cognitive* is reflected in Mahoney's remark that "the tools and techniques of a field embody its

ARPA and Intelligent Computing," *Social Studies of Science* 28 (1998): 103-38. For a complex discussion of the wider context of computing (and of boundaries such as that between *hardware* and *software*), see Richard Hull, "Governing the Conduct of Computing: Computer Science, the Social Sciences and Frameworks of Computing," *Accounting, Management & Information Technology* 7 (1997): 213-40. A full treatment of Hull's paper is beyond the scope of this Commentary.

[3] See Robert Evans, "Soothsaying or Science?: Falsification, Uncertainty and Social Change in Macroeconomic Modelling," *Social Studies of Science* 27 (1997): 395-438.

agenda." It is easy to see TCS as 'artificial', not 'natural': yet, as Stefan Helmreich has argued,[4] the routine techniques of those who develop the so-called *genetic algorithm* are pervaded by hidden metaphors of 'nature'. The dialectical
relation between research techniques and definitions of the problems to which
those techniques are addressed is by now a familiar theme.[5] As Alexandre Mallard
has recently said, "instruments and their metrology are elaborated simultaneously."[6] And, as Judith Schlanger put it in 1970, in discussing the technical origins
of metaphors which are central to the advances in molecular biology then emerging, "the concept of cell regulation establishes the field for which it sets the
boundaries and is the coordinator."[7] Historians could usefully explore the extent to
which such insights surfaced within TCS, and how the practitioners coped with
them.

Comparative Studies

I was puzzled as to why I had been invited to be a Commentator at this Conference until Arthur Norberg assured me that I was an expert in studying emerging
disciplines. He rested this claim mainly on the book Michael Mulkay published in
1976 on the emergence of radio astronomy in Britain (to which I have already
referred). He might have added that I also played a role in the institutionalisation
of 'science studies', and so I have just two cards in my hand. I will play the reflexive one first.

I am impressed by Mahoney's emphasis on the importance of agendas in scientific innovation, and in particular to his remark that "the standing of a field may be
measured by its capacity to set its own agenda." In science studies, we're still
struggling with this one! However, there are some similarities here with TCS: like
TCS before 1955, the agenda of science studies did not exist (as such) before
around 1970; its emergence strongly reflects local interests (and this affects both
teaching and research: curricula vary widely, and research aims have many hidden
agendas); there has been much hot air expended over its aspiration toward 'scientific' status; and achieving consensus over the definition of central problems (and
over "what a solution would look like") is difficult. But perhaps the main reason
why a reflexive history of science studies would be worthwhile (and a suggestive
parallel to that of TCS) is contained in Mahoney's comment: "Evidently, the picture which people have of a subject can significantly affect its subsequent devel-

---

[4] Stefan Helmreich, "Recombination, Rationality, Reductionism and Romantic Reactions: Culture, Computers, and the Genetic Algorithm," *Social Studies of Science* 28 (1998): 39-71. This
is a study of work at the Santa Fe Institute for the Sciences of Complexity on 'Artificial Life',
an advanced species of theoretical biology.
[5] My own introduction to the topic was in drafting David Edge and Michael Mulkay, *Astronomy
Transformed: The Emergence of Radio Astronomy in Britain* (New York, 1976), but the notion
is now almost banal. For a massive data-base on the topic, see Peter Galison, *Image and Logic:
A Material Culture of Microphysics* (Chicago, 1997).
[6] Alexandre Mallard, "Compare, Standardize and Settle Agreement: On Some Usual Metrologi-
cal Problems," *Social Studies of Science* 28 (1998): 571-601. Recent publications on metrology
offer much insight into "how practices travel."
[7] Judith Schlanger, "Metaphor and Invention," *Diogenes* 69 (1970): 21.

opment. ... Until a field gains autonomy over its own agenda, its development depends on what *other disciplines* think its practitioners *should* be doing." With recent brutal experience of the so-called 'science wars', my colleagues would empathise with that! Clearly, the extent to which emerging disciplines need to heed *outside* expectations and criticisms in order to survive may vary, but here is at least one criterion for selecting other disciplines for comparative historical study.

But, overall, my experience of radio astronomy (RA) is in sharp contrast with Mahoney's account of TCS (and of science studies). Briefly, RA always pursued goals set before its birth: it is located within physics and astrophysics (Ryle & Hewish won the Nobel Prize for *Physics*, essentially for their development of the 'aperture synthesis' technique for large aerial arrays, the foundations of which rest firmly on classical electromagnetic theory, Fourier transforms, and so on); its goals quickly elided with traditional astrophysical concerns (which gave RA its scientific credibility); and it came to public notice by offering empirical findings which could test the predictions of cosmological theory (which had a long history). And yet it was never beholden to "what *other disciplines* thought its practitioners *should* be doing." The development of radio techniques to sense astronomical emissions in that part of the electromagnetic spectrum had its own, *autonomous* drive: RA's *tools and techniques* embodied its own *agenda*. As Martin Ryle once said to me, in justifying his early observational strategy: "it didn't matter whether these radio stars were distant galaxies or Little Green Men we had to get on and map them as accurately as we could", i.e. "get on with *doing* it." But I recognised the complexity of Mahoney's 'Agendas' (Figures 1 & 2). When I interviewed a veteran radio astronomer in the Cambridge group (which was characterised by a notably coherent research strategy) and asked him to sketch out the development of his own research career, the result looked much like Mahoney's Figures! Even where the meaning of 'doing it' seems most clear, the development of instruments and the agendas they stimulate are "elaborated simultaneously."

There were, of course, many early *local difficulties* in RA in reaching some agreement over the validity of observations, but there was no significant doubt as to how these could be settled—as to "what a solution would look like." The closeness of RA's techniques to (established) physical theory, and its aims to (preexisting) astrophysical goals, largely removed the kind of uncertainty and angst that seems to have so afflicted TCS. And no-one was in any doubt as to the scientific status of RA: Ryle used his mastery of (established) physical theory and technique to remind everyone of that fact (and to exert control and leadership). To him (and many others), no radio astronomer need be beholden to anybody when it came to setting agendas! Although RA's early development exhibits much of the *local variation* that beset TCS, it would not be my best bet for a discipline with which to compare TCS.

Comparative studies of TCS (and related innovations) at the national level are likely to be productive. For example, Brigitte Chamak has recently published a study of the emergence of cognitive science in France.[8] This is not only a field close to TCS, but her paper contrasts developments in France and the USA, and

---

[8] Brigitte Chamak, "The Emergence of Cognitive Science in France: A Comparison with the USA," *Social Studies of Science* 29 (1999): 643-84.

she (briefly) compares the development of cognitive science with molecular biology (a topic mentioned by Mahoney). And Larissa Adler Lomnitz and Laura Cházaro have studied the development of computer science and applied mathematics at the National Autonomous University of Mexico,[9] stressing the significance of local contingencies. These may be useful studies on which to model comparative research.

Another potentially fruitful approach employs rhetorical analysis to reflect on many of the emergence and 'survival' strategies Mahoney describes in TCS. For example, Harro van Lente and Arie Rip have studied the establishment of membrane technology.[10] As they say in their Abstract: "The key step is the way promises put forward, and expectations being voiced, require actors to position themselves with respect to a future technology." Benoît Godin has conducted a similar study on the adoption of the microprocessor patient card in the Canadian health services.[11] There are resources here to guide and inform historical studies of TCS.

And then, of course, studies of controversies are always a fruitful source of theoretical and empirical insights. For instance, the controversy within Artificial Intelligence surrounding the 'perceptron' project (and neural nets in general) has attracted at least two recent analyses, by Mikel Olazaran and Jon Guice.[12] Those looking for "an agenda for history of computing viewed as science" may soon be embarrassed by an abundance of theoretical options!

Conclusion

In commenting on Mahoney's paper, I have added a few 'footnotes to Plato'. Mahoney has laid out the extent of the field. In focussing on the problems of *boundary-work*, and meditating on the criteria we may adopt in selecting topics for comparative analysis, I hope I have been able to strengthen his case.

---

[9] Larissa Adler Lomnitz and Laura Chárazo, "Basic, Applied and Technological Research: Computer Science and Applied Mathematics at the National Autonomous University of Mexico," *Social Studies of Science* 29 (1999): 113-34.

[10] Harro van Lente and Arie Rip, "The Rise of Membrane Technology: From Rhetorics to Social Reality," *Social Studies of Science* 28 (1998): 221-54.

[11] Benoît Godin, "The Rhetoric of a Health Technology: The Microprocessor Patient Card," *Social Studies of Science* 27 (1997): 865-902.

[12] Mikel Olazaran, "A Sociological Study of the Official History of the Perceptrons Controversy," *Social Studies of Science* 26 (1996): 611-59; Guice (n. 2 above).

Software as Science?
Commentary on Michael S. Mahoney,
"Software as Science"

Gerhard Goos

Universität Karlsruhe
Institut für Programmstrukturen u. Datenorganisation
76128 Karlsruhe
Germany

E-mail: ggoos@ipd.info.uni-karlsruhe.de

> A scientist builds in order to learn,
> an engineer learns in order to build.
> M. C. Walters[1]

Data and Information

Informatik or *informatique* are the terms used instead of *computer science* in Germany and France. The Académie Française defines it as "Science de traitement rationel, notamment par machines automatiques, de l'information considérée comme le support des connaissances humaines et des communications, dans les domaines techniques, économiques et socials."

Compared to *computer science* or the British *computing science* the notion *informatics* stresses much more the intellectual challenge of handling information in a systematic and rational way. Information in this context is the result of interpreting data encoded in writing, preferably in digital form, or in any other physical form such as acoustic or electric waves or by other electronic or magnetic means.

The methodology is based on viewing data as syntactic elements within a formal calculus and the interpretation refers to the mappings by which mathematical logic formally associates semantics with syntactic data. The result of such an interpretation may again be an element of a syntactic domain which may be subject to further interpretation. Interpretation is thus a multistep process; some early steps may be done by "des machines automatiques;" for controlling a machine these steps might already suffice; in all other cases the final interpretation of the results rests with human beings.

The data considered may be roughly grouped into two classes: the class of data which represents the process of information gathering, processing and transmission itself and the data which stem from applications and are processed for gaining insight and new information about the application area. The first class leads to insights into methodologies of information processing and their further develop-

---

[1] Meredith C. Walters, "Letter to the Editor," *IEEE Software* 15/1 (1998): 11.

ment; these methodologies are then applied to the second class in order to gain a better understanding and to create new ways of handling the application field. Informatics (or computer science) mostly deals with the first class; however, in practice the applications can be found in almost every field of science and engineering. After all, whatever human beings attempt to achieve, they achieve it by the information processing capability of their brain; even if the result was physically tangible it would have been previously conceived as well as its properties predicted by information processing based on physical or chemical laws.

Analytic and Algorithmic Knowledge

Traditionally science is the accumulation of factual knowledge and knowledge about processes in order to satisfy human curiosity and especially to predict future behavior based on past experience. In this respect informatics is not different from other sciences.

However, when it comes to applying this knowledge there is a striking difference: Informatics is considering constructive processes which achieve results *algorithmically*, i.e. in a finite number of steps. The steps represent elementary operations which may be implemented based on physical or chemical processes. In the field of hardware design informatics is concerned with the implementation of these elementary operations (which may be rather complex when viewed in the physics and engineering perspective). However, software represents this *algorithmic knowledge* in pure form: It solely consists of data which when interpreted in an appropriate context describe algorithms. Computers, also in the form of embedded systems, and humans are equally qualified for the interpretation of these data although the machinery interprets much faster and with less errors.

Software represents algorithmic knowledge in contrast to the analytic knowledge which we are used to in many other sciences. Herbert A. Simon[2] discusses at length that algorithmic knowledge is seen as a relative newcomer amongst scientists although the concept goes back to Euclid. When we describe behavior in nature or society we are not used to consider such behavior as a step by step process based on causality. This is the reason why "software as science" is increasingly considered as a model for arguing about many engineering disciplines.

Criteria

Michael S. Mahoney[3] and others make a subtle difference between "theoretical computer science" and "computer science" itself as seen by its respective proponents. This difference seems to stem from differing yardsticks for success: Theorists strive for establishing "eternal truths" similar to mathematicians; computer science as a whole is much more bound to the technical conditions on which computing and information processing are taking place, such as the von-Neumann computer, distributed computer systems, the internet, etc.

[2] Herbert A. Simon, *The Sciences of the Artificial,* 3rd ed. (Cambridge, Mass., 1996).
[3] Michael S. Mahoney, "Software as Science – Science as Software," *This volume* (2000).

In both cases correctness of results is mandatory like in any other science. A theory does not make any assumptions about the context in which a result is considered; logical consistency is the sole correctness criterion. Practical computer science adds optimality and other criteria for quality which have no counterpart in theory: whether the solution to the problem of a traveling salesman is at an optimum may be judged independently of technology; but the usefulness of a solution to a real-time problem depends on whether the externally given time limits are met or not; if not the solution may cause damage even if it is correct in the logical sense.

Additional criteria such as usefulness become particularly significant when they depend on economics: Systems such as medical patient control systems on which the well being of humans depend should function correctly (or nearly correctly) no matter how the conditions of use are disturbed. For example, correct functioning of hardware under all circumstances and protection against all kinds of accidents potentially caused by overstressed or tired nurses is required. However correctness is becoming extremely expensive if the usual preconditions are no longer met; at the latest failure is unavoidable if electricity is turned off (and the replacement by batteries also fails and the replacement of the replacement fails ...).

Models and Reality

Michael S. Mahoney[4] rightly states that software is an artifact; there is nothing natural about software except that nature is sometimes also executing algorithms, i.e., to a certain degree nature produces software. To be more precise: we do not know whether nature is really executing algorithms; we only state that algorithms are sometimes a good conceptual model for explaining natural behavior.

This issue of modeling leads to the most fascinating aspect of software. We could model the falling of a series of dominoes as an algorithmic process and in this way predict the behavior of complicated domino patterns. However such explanations could be replaced by other ones which do not use the notion of an algorithm. On the other hand, if software engineers invent models of possible behavior, then create software for representing such a model, together with appropriate hardware, they will create a system which exclusively shows exactly the behavior of the underlying model; any other explanation will fail in its attempt to correctly and fully describe the system in this respect. Whereas the model originally represented an object in the Platonian world it is becoming reality when it is represented in software: a radio, TV-set or the internet nowadays only consist of 10-20% hardware, the remainder is software.

Turning a conceptual model into reality is in my opinion the fundamental change when we consider software as science: whereas science is traditionally used to analyze reality and to predict its future behavior we have in this case a methodology to force predictions to become true. It is true that this methodology can also be found in other engineering disciplines: the invention of the railway, of cars and of airplanes has had deep social and even cultural implications and has changed reality. However the creation of software has been representing this

---

[4] *Ibid.*

methodology in its purest form so far. Of course, social and cultural implications often turn out to be different from forecasts also in the case of software; forecasts becoming true mostly apply to technological forecasts. This restriction, however, does not fundamentally change the picture.

The Agenda

Michael S. Mahoney[5] asks for the agenda when exploring software as a science.

We should first mention that the whole title "software as science" of the undertaking may be questioned: software is commonly viewed as a product; practitioners know by experience that the hidden work required for documentation, packaging, adequate user interfaces, etc. is comparatively higher than what is required for developing the underlying algorithms. Thus "algorithms as science" seems to be a better title leaving software totally as a subject to the engineers.

However the latter title would ignore that in our days most of the software systems are in fact *reactive systems*: They process one or more flows of input data in order to create flows of output data. The main difference to pure algorithms consists in feedback-loops by which outputs of the system and reactions to these outputs by the environment may influence future inputs. Algorithms may be viewed as implementations of mappings in the sense of mathematics and thus can be based on a large frame of mathematical knowledge. Compared to algorithms the modeling and exploration of reactive systems represent a far more difficult task. Already the notion of correctness may be difficult to define due to environmental dependencies.

Besides we should also mention the so-called *software science*[6] which bears no relation to the notion of science used so far. It proposes some formulae for measuring the complexity while dealing with modifications and corrections of malfunctioning during the maintenance phase, i.e., it solely belongs to the sector of software engineering.

A software engineer might not be the right person to propose the agenda for historians. However, if I have a try the following points seem to be important:

- What makes the fundamental difference between software (or algorithms, or reactive systems) considered as science and other sciences? Certainly it is not only the fact that we consider artifacts since this is a matter we share with many other engineering disciplines.
- What actually is the relation between the subjects studied by computer scientists and the subjects introduced by applications? Why doesn't public opinion measure progress in informatics in terms of scientific progress as in other scientific disciplines but in terms of improvement of applications or invention of new applications?
- How did the relation between syntactic data and their semantic interpretation develop in the course of time? This is closely connected to the development

---

[5] *Ibid.*
[6] Maurice H. Halstead, *Elements of Software Science* (New York, 1977).

of the notions of computability and decidability as well as the development of
semantic theories and mathematical logic.

- What are the leading means and tools for developing software such as formal
  specification methods, programming languages, configuration tools, algorithms and data structures, etc. and how did they develop?

Discussion following "Software as Science"

Thomas Haigh

University of Pennsylvania
Department of the History and Sociology of Science
303 Logan Hall
Philadelphia, PA 19104-6304
USA

E-mail: thaigh@sas.upenn.edu

A central topic of discussion was the extent to which Mahoney's paper had covered the whole range of sciences associated with software. Some speakers suggested that it devoted undue attention to narrow areas within mathematical science concerned with automata and formal languages. Both other areas of mathematical computer science (particularly the study of algorithms and data structures) and other fields of science (such as psychology) were suggested as alternatives deserving careful study. Did an exclusive focus on theoretical computer science as the science of software take what might have been a valid conclusion and embed it as a premise? Another interesting suggestion for a "software science" was the body of study concerned with establishing quantitative measures of different software characteristics such as quality, reliability and maintainability.

Mahoney acknowledged the tight focus of his paper, but argued that his research suggested that this reflected dominant use of the idea of "science" by early computer scientists. He also suggested that a properly historical understanding of the relationship between computer science and psychology would reveal that modern psychology was itself fundamentally shaped by the emergence of the computer.

Other discussants followed Goos in questioning the extent to which software could be said to be scientific in the first place. This stream of discussion followed two basic paths. In the first discussants questioned the connection of computer science to the craft activity of programming and hence to software. In the second, the scientific credentials of computer science itself were questioned from a philosophical view point—if it doesn't make predictions or provide laws about the natural world can it be a science? A similar question, directed to the "science as software" part of the paper, asked whether we should question the scientific status of modeling work performed with no direct correspondence to reality.

Mahoney dealt with all these questions by asserting his neutrality as a mere reporter of the ideas of practitioners. He suggested that trying to define whether or not software was science was the wrong issue. There were different definitions for different times, circumstances and locations. The question really is WHY is computer science called science and WHO is adopting the term computer science. Mahoney reminded the participants that historians want to avoid definitions—that debate is for the pioneers/practitioners of a specific time. Historians do not need to comment upon whether software is science or not but to watch other people doing so, look at what actually went on and how it was connected to advancement. They need to look at what practitioners said and ask "What did they have in mind?" It was important for historians to have no stake in whether software was science or not otherwise they would prejudge the results of their research.

Like Edge, Mahoney felt that boundary work was a crucial part of science and must be performed by the scientific communities themselves. Edge remarked that he wished to thank conference participants for their practical example of boundary setting in action during the discussions on is software science? Mahoney also found Simon's formulation of "the sciences of the artificial" to be a salient framework for contemplation of these issues. He suggested that the correspondence of mechanical models to the natural world was not a new concern for science, but could be traced back to the Enlightenment.

This led to a stream of discussion on whether the particular types of theoretical knowledge used to establish software as science had changed over time. In general an early concern with automata theory gave way to a later focus on algorithmics. One participant asked whether both of these could now be seen as "fads," given that each enjoyed a comparatively short vogue at different times in different parts of the world. Goos replied that this shift reflected not mere fashion, but a success in putting some kinds of software (such as compilers) onto firm theoretical ground that had yet to be matched in other areas such as operating systems.

Part 2
Software as Engineering

Software as Engineering

James E. Tomayko

Director
Master of Software Engineering Program
and
Department of History
Carnegie Mellon University
5000 Forbes Avenue
Pittsburgh, PA 15213
USA

E-mail: jet@cs.cmu.edu

Introduction

> "The phrase 'software engineering' was deliberately chosen to be provocative ..."[1]

Those words, in the introduction to the proceedings of the first NATO conference on software engineering, unleashed a veritable storm of often acrimonious debate on the viability of software as engineering. The inconsequence of this debate of more than thirty years is evident from an announcement of Pittsburgh's Carnegie Science Center's activities for this year's National Engineer's Week. The note said that, "engineers from all disciplines—chemical, electrical, mechanical, civil" would participate.[2] It is somewhat strange that in the year 2000, aeronautical, bio, hydraulic, computer, and software engineers have no place even under the seemingly comprehensive umbrella of "all." The "other" engineers may take solace that the premier engineering institution in the region, Carnegie Mellon University, celebrating one hundred years in 2000, has only those four disciplines plus materials science and engineering in its engineering school. The Electrical Engineering Department, in a concession to the fiscal tail that wags the dog, renamed itself the Electrical and Computer Engineering Department, but otherwise the departments are as founded nearly a century ago. Meanwhile, across town at Robert Morris College, the school is trying to carve a niche with logistics engineering and software engineering, as neither program exists for undergraduates at any of the plethora of Pittsburgh colleges and universities. Of course, many critics would comment that neither program should exist at *any* college or university. On one hand, some would say that logistics engineering is some collection of activities

---

[1] Peter Naur and Brian Randell, eds., *Software Engineering: A Report on a Conference Sponsored by the NATO Science Committee, Garmisch, Germany, 7ᵗʰ to 11ᵗʰ October 1968* (Brussels, Scientific Affairs Division, NATO, 1969), 13.

[2] *Carnegie* 65/1 (January-February 2000): 35.

that are hardly engineering in nature, resulting in a kluge like "maintenance engineering," which further dignifies janitorial work. On the other hand, some regard software engineering as subordinate to computer science, or merely practiced by "real" engineers as part of their daily work. Such is the nature of the debate.

The purpose of this paper is to set the context for a research agenda for examining software practice as engineering, not to resolve the debate. My own contributions to finalizing this discussion are elsewhere.[3] The reason why we have so much difficulty recognizing the engineering aspects of software development is that there is no obvious relation to natural science. The older engineering disciplines enumerated in the Science Center advertisements are all based on physics (if we accept breaking up chemistry into its component parts). Even bioengineering disciplines such as genetic engineering are grounded in physics. All these fields, including software engineering, claim mathematics as their "language." Software engineering is challenged as an engineering discipline because its seems to lack a physical basis. Mathematics is indeed its language, but the absence of something to physically touch is a problem for its adherents seeking legitimacy.[4] It seems that the distance from nature exacerbates the problem. One can reason that physics underlies electronics, which enables the physical medium (computers) on which software resides, but that is a long way to go. Basically, science is the study of natural phenomena in the natural world, and computer science is the study of phenomena surrounding an artifact, so there is no actual help there. The distance is still too great for comfort. The interesting challenge for historians is to recognize the activities of software engineers and differentiate them from the activities of computer scientists.

The History of Engineering

So, let us try to make more sense of software as engineering. The best way to examine software engineering is to first identify the basic themes of traditional engineering, and put software into that context. How do we study engineering? There appear to be three major themes, independent of the type of engineering discussed. The first broad theme is, in apparent contradiction, the "art of engineering," the collection of compromises that an engineer makes, most often expressed in design. The second theme is the acquisition and application of engineering knowledge, in which resides the claim of "engineering as applied science." The third, fairly recent, theme is the role of failure. This may be related most closely to the second theme, as it is a way of acquiring knowledge, but for now we shall keep it separate for the reason that it provides a contrast: acquiring knowledge through a negative, while the second theme stresses the positive.

---

[3] James E. Tomayko, "An Historian's View of Software Engineering," *Proceedings of the 13th Conference on Software Engineering Education and Training*, IEEE, March 2000; "Forging a Discipline: An Outline History of Software Engineering Education," *Annals of Software Engineering* 6 (1998): 3-18.

[4] Michael Davis used the lack of physicality as one of his central arguments against the existence of software engineering in Michael Davis, "Defining 'Engineer:' How to do it and Why it Matters," *ASEE Journal of Engineering Education* (April 1996): 97-101.

The next sections examine these three themes in turn, to discover what we gain from them about the history of engineering. The following sections revisit the three themes in the context of software engineering. We try to suggest the location of fallow fields of research for each of these areas in software engineering.

The Art of Engineering

Thirty years ago two professors at Carnegie Mellon produced a text unselfconsciously entitled *An Introduction to the Art of Engineering* to accompany a survey course in engineering and its sub-fields for young, inexperienced engineers. The authors continuously stressed that engineering products require compromise, what later would be called "satisficing." They write,

> The engineer must deal in realism; and whether it is because of the economics of time or money or simply because of the sheer complexity of the problem, a "perfect" solution can rarely, if ever, be achieved or even justified in practice.[5]

They also discuss the aspects of art related to what they term the "creativity gap." This is the vast chasm between idea and physical reality. An example is the idea of building a rocket to go the moon and its physical result in the Saturn V, winner of a mechanical engineering achievement award. The authors point out that even though there are many engineering handbooks (even a *Handbook of Astronautical Engineering*[6]), there was, and is, no *Handbook for Going to the Moon*. It remains too complex a problem for stock solutions. Intuition is honored as a means to cross the creativity gap. Yet still, when there was a Chief Scientist of the Software Engineering Institute (a contradiction of Orwellian caliber), there was a project that became a diversion into "Handbook Engineering." The software engineers of ten years ago saw the development of handbooks as a necessary sign of maturity (after all, the first engineering handbooks appeared in 1853![7]). However, "it is usually a shock to (engineering) students to discover what a small percentage of decisions made by a designer are made on the basis of the kind of calculation he has spent so much time learning in school," or finding in a handbook.[8] Still, software engineers find this part of engineering knowledge compelling, even calling for the development of a handbook for software architectures, a sub-field of software engineering where art should dominate.[9]

Historians of engineering and many thoughtful engineers agree that, "the successful design of real things in a contingent world will always be based more on art than on science."[10] Designers bring "feel" to their work that is used to bridge

---

[5] Alvin S. Weinstein and Stanley W. Angrist, *An Introduction to the Art of Engineering* (Boston, 1970), 5.

[6] Heinz H. Koelle, *Handbook of Astronautical Engineering* (New York, 1961).

[7] James Kip Finch, *Engineering and Western Civilization* (New York, 1951), 89.

[8] "Report on Engineering Design," *Journal of Engineering Education*, April 1961, 645-60.

[9] Mark Klein and Rick Kazman, *Attribute-Based Architectural Styles* (Pittsburgh, Pa., Carnegie Mellon University Software Engineering Institute, TR-022, October 1999), 2.

[10] Eugene S. Ferguson, *Engineering and the Mind's Eye* (Boston, 1992), 194.

the creativity gap.[11] These solutions are often in visual form, ranging from back-of-an-envelope sketches to complex computer-aided designs.

Engineering as Applied Science

A healthy line of inquiry has been the acquisition of engineering knowledge. Many contend that engineering science (that part of science specifically facilitating engineering practice) is the basis of all engineering knowledge. How, then, was this knowledge acquired? Some argue that it is discovered through practice.[12] Even those who support the notion of engineering science as the source of knowledge acknowledge art in engineering practice is still important.[13] Nevertheless, the common knowledge of engineering science (taught in school and perhaps captured in handbooks) makes it possible for engineers of lesser talents than an acknowledged "Great Designer" to make contributions.[14] Average engineers can apply the principles of engineering and create artifacts that would be beyond their abilities if it were not for the quantification of engineering knowledge and the capture of successful art. This theme developed because there seems to be a body of knowledge between science and technology. Recent bibliography supports this view.[15]

Quite frankly, I have opposed establishing the legitimacy of software engineering by the development of underlying science.[16] I agree with the notion that "we are what we do," and that "society classifies a member according to his or her role in it."[17] Therefore, doing engineering activities is enough for engineering to be recognized as happening.

The Role of Failure in Engineering

Henry Petroski wrote two books over the last fifteen years that assert that engineering is a process of finding the limits of successful designs through failure.[18] The second book is entitled *Design Paradigms*, and contains an argument similar to that independently made by David Wojick twenty years ago (and myself more recently in talks at several places).[19] The essence of this argument is that the use of paradigms, even if captured merely in folklore instead of handbooks, indicates some engineering maturity. The acquisition of new engineering knowledge is

[11] Louis Bucciarelli, *Designing Engineers* (Cambridge, Mass.,1994), 76.

[12] Walter Vincenti, *What Engineers Know and How They Know It* (Baltimore, 1990).

[13] Finch (n. 7 above), 88.

[14] Finch, 93.

[15] David F. Channell, *The History of Engineering Science: An Annotated Bibliography* (New York, 1989).

[16] Most recently in James E. Tomayko, "An Historian's View of Software Engineering."

[17] Ervan Garrison, *A History of Engineering and Technology: Artful Methods* (Boca Raton, Fla., 1991).

[18] Henry Petroski, *Design Paradigms* (New York, 1994); *To Engineer is Human: The Role of Failure in Successful Design* (New York, 1985).

[19] David Wojick, "The Structure of Technological Revolutions," in *The History and Philosophy of Technology*, ed. George Bugliarello and Dean Doner (Urbana, Ill., 1979), 238-61; James E. Tomayko, "Paradigm Shifts and the Maturity of Engineering Practice," The Society of the History of Technology Annual Meeting, London, The University of Ulster, Belfast, the Dagstuhl Conference on the History of Software, Germany, all in 1996.

accelerated when these paradigms fail. This is precisely the argument made by Thomas Kuhn in *The Structure of Scientific Revolutions*. He uses the term "normal science" for a paradigm of scientific understanding.[20] The practice of "normal engineering" (in Wojick's understanding) is what our "average engineer" is doing applying the engineering knowledge he learned in school. The fact that he did learn it in school is evidence that it forms a paradigm. Unfortunately, the word "paradigm" is crippled by what computer scientists' call "overloading," or using the same name for different parameter lists. Suspend criticism of our (mis)understanding of the term for a moment and consider this: the Tacoma Narrows bridge had a certain amount of strengthening in its deck. How much strengthening to use was a function of the designer's notion of the paradigm of a suspension bridge, and the details of strengthening, over a large gap. The bridge collapsed. The paradigm of suspension bridge design survived intact. The notions of bridge deck thickness relative to length and environment did not; new knowledge replaced it. Petroski details this and a host of other examples of acquiring new engineering knowledge in his two books.

We see that engineering can be considered an art and a science. It acquires new knowledge by success and failure. It creates with or without scientific knowledge. It is a mass of contradictions, and yet has been around as a recognizable discipline for millennia and as a formal body of academically transmittable knowledge for a couple centuries. Should software engineering have it any easier?

The History of Software as Engineering

There have been very few attempts to collect the history of software, which is why we are having this meeting. William Aspray prepared a bibliography concentrating on secondary sources in the history of software in 1988.[21] He believed by this time that software had "attained the same level of historical study and interest as had the wider subject of computing in 1979." There was an enormous increase in the number of studies of computing history at about that time. Figure 1 shows the increase of works of computer history indexed in *Technology and Culture's* annual bibliography. It illustrates the rapid upward turn in the production of computer history beginning about 1979. However, studies of software within those totals have remained static at between ten and twenty or so annually since 1984. With a wider definition of software, James W. Cortada published a guide to the history of computer applications.[22] He grossly divided the references between 1950-1965 and 1966-1990. Within each division there is a plethora of finer grains, such as "Computer Dating," perhaps of interest to social historians but hardly of the same import as the development of subroutines. His decision to cast a wide net resulted from his opinion that a big gap in the history of computing was the consideration of what the machines were for. Where his 1990 bibliography had only a relatively small section on applications, here he devoted 1600 entries to them. Our

---

[20] Thomas S. Kuhn, *The Structure of Scientific Revolutions*, 2nd ed. (Chicago, 1970).

[21] William Aspray, "An Annotated Bibliography of Secondary Sources on the History of Software," *Annals of the History of Computing* 9 (1988): 291-343.

[22] James W. Cortada, *A Bibliographic Guide to the History of Computer Applications, 1950–1990* (Westport, Conn., 1996).

intent lies somewhere in between: slightly over a decade later, we still stand at Aspray's takeoff point, but we are not interested in every application of software, just those that can cast light on the development of software within the three themes of the history of engineering.

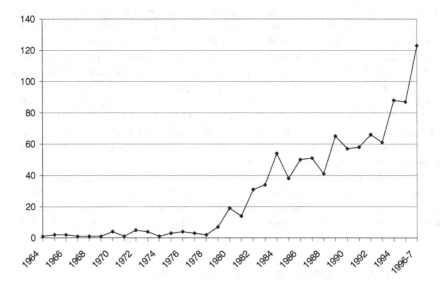

Fig. 1. Paper production—computer history

The Art of Software Engineering

We are not even sure when to date the realization that software development required design knowledge. Early programming was function-based and more closely resembled the forms of its underlying mathematics. Maurice Wilkes' team at Cambridge created the notion of subroutines while working with the EDSAC.[23] This was an important first step toward the ability to design programs by functional decomposition, but the entire field stagnated for a decade while programs were tied to idiosyncratic machine languages. The nearly simultaneous advent of higher level languages and large applications resulted in some new uses of design tools such as means of visualization (flow charts). These showed both structure, logic, and flow. Several additional visualization tools accompanied the further development of functional decomposition. These included data flow diagrams,

---

[23] Maurice V. Wilkes, David J. Wheeler, and Stanley Gill, *The Preparation of Programs for an Electronic Digital Computer* (reprint, Los Angeles,1982).

IBM's HIPO diagrams, Warnier-Orr, and the like.[24] When used in concert with simple structure charts, design abstractions could be shown.

In the 1970s, there was an explosion of conscious thinking about design, which yielded David Parnas' concept of information hiding, work on abstract data types, and the general realization of the importance of coupling and cohesion.[25] These concepts led to object oriented design in the 1980s and the idea of software architecture in the 1990s.[26] Study of software architecture has resulted in the recognition of design patterns such as "pipe-and-filter," "blackboard," "object," and the like. There is even a movement to discover and use design patterns on a scale smaller than that of a system.[27]

Threads of historical research in this thematic context could be the development of visualization, development of individual design methods inspired by stepwise refinement and functional decomposition, and the concepts surrounding objects. There will always be voluminous technical documentation to serve as a springboard for framing historical questions.[28] However, what is needed here is some work in oral history and the farming of notebooks and other diary-like sources to find the origins of these design ideas. Except for technical surveys that have a brief historical note to set context, there is little. In fact, histories of the origins of programming languages come close in that they usually have an underlying design paradigm (there is that word again!) that they implement, such as objects and C++, data abstraction and Ada, and so on. There have been conferences and books about the history of languages, but not about design ideas.[29]

Software as Applied Science

The second theme that pervades engineering history is the application of scientific principles. Michael Mahoney is dealing with the role of science in the development of software in this conference, and I will leave this topic in his able hands.[30] Here, however, we can briefly mention some times where science was self-consciously applied to software engineering. Some have argued that the underlying science is still not complete enough to truly support software engineering in the same way as it does in older engineering disciplines.[31] On this point we agree, but engineering knowledge is gained by practice first, then later by scientific ex-

---

[24] Roger S. Pressman, *Software Engineering,* 2nd ed. (New York, 1987); older editions such as the second and third of this venerable survey text have excellent brief descriptions of these visualization tools.

[25] David L. Parnas, "On the Criteria to be Used in Decomposing Systems into Modules," *Communications of the ACM* 12/15 (1972):1053-8.

[26] David Garlan and Mary Shaw, *Software Architecture: Perspectives on an Emerging Discipline* (Upper Saddle River, N.J., 1996).

[27] Erich Gamma et al., *Design Patterns* (Reading, Mass., 1995).

[28] Edward N. Yourdon, ed., *Classics in Software Engineering* (New York, 1979); *Writings of the Revolution: Selected Readings in Software Engineering* (New York, 1982).

[29] Jean Sammet, *Programming Languages: History and Fundamentals* (Englewood Cliffs, N.J., 1969); Richard L. Wexelblat, *History of Programming Languages* (New York, 1981).

[30] Michael S. Mahoney, "Software as Science—Science as Software," presented at the International Conference on the History of Computing 2000, Paderborn, Germany, 5-8 April 2000.

[31] Mary Shaw, "Prospects for an Engineering Discipline of Software," *IEEE Software* 7/6 (1990): 15-24.

planation of successful practice. The fact that there are not scientific explanations of all of software engineering fits a nascent field. There are still examples where science has risen to the support of software engineering. These examples are uniformly from mathematics, which has turned out to be software engineering's language and also its foundation.[32]

A specific example is the development of the "Cleanroom" technique. The historical study of its development has already lost some focus because of the death of one of its most accomplished originators, Harlan Mills. The scientific basis of Cleanroom was developed by Mills and enlarged into a book on the mathematical basis of structured programming.[33] Mills started by declaring that each module of a program is a mathematical function, subject to proof. In *Structured Programming: Theory and Practice,* he and his co-authors developed the "function-theoretic" view of programs and made proofs of program structures. The program structures were the same "sequence, selection, iteration" structures that had been earlier proved by Böhm and Jacopini to be the only structures needed to program a Turing machine.[34] Thus there is a line of scientific principles originating in 1930s computability theory running through the 1960s proofs of program structures to Mills' provable programs-as-functions. Note that programmers wrote software containing these structures before the proofs existed. In fact, languages were designed with these structures before the proofs. However, after these proofs were discovered and the application of program structures was more rigorous, the resulting software has been of much higher quality.[35] The Cleanroom technique is still being refined by the inclusion of process principles, but its scientific basis is twenty years old and unchanged.[36] It remains an example of the use of "timeless" science to make engineering stronger. The provable program structures are building blocks so basic that they rival the science applied to civil engineering, such as the strength of materials. There the most fundamental principles are those of physics, whereas mathematics serves software. Dr. Mahoney's contribution to this discussion will help set the research agenda for this theme.

The Role of Failure in Software Engineering

The Cleanroom example is the creation of high quality software through principles discovered and applied in a constructive way. The third theme in the history of engineering is the development of knowledge by learning from failure. There seems to be many opportunities to derive such knowledge in software engineering. The field seems riddled with failures: projects fail and products are delivered with

[32] Michael S. Mahoney, "The History of Computing in the History of Technology," *Annals of the History of Computing*10/2 (1988): 113-25.

[33] Richard C. Linger, Harlan D. Mills, and Bernard I. Witt, *Structured Programming: Theory and Practice* (Reading, Mass., 1979).

[34] Corrado Böhm and Giuseppe Jacopini, "Turing Machines and Languages with Only Two Formation Rules," in *Classics in Software Engineering*, ed. Edward Yourdon (New York, 1979), 13-28.

[35] Harlan D. Mills, Michael Dyer, and Richard C. Linger, "Cleanroom Software Engineering," *IEEE Software* (September 1987): 19-24.

[36] Stacy J. Prowell et al., *Cleanroom Software Engineering: Technology and Process* (Reading, Mass., 1999).

many defects. In light of this, some think that software can not be engineering because of the types and pervasiveness of "bugs," which are forms of failure. However, this seeming lack of quality is persistent in other forms of engineering. Petroski wrote, "the mass produced mechanical or electronic object undergoes much of its debugging and evolution after it is offered to the consumer."[37] Note the phrase "mass produced." Single or low-production items such as spacecraft have much higher quality than the average product of an automobile company, even though there is over a century of design and production experience in the latter. The software in the Space Shuttle certainly "crashes" less often than that of a mass-consumer word processing package, certainly the one that I am using. First of all, these defects are not the types of failure Petroski describes. They are not the sort that can serve to fix the boundaries of engineering. Most bugs are preventable, but their prevention is economically prohibitive. One of the reasons that the cost of a spacecraft is so great is that it must be as close to perfect as possible. The frequent failures of NASA's recent "better, faster, cheaper" programs, which are all invariably cheaper first, prove the economic argument.

The kinds of failures that need to be studied are the kinds that reveal the boundaries of possibility. The trouble is, the boundaries to software engineering are constantly changing, like the world map in the twentieth century. Over the history of, say, civil engineering, designs have become more elegant as a result of incrementally courting failure. Massive stone bridges give way over the centuries to ethereal suspension bridges. Economy in materials and cost are gained until a bridge winds up in a ravine, and the subsequent investigation reveals a trifle too much acceptance of risk than engineering knowledge justified. The failure of a bridge due to shortcomings in materials or workmanship can be repeated if one were foolish enough to do so. This is because the laws of physics do not change. Something about gravity is true today *and* tomorrow. However, a software engineer designing a system with strict performance constraints may come up against limitations in using structures that require context switches one day, and these constraints may be lifted the next due to the advent of a faster processor. Once I was studying the best means to construct a system using a 32-bit processor, while the main development group built the system for 16-bit machines. It was a decades-long project, and we had every right to expect the larger machines to be ubiquitous by the time we neared production, and we wanted to be ready with a design optimized for them. At that level, it was like expecting the replacement of stone with steel as a bridging material. This potential for revolutionary change makes the use of failure to find boundaries more difficult, but not impossible. Going down a level, the speed of light is still the same, but as we have noted, software engineering is not that close to nature, meaning that there are very few immutable principles.

So, what are the uses of this theme in the history of software engineering? One use is helping to understand the kinds of restraints on engineering practice at different times; another use is capturing lessons learned. The ways that avionics software has been implemented over the years were driven by the limitations of processors and strict performance constraints. For instance, how much of the development of time-sliced, cyclic operating systems was due to a desire to avoid

---

[37] Petroski, *To Engineer is Human* (n. 18 above), 26.

starvation of processes on barely-capable computers and how much was a desire for simplicity or elegance? The Charles Stark Draper Laboratory has consistently designed their embedded systems with such operating systems even after computers powerful enough to more easily run the more efficient asynchronous priority-driven operating systems became available. Did Draper Lab have a failure or predict a failure that steered them away from priority-driven systems? Did they find a boundary and decided to stay within it even though it is now less restrictive?

The study of stillborn software systems ought to be fruitful from both the historical and practical software engineering angles. For many years, most software projects had little prospects for full success. The users of software have demonstrated the patience of Job, both in terms of waiting for delivery and actually using what is delivered. Now in its fourth decade, the "software crisis" evidenced by schedule and budget overruns begs explanation. It is the software equivalent of the Hundred Year's War, very lengthy with sporadic hot flashes. Does it persist because software engineers are blind to boundaries? In many cases, software engineers go boldly forward into thickets of risk that would halt engineers in more established disciplines. Why? What is the real effect of software engineers not having to worry about erasing their mistakes with jackhammers? Does ease of failure actually promote failure? Aside from the lack of historical studies of successful projects, there is a void in the literature of failed projects.

Summary

The history of software engineering seems to fit the themes of the history of engineering. There is much to do related to the art of engineering. Software engineers, in a misguided attempt to gain legitimacy, deny the artistic aspects of their field. However, Fred Brooks found a truism that indicates that art, rather than handbook engineering, is clearly dominant. He points out that the systems that people have grown to dislike (COBOL, the VMS operating system, the Ada language), were done by committees using the "leading" principles of the day. Those that people like (the C language, the Unix operating system, Java) are the products of one or two minds. This seems to indicate that the elegance coming from an idea carefully husbanded by the originator has pleasing qualities even in software. However, this art is poorly explained. Literature focused on the acquisition of software engineering knowledge through science is quite sparse. Finally, software engineering knowledge acquired by failure is voluminous, though poorly documented. There appears to be plenty to do.

Let us discuss the key source materials of software engineering history. The traditional primary sources of institutional history, oral histories and organizational records, have their place in studying the history of software engineering. In the case of the development of a new language or system by a single virtuoso, oral history is all that there is. Very rarely do such people keep the types of notebooks that capture the genesis of ideas in the laboratory sciences. In the case of the histories of large projects, memos and project plans (if available) are useful, but in the case of projects that are considered failures, even if they result in new knowledge, institutions are reluctant to share their records. The historian is forced into becoming almost exclusively an oral historian interviewing engineers and managers who have retired or left the organization. There is a movement in the industry for projects to capture "lessons learned" in a post-mortem document for each project. The NASA standard for project documentation even requires these. This is a fine way to record the discovery of new engineering knowledge. However, companies are very reluctant to share these reports with any customer, let alone the government, because they seem overly negative. Even though the positive results of engineering decisions are recorded as well, the organizations are highly sensitive about publicly revealing decisions that brought little success. Thus new engineering knowledge becomes proprietary to the originating company. However, if available, these documents are a basis for fruitful research and generally lead down other useful paths. They are also becoming more common, so there is hope for future historians.

One additional source that can be considered as primary is technical reports. These often have a paragraph or two of historical context followed by insights into specific instances of gaining engineering knowledge. However, they are difficult for many historians to use because of their abstruse nature. Even though they may be the only source, how they are used depends on how much the historian plans to "open the box" and show the inner workings of the technology. Alex Roland made an insightful presidential address to the Society for History of Technology on the question of how much technical detail historians of technology should reveal.[38] In the case of the history of computing in general, the discussion of important milestones often requires technical insight. The question is how much to share with the reader. My personal experience provides an example of two levels of sharing. *Computers in Space Flight: the NASA Experience* is a comprehensive history of NASA's use of computers in all aspects of space flight, including ground-based control and checkout systems as well as computers embedded in piloted and unpiloted spacecraft.[39] In my youthful enthusiasm, believing that the evolution of the technology was equally important as the institutional history, I opened the box very widely to the readers. My NASA editors clearly preferred the institutional history and relegated the exposition of technical details of the engineering history to sidebars and appendices. More than a decade later, my editor, J. D. Hunley, guided me to be very judicious in opening the box in *Computers Take Flight: A History of NASA's Pioneering Fly-by-Wire Project.*[40] In military history, an exposition can be bogged down in a discussion of the gun calibers of ships in a naval engagement instead of what went on in the mind of the commanding admiral. The history of computing also has such dangers. One can argue that it is impossible to read the admiral's mind, but that the gun calibers are well documented facts. The counter argument is that histories are interpretations of events, stories built on the foundation of the facts. In *Computers in Space Flight*, the technology stood on its own and was difficult for the general reader. In *Computers Take Flight*, under-

---

[38] Alex Roland, "What Hath Kranzberg Wrought? Or Does the History of Technology Matter?" *Technology and Culture* 38 (July 1997): 697-713.

[39] James E. Tomayko, *Computers in Space Flight: The NASA Experience* (New York, 1987). Also published as NASA Contractor Report 182505, March 1988, reprinted on the NASA website: http://www.hq.nasa.gov/office/pao/History/computers/Compspace.html.

[40] James E. Tomayko, *Computers Take Flight: A History of NASA's Pioneering Fly-by-Wire Project*, NASA SP2000-4224 (Washington, D. C., 2000).

standing the technology led to (hopefully) a better story, but its development is not the dominant part, even though it is the central reason for the project.

Basically, then, technical understanding of the engineering is good, and is the basis for the history of software engineering. However, many ostensibly non-technical historians have done quite well in this field. Practitioners have produced much of the history of computing since they easily understand the technology and are motivated to set down their own stories. They make prevalent the overly-technical history. What is needed are more trained historians to enter this area of the history of technology. Hopefully, they can write the history of this exciting field and make it interesting and useful to practitioner and layman alike.

Addendum

I would like to thank the commentators and those at the conference itself who commented and had questions. They contributed a lot to my further understanding of this topic. Bruce Seely had the most insights of any of us, which is a tribute to his keen analytical ability while applied to an unfamiliar area. I especially appreciate his comments about the undervalued "procedural knowledge" and later material about industrial engineering. I sought out an industrial engineering department head who immediately confirmed that industrial engineers suffer from an acceptance problem among other engineers. This is despite MIT, a highly respected school, originating industrial engineering. The situation has a parallel in software engineering in that Carnegie Mellon, an outstanding computer science school, offers one of very few masters of software engineering and one of only two doctoral programs in the subject.

Commentators at the conference indicated that they expected more on the history of how software engineers actually work than whether or not software engineering is a discipline. This is a failing of either my oral presentation or the paper itself, as I thought that by demonstrating the three attributes of engineering and how software engineers accomplished these attributes, I was indicating how they worked. For example, the section on design told how information hiding became part of the software engineers' repertoire, the section on applied science showed how the Cleanroom technique was an application of mathematics to software development, etc. I have been suitably inspired to be more specific in the future, and this comment opened my eyes to a larger field of research. Another comment was that the paper failed to mention that dominant part of software development: maintenance. This is largely due to two things: First, my interpretation of the original instructions to authors seemed to favor the original production of software. Second, there are two forms of what is called maintenance activity: defect repairs and added functionality. Defect repairing I consider a special topic outside the present scope and enhancements are supposed to be done using the same techniques as original engineering (or so I tell my students).

Finally, I am grateful to the organizers for their invitation to participate in this effort.

Commentary on James E. Tomayko, "Software as Engineering"

Albert Endres

Iselerstr. 1
71067 Sindelfingen
Germany

E-mail: a.endres@computer.org

Introduction

Jim Tomayko's paper contains much of interest to me, and I think to others, too. It certainly provokes comments from an engineer who has made a livelihood of developing software products. The same questions have been posed to me again and again as the software man in an environment dominated by hardware people. I shall address only the three main themes of Jim's paper: the art of software engineering, its scientific basis and the role of failure.

The Art of (Software) Engineering

Engineering is about design and invention. Designs are solutions to problems using practicable methods and materials. The art is finding the creative answer to variety. In general terms, today's problem is both similar to and different from yesterday's. The problem may be important or less important. It may concern only a few (i.e., the engineers themselves) or all of humankind. It may be real or imaginary. It may have been solved in various ways before, a year ago or a hundred years ago. We may not know about all previous solutions or may be unable to use the same solution again. It may be necessary to come up with a new solution even when one equally good is known.

For similar problems, the same solution or solution elements may be applied. To find an (almost) optimal solution under given constraints is the essence of good design. With software, design and construction are not always clearly separated. As Maginnis[1] has pointed out, in other fields of engineering engineers do not build. That is done by technicians. This forces engineers to do a much more thorough design job. If they do the construction as well (as is typically the case with software), they often proceed with a sloppier design. In any case, a good design is usually a good compromise. It requires a trade-off between many conflicting factors. Despite thorough requirements analysis, it is impossible to specify all the

---

[1] Terri Maginnis, "Engineers Don't Build," *IEEE Software* 17/1 (2000): 34-9.

factors affecting the success of a product, or the criteria for trade-offs. It is therefore advisable to build prototypes (or models) and to iterate. To go from a waterfall to a spiral process in software is not really a shift in paradigms. A spiral process is a waterfall process preceded by two prototype stages. In every design decision, experience and judgement come into play, particularly the designer's judgement with respect to the users' tolerance.

For an identical problem, the variance may be in the solutions. If the solution is novel, it is called an invention. Inventions can be patented if the problem is economically relevant and the solution is superior to previous methods in terms of the materials or other resources (time, energy) needed. A patent application is the appropriate way for an engineer to write a publication. Few software people read these or any other (non-essential) publications. Also, not all inventions are patented. The patent process may not be considered cost-effective, or the invention may be "published" faster through a product. Several thousand software patents have been issued. There is currently intense debate on genetic patents. Today, engineering is being done with biological material as well as with software and older, more traditional materials.

Engineering cannot be contrasted with art. The more good art there is in design, the better. The more daring the design is, the greater the success (or failure). There is no reason why useful things cannot be aesthetically appealing. This ideal was pursued by a group of architects and painters between 1919 and 1933. The group was called the Bauhaus.[2] Their goal was to give artistic format to everyday objects. In their words, they attempted to "apply spirit to gadgets." Someday—I am sure—we will apply the Bauhaus approach to software, particularly to Web products.

It may be that English-speaking engineers derive the designation of their profession from engines (e.g., war machines). By contrast, we Germans (still) prefer to use the French word "ingénieur" as imported more than 300 years ago. It is closely related to the word for ingenious in French (ingénieux) for which Petit Larousse gives the following definition: full of spirit, inventiveness and skill.

(Software) Engineering as Applied (Computer) Science

In a narrow sense, science is natural science and concerns itself with the understanding of matter. Its aim is to make discoveries about the laws of nature. Following Popper,[3] either facts or theories may come first. Theories explain facts. In the process of scientific exploration, theories may either be verified or proved wrong. There are three methods of doing this, namely observation, experiment and proof. All three methods are used in computer science.

The main argument in our field is about which facts theory ought to explain. As Jim says, practitioners would like to have a scientific explanation of successful practice. It would, of course, also be very helpful to understand unsuccessful practice. If we scan the computer science literature, it is hard to find theories of this kind. We certainly cannot expect the scientific basis of software to come from

---

[2] Elaine S. Hochman, *Bauhaus: Crucible of Modernism* (New York, 1997).
[3] Karl R. Popper, *Conjectures and Refutations: The Growth of Scientific Knowledge* (London, 1963).

physics, as in the older engineering branches. It may come from mathematics or from biology. Mathematics has clearly been helpful already, be it in cryptology or in program proof automation. Biology is largely untapped. A better understanding of how the human mind works would remove some of the risks in software. For example, the distinction between short-term and long-term memory certainly helps in designing a better human interface.

The scientific approach and scientific methods can be used outside natural science. They have to do with the specificity of terms and the continuous integration of new knowledge with the old. Rigorous documentation of successful concepts and methods is of great value to any engineering field. This has lead to handbooks. Handbooks, written by acknowledged experts or by well-organized teams, give practitioners the confident feeling of being on safe ground. An example in software engineering is the Handbook on Software Reliability Engineering edited by Michael Lyu.[4] Following accepted paradigms saves time and money and often provides superior solutions. Well-structured knowledge can be taught by people who have not acquired the relevant experience firsthand. Of course, firsthand experience makes better teachers, but it is often not possible in today's world.

Software design has two aspects, external and internal design. External design is concerned with forms, sounds, colours, with dialogues and images, with usefulness and stress. Internal design addresses structure and dependencies. The science of these two aspects is different. Conferences on external design have titles such as human-computer interaction or computer graphics. Conferences on internal design have titles such as structured programming, object-oriented programming, or components and patterns. Now, the process of design is looking for a scientific underpinning with conferences and journals on design processes. The problem is that computer science is too new and has too many demands placed upon it by the accelerating pace of hardware technology and system use. Few, if any, can address the whole field, and specialists find it increasingly difficult to communicate with one another.

I fully agree with the position that engineering should not have to establish its legitimacy from the underlying science. In my view, it does not matter whether the science underlying engineering is physics, biology, mathematics, or some other. Scientific methods are used in all engineering fields to come up with a well-structured and easily accessible body of canonical knowledge. This knowledge helps the practitioner to distinguish between the application of known ideas and the invention of new ones. These foundations are not yet available in all fields of software and software engineering. Another argument why the definition of engineering cannot be made dependent on science is that technology and engineering precede science in most fields. This is as true for the Maltesian temple builders in 3600 BC and the constructors of the Egyptian pyramids one millennium later as for Marconi and the Wright brothers at the beginning of the last century. The latter two had to defy science in order to succeed. They had to prove wrong the prevailing scientific theories as expounded by such authorities as Poincaré and Lord Kelvin, respectively. I even venture to say that software engineering predates computer science and largely flourishes independently of it.

---

[4] Michael R. Lyu, *Handbook of Software Reliability Engineering* (New York, 1996).

The Role of Failure in (Software) Engineering

It is misleading to say that software is invisible. In almost all cases, a layman can judge whether software is involved, and whether it is doing a good job. Numerous criteria influence the decision as to which software to buy. Its quality must be "good enough" for the purpose in hand, but the price, the support, the future out-look have to be right, too. Because of their nature (communication—only one telephone set is of no value; it becomes more valuable the more sets it can com-municate with), many programs—including, for example, text editors—increase in value, the higher their market penetration. How would you feel with the best text editor on earth if nobody could access your text or you theirs?

Failures are important in that they show—provided they are not accidental—"the limits of current designs and methods." There are the big failures, such as those Bob Glass[5] tracks and tries to understand. A particular problem of our indus-try is the error projections that are being quoted by some major suppliers. If Win-dows 2000 is said to contain 60,000 errors, that certainly worries a lot of people. To me, it is mainly an indication of how big that system is and that their error-prediction methodology has not yet improved. I am sure their prediction model assumes approximately one error per thousand instructions delivered. What this tells me specifically is that we need more work on operational profiles. This is a term coined by John Musa[6] to indicate how our test coverage relates to the actual use of a system during its lifetime. If size and total amount of usage is the only measure, then we have the embedded assumption that the Italian version of PowerPoint interacts with the Japanese version of spell check in Excel in the same way as core functions of the system do. With the help of an operational profile one could try to express this relationship a little more accurately. It could show that no single user will ever experience more than one per mill of the errors quoted above. Which is quite a different message. By the way, Windows is not "mass-produced," it is "mass-used." It is produced once, augmented for each major language of the world, then copied and shrink-wrapped.

It is the lack of codified knowledge that makes it difficult for practitioners to distinguish accidental failures from systematic ones. It is only in the case of sys-tematic failure that existing paradigms must be re-examined. We sometimes change paradigms before credible evidence is produced. We seem to believe that change has value in itself. Changes to the status quo certainly create new business opportunities for somebody. When the dust has settled, we do the old things again, maybe better than before. Maybe this view of an ongoing revolution is the product of a somewhat short-sighted perspective. Here, we can probably learn from phys-ics to take multiple views: gas dynamics is more than Brownian movement of gas particles, and astronomy is different from quantum physics.

---

[5] Robert L. Glass, *Software Runaways* (Englewood Cliffs, N.J., 1997).

[6] John D. Musa et al., "The Operational Profile," in *Handbook of Software Reliability Engineer-ing*, ed. Michael R. Lyu (New York, 1996).

Some Hints for (Software) Engineering Historians

Finally, some hints for historians. New engineering knowledge is valuable, so do not look for it on the streets. Companies most often try to keep new engineering knowledge to themselves. Most engineering knowledge is either local or private anyway. The knowledge of engineers (including that of software engineers) is expressed more in products than in papers. Most private knowledge will eventually be documented—not by the designers and developers themselves, but by people who are willing to study designs and compare them with others. At the moment, there are not nearly enough researchers doing this type of work in the field of software engineering. They will be welcomed by both practitioners and historians.

Do not lump all software together and treat it as a single phenomenon. Software for a space flight, a text editor or a student's first trials in Java are quite different things. To do so, would be like treating an aircraft maintenance manual, a best-selling novel and graffiti in the subway as comparable works in writing. Too often, people who have written one type of program declare themselves experts on all types. You would not accept that for any other types of engineering or literary work. Nor does it make the teaching of software engineering any easier.

Commentary on James E. Tomayko, "Software as Engineering"

Bruce E. Seely

Michigan Technological University
1400 Townsend Drive Houghon,
MI 49931-1295
USA

E-mail: bseely@mtu.edu

James Tomayko has contributed a thoughtful paper that raises a number of interesting issues about software development considered as an engineering activity. He brings to this task the perspective of a scholar who has examined the topic for a period of years, observed it from the inside, and worked to develop educational aspects of the enterprise.[1] As a matter of truth in advertising, it should be understood that I am not as familiar with software development; my areas of historical research have been engineering education and the activities of engineers in transportation fields. My remarks will focus on comparing software as engineering with older, more traditional branches of engineering.

This paper opens with an interesting discussion of the fact that some observers do not consider *Software Engineering* to be a "real" engineering field. This is rather interesting. The current organizational structure of engineering schools would generally be recognizable to most late 19th century graduates, with their departments of civil, mechanical, electrical, chemical engineering, and metallurgy and materials. At the same time, many sub-specialties have emerged, most recently at the interstices between engineering and other realms of science or even business. For example, aeronautical, marine, nuclear engineering all emerged from mechanical engineering; municipal, railway, highway, and environmental engineering were, or are, recognized subfields within civil engineering; and radio, electronic, and computer engineering are the notable subsets of electrical engineering. Since 1950, inter- and multi-disciplinary topics have appeared, such as materials engineering or the current hot topic on many campuses, biomedical engineering. Tomayko also mentions logistics engineering, while there is some

---

[1] See Mary Shaw and James E. Tomayko, *Models for Undergraduate Project Courses in Software Engineering* (Pittsburgh, 1991); James E. Tomayko, ed., *Proceedings of the 5th Software Engineering Education Conference*, SEI Conference on Software Engineering Education, Pittsburgh, P.A., October 7-8, 1991 (Berlin, New York, 1991); James E. Tomayko, *Teaching a Project-Intensive Introduction to Software Engineering*, Technical report, Software Engineering Institute, CMU/SEI-87-TR-20 (Pittsburgh, Carnegie Mellon University, Software Engineering Institute, 1987); and Gary Ford, Norman Gibbs, and James E. Tomayko, *Software Engineering Education: An Interim Report from the Software Engineering Institute*; Technical Report, Software Engineering Institute, CMU/SEI-87-TR-8 (Pittsburgh, Carnegie Mellon University, Software Engineering Institute, 1987).

discussion on my campus about service sector engineering. In other words, fields of specialization come and go, with change both additive and destructive. Railroad or municipal engineering, along with radio engineering, exist now only as individual courses, not separate majors.

Given this pattern of constant change, assessing Tomayko's comment about software engineering *not* being seen as a field of engineering requires determining the elements that define a field of engineering and engineering activity. Tomayko suggests that one problem is related to the way that most engineering fields engage in work that is tangible and physical. This idea that engineering is about things we can touch has been reinforced by the historian Eugene Ferguson, who argues that engineers work in a nonverbal, visual fashion. This explains the pre-eminence of drawings, sketches, models, and other representations of nature within engineering since the Renaissance.[2] Thomas Edison's notebooks, model builders, and tests of real things provide classic instances of this engineering style of working.[3] Moreover, Ferguson emphasizes that experience in the physical world is central to the successful efforts of engineers to develop complex systems. This insight suggests why some might not consider software to be engineering, for Tomayko notes that a tight linkage does not exist between software designers and nature. He highlights the difficulty by asking whether software has to be understood as the holes punched out of cards.

To counter this approach to characterizing engineering fields, Tomayko then turns to three traditional themes in the history of engineering: the art of engineering or design; engineering as applied science, and failure in engineering. I will examine these out of order, since the first is potentially most fruitful for our discussion on the relationship of software to engineering. Let me start with the second, which presents engineering as an outgrowth of science. This idea has become strongly rooted in many places, thanks largely to the formulation of this idea by Vannevar Bush in his influential 1945 report to President Roosevelt, *Science, The Endless Frontier*.[4] But historians of technology have consistently debunked the premise that engineering flows largely from science. Even during the modern era, engineers often have been able to do things before they understood the scientific principles behind their accomplishments. Thus John Smeaton made huge advances in the efficiency of Newcomen atmospheric engines in the 1760s well before the Scottish engineer Rankine developed a mathematically-based thermodynamics.[5]

---

[2] Eugene S. Ferguson, *Engineering and the Mind's Eye* (Cambridge, 1994).

[3] The information on Edison shows best in the four volumes of his published papers: Thomas Alva Edison, *The Papers of Thomas A. Edison*, vol. 1; *The Making of an Inventor, February 1847-June 1873*; vol. 2, *From Workshop to Laboratory, June 1873-March 1876*; vol. 3, *Menlo Park: The Early Years, April 1876-December 1877*; vol. 4, *Wizard of Menlo Park 1878*, ed. Reese V. Jenkins et al. (Baltimore, 1989). Others who have discussed Edison's style include Paul Israel, *Edison: A Life of Invention* (New York, 1998) and Robert Friedel and Paul Israel, with Bernard S. Finn, *Edison's Electric Light: Biography of an Invention* (New Brunswick, 1987).

[4] United States, Office of Scientific Research and Development, *Science, The Endless Frontier* (Washington, 1945, 1960).

[5] On Smeaton, see J. S. Allen, "Steam Engines," in *John Smeaton, FRS*, ed. A. W. Skempton (London, 1981), 179-94; on Rankine, see David F. Channell, "The Harmony of Theory and Practice: The Engineering Science of W. J. M. Rankine," *Technology and Culture* 23 (1982): 39-52. For a general comment on the relationship of science and technology, see Derek de

But in the postwar period, the connection between scientific discoveries and new technologies has grown more apparent, as the lag between discovery and engineering exploitation has grown ever smaller. Thus even many engineers accept the subordinate relationship of engineering to science.

Yet the historian's understanding of the relationship between science and engineering may not influence the perceptions of other scientists and engineers. Perhaps there is "status" value in winning acceptance as a field of "real" engineering, if an activity possesses a scientific pedigree. For example, historian Stephen Johnson has argued in a recent analysis of the development of systems engineering and other management approaches to large-scale technical systems that a lack of respect in academic circles grew from the lack of a scientific basis. "Procedural knowledge," he wrote, "was (and is) consistently undervalued in the mathematically oriented curricula of science and engineering departments. There, the procedurally oriented disciplines of operations research and systems engineering struggled for existence among more scientifically oriented departments. To academics who valued mathematical theory, these disciplines were empty of content."[6] Clearly, there is a parallel here to the experience of software engineers, who also focus on procedural issues. Over and over, mathematics has been identified as a principle gatekeeper for entry into engineering, a base of knowledge that certifies membership, and a mark of professional status.[7] For that reason, Tomayko may be on to something in his assertion that the inability to connect to basic science has hurt the prestige accorded software design. Yet I hesitate, because software can claim a clear heritage to both computer hardware and to computer science, especially through programming issues where math was early-on a key attribute. In the end, the absence of a clearly articulated lineage between software development and science should not disqualify software activities from consideration as engineering from the historian's perspective. Whether it affects the relative prestige of software developers is more open to discussion.

Tomayko's next category—failure—is a more important point of reference for connecting software work to other engineering disciplines. Both Henry Petroski and Eugene Ferguson have drawn attention to the role of failure in engineering, highlighting the way that advances in many fields have emerged from the learning experiences failures provide. Ferguson quotes the editor of *Engineering News*, who in 1887 observed, "We could easily ... publish the most interesting, most instructive, and the most valued engineering journal in the world, by devoting it to only one particular class of facts, the records of failures. ... For the whole science of engineering, properly so-called, has been built up from such records."[8] Indeed,

---

Solla Price, "Is Technology Historically Independent of Science? A Study in Statistical Historiography," *Technology and Culture* 6 (1965): 553.

[6] Johnson examined the emergence of systems engineering and other approaches to managing large-scale systems, and found that the least scientific and quantitative approaches engendered the least respect from the academic world. See Stephen B. Johnson, "Three Approaches to Big Technology: Operations Research, Systems Engineering, and Project Management," *Technology and Culture* 38 (October 1997): 891-919; quotation on p. 915.

[7] See especially Sally L. Hacker, "Mathematization of Engineering: Limits on Women and the Field," in *Machina ex Dea: Feminist Perspectives on Technology*, ed. Joan Rothschild (New York, 1983), 38-58.

[8] Ferguson (n. 2 above), 173-74.

failures can be catastrophic like the Tay Bridge collapse, the Quebec City Bridge failure in 1907, or the "Galloping Gertie" suspension bridge disaster at the Tacoma Narrows site in 1940. More often, smaller and less publicized failures have been critical to the development of the state of the engineering art. As Walter Vincenti noted, one of the most basic methodologies of engineering—parameter variation—is predicated upon failure.[9]

But the intriguing point in Tomayko's paper is related to a situation that has been experienced by anyone who has worked with computers, namely that software failures are amazingly common! The challenges facing software designers certainly are enormous, for all of us expect smooth interfaces with peripheral devices not even conceived when programs were being written. Even when making allowances, though, it is clear that software fails a lot. You all know the waggish comparison of software and automobiles, that ends with the remark that no one would tolerate a car that occasionally stopped without warning while driving down an Interstate highway, forcing the driver to pull over, start the engine, wait for systems to come back up, and then drive away. Michael Mahoney examined another facet of this issue in a paper at the Dibner Institute a few years back, looking at the warranties provided by packaged software manufacturers, and found they basically warrant nothing about their products.

Failure, then, is an issue of special importance in understanding software as engineering. And my sense is that something different is going on here. From Vincenti's point of view, failure is important because it leads to greater reliability, higher performance, and better designs. Some of that is true with software, as anyone who has downloaded patches to resolve glitches and other headaches knows. But Tomayko suggests that software developers seem to view failure differently than designers in other realms of engineering. Most engineers use failure to reveal the boundaries of possibility, while computer hardware changes so rapidly that the boundaries facing software designers are themselves changing rapidly. Perhaps, suggests Tomayko, this is why software designers seem highly willing to take risks. Tomayko makes an important point when he asks: "What is the real effect of software engineers not having to worry about erasing their mistakes with jackhammers? Does ease of failure actually promote failure?" The scary point for me is that software failures can be every bit as catastrophic as a bridge or dam failure. Indeed, one of the most unsettling aspects of the Star Wars missile defense system were the debates about software performance and reliability in a system that could never be fully tested. So to Tomayko's question I will add another query: how can we reconcile the stereotypical image of engineers as precise perfectionists with the imprecise performance of software?

The last of Tomayko's categories seems to me the most essential element in understanding engineering, for design is, I believe, the distinguishing feature of this profession. I claim no originality for this conclusion, which rests upon the work of Eugene Ferguson, who showed that design and problem solving is what engineers do. It is fascinating that over the past two decades, engineering schools have remade themselves in order to place this understanding back at their center after a forty-year hiatus. Since the end of World War II, engineering educators had

---

[9] Walter G. Vincenti, *What Engineers Know and How They Know It: Analytical Studies from Aeronautical Engineering* (Baltimore, 1990), 59.

embraced an analytical and scientific approach and forced design to the sideline of most engineering curricula.[10] The restructuring effort has been intended to re-connect engineering education to the real world within which engineers operate by including project courses in the first year and capstone design sequences in the senior year. Compared to this emphasis upon problem-solving, the design efforts of software developers certainly look like engineering. Like other engineers, soft-ware developers face the challenges of making systems work. And they clearly share the desire to produce elegant solutions to problems, as Ferguson noted.[11] How can this *not* be engineering?

Louis Bucciarelli further reinforces this sense that design is the central feature of what engineers do. He makes clear, moreover, that this not just an art, as Fergu-son describes it, but also "a social process. Executive mandate, scientific law, marketplace needs—all are ingredients of the design process, but more fundamen-tal are the norms and practices of the subculture of the firm where the object serves as icon."[12] This sounds like the environment within which most software designers operate! Indeed, Bucciarelli offers one case study that clearly shows that those engaged in software activities pursue their work in a fashion little different from other engineers. He followed closely the development of a component of a photoprocessing machine. And just before the actual device was to be tested, the team discovered that the processing time was too long—2 minutes instead of the hoped-for 30 seconds. To deal with this,

> Mark spent fifteen hours ... sitting at a computer console, wrapped up in an object world. He methodically went through every block of computer code, timing each phase and segment, looking for unnecessary operations ... for ways to restructure segments in order to achieve the sorely needed time savings. Life is intense within the worlds of bits and bytes, where a characteristic event such as the execution of one line of machine code takes a millionth of a second, where data bytes from 512 detectors, sampled at thou-sandths of a second, mount up in a queue to be processed, and where the code that does the processing marches through its programmed operations millions of times to yield the correct gray tone of each and every one of a thousand pixels that, all together, distributed over the monitor screen, constitute an image. ...
>
> Mark has the specific tools at hand for his diagnostic work—software development pro-grams that allow him to step through the code line by line or run through a subset of in-structions over and over again in order to obtain a measure of the "real time" the subset consumes. Using these, he develops a feel for the machine's response time at the level of microseconds. With these tools, he appropriates the whole line of code, or eliminates a section altogether, runs the program, and notes the difference in execution time. He in-ventories microseconds; they absorb all of his attention as he tracks down and conserves these intervals as objects. Backing and filling, he labors to reduce the overall time to produce an image. Alone in the building, he hardly notices the hum of the heating sys-tem as the time flies by.[13]

[10] See my articles, Bruce E. Seely, "The Other Re-Engineering of Engineering Education, 1900-1965," *Journal of Engineering Education* 88/3 (July 1999): 285-94; and "The 'Imbalance' of Theory and Practice in American Engineering Education: Reforms and Changes, 1920-1980," *ICON* (forthcoming).

[11] Eugene S. Ferguson," Elegant Inventions: The Artistic Component of Technology," *Technol-ogy and Culture* 19 (July 1978) 450-60.

[12] Louis L. Bucciarelli, *Designing Engineers* (Cambridge, 1994), 20.

[13] Bucciarelli, 192-93.

This extended quotation highlights a couple of understandings for me. First, Bucciarelli's description demonstrates, as did Tracy Kidder's *Soul of a New Machine*, the all-consuming passion of a software design effort.[14] This passion is hardly limited to engineers. It matches Edison, of course, but applies to many others as well. The enthusiasm of intense tinkering strikes me as one of the most important ways software looks like engineering. Second, this account shows that software is always keyed to the operation of some machine or a process. This recognition may provide the element of physicality, the connection to the real world, that was identified above as central to engineering.

All of this serves to show that software development IS—or at least can be—an engineering activity. Yet there is one element that may pose a potentially disturbing question for those who seek to define software development as engineering. Walter Vincenti quoted a British engineer's definition of engineering: "'Engineering refers to the practice of organizing the design and construction [and I would add operation] of any artifice which transforms the physical world around us to meet some recognized need.'" He goes on to note, "A key term for present purposes is the word *organizing*, for which we could also read *devising* or *planning*. This word selects engineering out of the more general activity of 'technology,' which embraces all aspects of design, production, and operation of an artifice. Draftspersons, shop workers, and pilots, for example, though all are technologists, do not organize in the engineering sense and are therefore not engineers. ... Not all technologists count as engineers."[15]

Given Bucciarelli's account, then, where should we place the software people? Is Mark organizing in the engineering sense? Is software development a craft skill, or is a college degree and the possession of mathematical skills a requirement for success? Can software work be reduced to formal rules and algorithms? How important is the tacit knowledge that comes from experience? How important are the theoretical principles that furnish a higher-level guide to the software engineer? Interestingly, the stereotypical software designer is a young man with a less than well-adjusted social life who has an intrinsic feel for what he is doing—at the bits and bytes level. Often such individuals do *not* require a college education in order to enter this field and achieve success. Perhaps I should not blindly embrace this stereotype. But we need to know more about this situation, for the generalization endorses a definition of software work as art more than as a routine design exercise. In attempting to answer all the questions posed above, comparisons between software work and other engineering endeavors ought to be useful.

This line of inquiry leads to a much more general question that underlies the discussion of software and engineering. Why is it important that software work be considered a form of engineering? In his recent history of computing, Paul Ceruzzi discussed the 1968 Garmisch conference, which rested on the assumption that better software could be developed if a theoretical base for such work could be established, and if the day-to-day discipline of engineering could be imposed on software developers. Yet Ceruzzi reported that another conference in 1996, with many of the same actors present, concluded that the profession had shown no

[14] Tracy Kidder, *The Soul of a New Machine* (Boston, 1981).
[15] Vincenti (n. 9 above), 6, 14.

ability to control entrance to the field or to set norms. Ceruzzi concluded that "the attempt to establish software engineering on the whole had failed."[16] The key question remains: Does this matter?

Here a comparison with other realms of engineering may prove quite useful. Specifically, let us turn to the engineers themselves and their perennial concern about social status, prestige, and recognition. We know from the work of historians of engineering such as Edwin Layton and especially Bruce Sinclair that enhancing social prestige was a central purpose for professional organization in the first place. Identifying techniques and patterns that can be taught, and that rest upon a base of formal knowledge, can permit those engaged in a given activity to claim to be professionals, and then to build a common identity. That identity can spawn conferences and journals that spread information about the field, bringing recognition as an professional engineering subdiscipline and improved remuneration for special expertise.[17] My own research has suggested that similar concerns about social status were pivotal in shaping academic engineering education after 1880, including the content of curricula, for engineering educators above all wanted the social recognition given other professionals and later scientists. The histories of every professional engineering society deal with this issue in some way, shape, or form.[18]

So are software developers repeating this pattern in their desire to be called software engineers? Mike Mahoney hinted at this earlier in this conference, when he discussed the desire of software developers and programmers to gain professional autonomy. But can the title "engineer" actually provide them with professional autonomy and control over a professional agenda? I am doubtful in this case, for a couple of reasons. First, although software is becoming increasingly the center of the computer world, the traditional arrangement of work in this industry has been for hardware to be developed first, with the software following and operating within the constraints imposed by the machines. (Windows may be overcoming this tendency, forcing machines to meet the demands of existing packaged software.) Second, the structure of corporations will pose the same limitations on the professional activities of software developers that it has upon engineers, for both are problem-solvers in the corporations' employ rather than professional free agents. Finally, as Peter Meiksins has shown, not all engineers automatically achieve their desired level of professional status. Some end up in that "other" category noted by Vincenti, not automatically recognized as members of the engineering guild. Peter Meiksins, for example, studied engineers who turned to labor unions during the 1930s, in part to avoid second-class citizenship, when they found themselves at the lower levels of business and technical organizations.[19] Today draftsmen, surveyors, and engineering technicians fall into this group. Are

---

[16] Paul E. Ceruzzi, *A History Of Modern Computing* (Cambridge, 1998), 105.

[17] See Edwin T. Layton, Jr., *Revolt of the Engineers: Social Responsibility and the American Engineering Profession* (Baltimore, 1986); Bruce Sinclair, *A Centennial History of the American Society of Mechanical Engineers, 1880-1980* (Toronto, 1980).

[18] See A. Michal McMahon, *The Making of a Profession: A Century of Electrical Engineering in America* (New York, 1984); and Terry S. Reynolds et al., *75 Years of Progress: A History of the American Institute of Chemical Engineers, 1908-1983* (New York, 1983).

[19] Peter Meiksins, *Engineering Labour: Technical Workers in Comparative Perspective* (London, New York, 1996).

software developers more like engineers or surveyors? Are those who seek to label software an engineering subfield seeking assurance that they are not considered like the latter? American engineering has been through this before, and the legacy has been visible in the politics of professional organizations ever since.

From this perspective, it may be better to claim to be a *scientist* than an engineer. To be sure, science like every other profession, including law, has been domesticated by business corporations, but engineering has seemed especially limited in developing professional autonomy and recognition. Moreover, laying claim to the authority of science also removes the difficulty posed by a lack of tangibility in the work of software designers.

Interestingly, another group of engineers that had similar difficulty winning acceptance as a "real" engineering field reacted in ways not much different than some software developers. Industrial engineers also cannot easily tie their work to physical design problems. Like software engineers, industrial engineers often produce only written information, diagrams, and organizational charts, not artifacts and machines. They don't "make" anything directly. Industrial engineering began to establish an identity in the 1880s at places like MIT, and after 1900, it began to develop independence from mechanical engineering. Courses and programs appeared at a number of schools, including Penn State, Cornell, Carnegie Institute, Rensselaer, and Purdue, but the leader was still MIT, which started a Department of Engineering and Business Administration in 1913. The practitioners in this subfield focused on organizational activities and efficiency within factories, with Frederick Taylor and other leading mechanical engineers as founders of the field. A professional organization—the Society of Industrial Engineers—took form in 1917, building upon the attention given to scientific management and others techniques used to improve the efficiency of manufacturing operations—Taylor's time-motion studies, and Gilbreath's films.[20] Some have disparagingly labeled industrial engineering "imaginary engineering;" perhaps it was no accident that Frederick Taylor labeled his work "scientific management," seeking a patina of science that went further than claims to be an engineering activity.

So in seeking to close the conversation about software as engineering, let me propose that we adopt a typology that historians of technology and engineering have been using. Under this structure, we have to recognize that not all software work is the same, just as engineering work varies enormously. There are very distinct differences, as Albert Endres pointed out in an earlier comment, along the spectrum of software activities. At one end we can place the theoretical workers who Mike Mahoney examined, folks who rely very heavily on mathematics as the basis of their knowledge and discourse. At the other end are practitioners who seem to need almost no science, only but a feel for and experience for their systems and the code. These are the people about whom one academic software engineer commented disparagingly, "the popular literature continues to suggest that

---

[20] The best overview of the emergence of industrial engineering is in Lindy Biggs, *The Rational Factory: Architecture, Technology, and Work in America's Age of Mass Production* (Baltimore, 1996), 36-54.

software developers can be 'engineers' without knowing or using mathematics."[21] Between these poles are activities that correspond to engineering science in the classic sense of that term as laid out by historian Edwin Layton. This work focuses on adopting the language, tools, and attitudes of science to solve design problems rather than to develop idealized understandings of nature for its own sake.

In this middle ground falls the work of individuals such as noted software designer David Parnas, who received the SIGSOFT Outstanding Research Award in 1998. Parnas used his award address to comment on the differences in the concerns of software developers and researchers and theorists. He observed what he thought was a substantial difference between software activities and work in other fields of engineering. "Whereas practicing engineers find things of value in research publications, most software developers do not."[22] As a result, Parnas found that "the developers" major problems were problems that I had never considered, problems that none of my professors or colleagues thought worthy of discussion."[23] Parnas assumed—incorrectly—that this gap between research and the real world was unique to the software field. In fact, differences like this have emerged in many academic engineering fields since 1945, as researchers and theorists go separate ways. Parnas, however, proposed a solution that offers one way of grounding many software activities firmly in the camp of engineering. He argued, "I believe the role of the successful engineering researcher is to understand the developers' problems, but to use the luxury of not having to meet short-term deadlines, to look for the underlying causes and fundamental cures rather than immediate, symptomatic relief. Developers, who must meet pressing market driven deadlines, do not have the time to look for long-term solutions, that is the researchers job." Parnas' view of research not only defines a relationship between theory and practice in software development that matches that used in other fields of engineering, but also positions academic software engineers (who are more likely to have the time to pursue fundamental research problems) in the realm of engineering science. Both moves make it easier to identify software activities as engineering.

The dilemmas that Parnas observed are part of the growing pains of the field of software engineering. Like industrial engineers, part of the difficulties may stem from the nature of their work—the seeming lack of ties to the physical world, or to an underlying physical science. As noted in the various comments, another problem lies in the amorphousness of the term, for software has come to cover a multitude of different activities. Some precision of meaning might help, or better definitions of the specific activities that are part of the word software. Perhaps attention to events in other fields of engineering will prove useful in starting to sort out the questions that James Tomayko has raised in this thoughtful paper.

---

[21] David Lorge Parnas, "Successful Software Engineering Research," *Software Engineering Notes* 23/3 (May 1998): 64-8.
[22] Parnas, 64.
[23] Parnas, 65.

Discussion following "Software as Engineering"

Mary Croarken

National Maritime Museum
Centre for Maritime Research
Greenwich, London, SE10 9NF
UK

E-mail: meroarken@nmm.ac.uk

The initial discussion predominately focused on whether or not software engineers were engineers in the traditional meaning of the word. It began with the question of patenting being that traditional means of engineering publication and the difficulties of patenting or copyrighting software. Several speakers commented on the term "software engineering" and what it might include. For example, it was suggested that the view of software engineering relating to computer systems tools was too narrow and sub disciplines such as compiler design, data base construction and operating systems be included as well as the lower status application programming. Tomayko responded that some computer scientists do software engineering but would not want to be called engineers.

The relationship between the self-conscious evocation of the term software engineering (confined mostly to universities) and the broader world of people actually creating programs was discussed. One speaker pointed out that within industry the term software engineer was not widely used. In Microsoft, for example, staff were called developers, architects, testers, etc., while in other companies with more engineering oriented cultures, such as Hewlett-Packard, the term software engineer would be used. Job titles were reflections of individual corporate models of what constituted a "good" programmer, not descriptions of the work actually carried out. While these kind of issues obviously overlapped with the software as labor process workshop, one participant stated that it was important to note that engineering was not the only model which could be used to describe the software process.

One practitioner described how industry needed three different kinds of software people: those educated in using software tools trained within a company; those educated in using software methods and typically trained at a technical university or polytechnic; and those with the foundations of the subject trained at universities. While there was some advantage in hiring university trained people because they had the skills to adapt in times of change, all three types of worker were needed in a company. This example illustrated that industry was interested in skills not titles.

The question of whether software was a trade or a profession was raised and a lively discussion about the professionalization of software engineering began. It was suggested that the term "engineer" was used to imply status and was part of the boundary drawing process. Considerable attention was given to the comparison of programmers to other modern day engineers. It was suggested that one way in which software engineering could be professionalized was through certification. Seely commented that most engineers working in US corporations were no longer state certified and that certification could only be *one* measure of professionalization. Another speaker stated quite bluntly that software engineers did want certification and that there was already a professional body in existence.

The theme of professionalizing software engineering through warranty was then explored alongside the idea of accreditation. It was noted that civil engineers could be sued if the bridge fell down but that software engineers were not sued because their software failed to work. This therefore undermined the idea of software engineers as engineers. Some participants felt that because software was often licensed and not bought that this was a barrier to software engineers offering warranties. Other contributors countered this by saying that warrantees are ubiquitous for contract software and that personal experience of packaged consumed software could not be generalized.

Current attempts by professional societies to accredit computer science and software engineering degree programs were discussed. Accreditation was seen, by some speakers, as a reflection of the need for academic software engineering departments to gain status. The consensus was that although interest in accreditation was growing it had not yet spread to elite schools. Rather it was used by mid-tier institutions seeking to separate themselves from the lowest tiers.

Norberg stated that, while the comments made had been interesting and that he had found it useful to learn about professionalization, he was concerned that the debate about software as engineering as a counterpoint to software as science had not been addressed. Norberg had hoped that this session would concentrate on the rapid changes in software development that had occurred over time as he had outlined in his "Themes and Objectives" statement given at the beginning of the conference. As a counter argument some practitioners suggested that the process of producing and maintaining software was a well defined and straightforward process and that engineers solve the problems they are presented with. The ideas concerning what abstractions were used, what was in the mind of practitioners and what were the important decisions could not be done by engineers and needed outside analysis. This statement illustrated the gulf between what practitioners meant by looking at software as engineering and what historians expected from the workshop.

Overall the debate focused on software engineering's claim to engineering status. Much of the discussion illustrated that the process of boundary setting (as discussed in the Software as Science workshop) was still going on among software engineers.

Part 3
Software as Reliable Artefact

A View from the Sonnenbichl:[1] On the Historical Sociology of Software and System Dependability

Donald MacKenzie

University of Edinburgh
Department of Sociology
18 Buccleuch Place
Edinburgh EH8 9LN
Scotland, UK

E-mail: D.MacKenzie@ed.ac.uk

Introduction

In October 1998, I went on a minor personal pilgrimage, to the Hotel Sonnenbichl, on the outskirts of the little town of Garmisch in the Bavarian Alps. It is a pleasant provincial hotel, comfortable without being over-imposing, and in the early Autumn it was quiet, except when a bus-load of package tourists stopped for the night. Two things, however, lift the hotel out of the ordinary. The first is the view of the mountains: the Wetterstein range and Germany's highest peak, the Zugspitze. To open one's curtains in the morning was to feel a towering physical presence that no photograph can quite capture. The second is the Sonnenbichl's place in the history of human thinking. Exactly thirty years before my visit, on October 7-11, 1968, it hosted the NATO Science Committee's conference on "Software Engineering," at which, famously, a "software crisis" was diagnosed and "software engineering" proposed as its solution.[2] I need not labour the conference's significance to the history of computing: others have pointed that out.[3] Its more general importance, however, goes beyond the history of computing as narrowly conceived. The second half of the twentieth century witnessed a growing love affair between industrial societies and the digital computer, a romance that is intensifying as we move into the new millennium. Neither the many benefits of computerization, nor the growing power and declining relative cost of the hardware upon which these benefits rest, needed labouring in 1968, nor do they now. The historical significance of the Sonnenbichl meeting was the way it provided the single most influential early diagnosis of one of the two fundamental problems that are the obverse of hardware's success: the deeply intractable difficulty of

---

[1] Fig. 1 shows this view.

[2] I am grateful to Brian Randell for recovering for me, via the photographs he took at the time, the information that the conference was held in the Hotel Sonnenbichl. "Bichl" is local dialect, not high German: roughly translated, "Sonnenbichl" means "sunny little hill."

[3] See, for example, Andrew L. Friedman with Dominic S. Cornford, *Computer Systems Development: History, Organization and Implementation* (Chichester, 1989), 101-6.

achieving dependable software. Since that problem is still far from solved, the intellectual, as distinct from the physical, view from the Sonnenbichl remains one that our increasingly computer-dependent societies would be wise to contemplate. The view may need to be broadened—I discuss some possible broadenings below—but its formulation remains an important historical moment.

Fig. 1. A view from the Sonnenbichl (Picture: courtesy Grand Hotel Sonnenbichl)

The story of the Sonnenbichl meeting has been well told elsewhere,[4] and need only be recapped briefly here. The idea for the conference came most centrally from Professor Friedrich Bauer of the Technische Hochschule München, and the invitation list was carefully constructed to include key figures in academia, in the computer industry, in the emerging "software houses," as well as a small number of important computer users. "Our goal this week," Alan Perlis of Carnegie Mellon University told participants, "is the conversion of mushyware to firmware, to transmute our products from jello to crystals." A confessional atmosphere developed, with participants being open about the difficulties being encountered in software development. Not all of them agreed with the diagnosis of "crisis:" "It's a very emotional word," said K. Kolence, of Boole and Babbage Inc. There was, however, widespread agreement that the techniques of software production were "backward" by comparison with those of hardware, that delays and cost over-runs were common, and that the final products were less dependable than they should

---

[4] For example, Eloína Peláez, *A Gift from Pandora's Box: The Software Crisis* (PhD thesis, University of Edinburgh, 1988), chap. 6.

be. Particularly worrying to several participants were the possible consequences when human safety rested upon computer systems. In their position paper for the meeting, E. E. David of the Bell Telephone Laboratories and A. G. Fraser of Cambridge University wrote: "Particularly alarming is the seemingly unavoidable fallibility of large software, since a malfunction in an advanced hardware-software system can be a matter of life and death, not only for individuals, but also for vehicles carrying hundreds of people and ultimately for nations as well." The spirit of the meeting was not, however, the gloom such warnings might suggest: it was positive, even liberatory. The Dutch theoretical computer scientist Edsger W. Dijkstra told the meeting that "The general admission of the existence of the software failure in this group of responsible people is the most refreshing experience I have had in a number of years, because the admission of shortcomings is the primary condition for improvement." For Dijkstra, even the Autumn weather symbolized the mood. "For me," he recalled, the Garmisch meeting, "was the end of the Middle Ages. It was very sunny."[5]

There is, perhaps, a sense in which "software engineering" has never left the Hotel Sonnenbichl—a subsequent meeting in Rome to take the subject forward was divided and acrimonious, and a meeting on the history of software engineering 28 years later revealed no consensus as to what it consisted in—but I have no conceit that ghosts spoke to me on my Autumn visit.[6] As the defining moment of self-reflection in the history of software, however, the Sonnenbichl meeting offers a useful entry-point to the history of dependability. Software's history is a short one—by any reasonable definition of "software," more than half that history has unfolded since October 1968—and the Sonnenbichl meeting thus offers an interesting perspective from which to view the subsequent decades.

Dependability

Let me begin, however, with terminology. Our meeting's organizers asked me to speak about "reliability," but I have chosen to frame these remarks around the notion of "dependability." An IFIP Working Group worked for several years to clarify these slippery words, and the results are available to us in a 1992 volume edited by Jean-Claude Laprie. It would, I think, be ungrateful of the rest of us not to adopt their suggested usages. They propose "dependability" as an overarching term subsuming availability ("readiness for usage"), reliability ("continuity of service"), safety ("avoidance of catastrophic consequences on the environment") and security ("prevention of unauthorized access and/or handling of informa-

---

[5] Peter Naur and Brian Randell, eds., *Software Engineering: Report on a Conference Sponsored by the NATO Science Committee, Garmisch, Germany, 7-11 October 1968* (Brussels: NATO Scientific Affairs Division, 1969), 17, 120-1, and 138; Edsger W. Dijkstra, interviewed by Eloína Peláez, as quoted in Peláez,175. On matters like weather, memory can play notorious tricks, but Randell's photographs do indeed reveal sunshine.

[6] John N. Buxton and Brian Randell, eds., *Software Engineering Techniques: Report on a Conference Sponsored by the NATO Science Committee, Rome, Italy, 27-31 October 1969* (Brussels: NATO Scientific Affairs Division, April 1970), Conference on the History of Software Engineering, Schloss Dagstuhl, Wadern, Germany, August 1996; see also Michael S. Mahoney, "The Roots of Software Engineering," *CWI Quarterly* 3 (1990): 325-34.

tion").[7] While there is some anachronism involved—in the years around 1968, "reliability" often had a more general meaning as "the trustworthiness of the results produced by a system"[8]—the advantage of the more general terminology is that the weights given to the particular aspects of dependability will vary from context to context (availability and reliability are arguably pervasive concerns, while safety and security are more context-specific). The communities of people that pursue each of the attributes are to a certain extent distinct, but there is sufficient common ground for dependable computing, and perhaps dependable software, to be a meaningful object of inquiry.

Laprie and his colleagues also usefully distinguish three classes of "impairments" to dependability: failure ("when the delivered service no longer complies with the specification, the latter being an agreed description of the system's expected function and/or service"), error ("that part of the system state which is liable to lead to subsequent failure") and fault ("[t]he adjudged or hypothesized cause of an error"). They also distinguish two means of achieving dependability: procurement (fault prevention and fault tolerance, "how to provide the system with the ability to deliver a service complying with the specification") and validation (fault removal and fault forecasting, "how to reach confidence in the system's ability to deliver a service complying with the specification").[9] The result is the tree of concepts reproduced here as Fig. 2.

The tree provides a useful, if humbling, guide to the tasks faced by the history of software dependability. Do we know the histories of faults, errors, and failure in software systems; of the procurement and validation of dependability; of the availability, reliability, safety and security of software systems? I could simply answer this composite question by the word "no," and end the paper at this point, but that would be too negative: it would sketch a huge historical agenda, without indicating either priorities or intellectual resources that are available for the task. Above all, it would not convey the task's importance: why it might matter not just to the historian, but to the software practitioner, and perhaps even to the general citizen.

---

[7] Jean-Claude Laprie, ed., *Dependability: Basic Concepts and Terminology in English, French, German, Italian and Japanese* (Vienna, 1992), 3-4, emphases deleted. I am grateful to Brian Randell for pointing me to this work, and more generally for convincing me of the virtues of treating "dependability" as an overarching concept.

[8] Brian Randell, "Operating Systems: The Problems of Performance and Reliability," in *Information Processing 71: Proceedings of the IFIP Congress, Llubjana, Yugoslavia, 23-28 August, 1971*, ed. C. V. Freiman, vol. 1 (London, 1972), 281-90, at 282. See, however, John E. Hosford, "Measures of Dependability," *Operations Research* 8 (1960): 53-64, in which "dependability" is treated as a higher-level concept than "reliability," albeit not in a context specific to computing.

[9] Laprie, 4, emphases deleted.

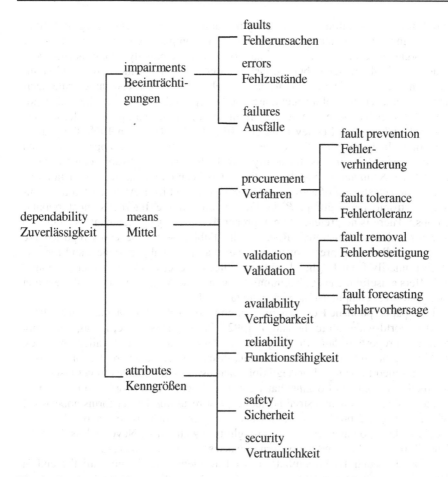

Fig. 2. The dependability tree. Based upon J.C. Laprie, ed., *Dependability* (Vienna: Springer, 1992), 5 and 104

Safety Failures

In sketching some intellectual resources available for the historiography of software dependability, I will not attempt systematically to work through the branches of the dependability tree, and I will be influenced by my disciplinary background as a sociologist. I will emphasize failures that impinge upon the wider society, and ways in which a sociological perspective can throw light upon the history of dependability.

The most obvious and most important form of impaired dependability is in the sphere of safety, particularly if failure leads to death. The history of failures of security, in contrast, is murky. The most successful breaches of security are those that go unnoticed, and even those that are noticed may not be reported, in order to avoid drawing attention to the underlying fault (and thus encouraging its further exploitation) or to protect the reputation of the company, government agency, or other organization involved. There may, of course, be equally strong incentives to "hush up" fatal accidents, but the task is more difficult. In most advanced countries, an accidental death leads to an official investigation, and large-scale accidents (such as crashes of airliners) are widely reported worldwide. The undependable computer has been a modestly prominent theme in our culture at least since Arthur C. Clarke and Stanley Kubrick's film *2001* (released in 1968, the year of the Sonnenbichl meeting),[10] and the media show considerable appetite for such stories. Since 1976 (that is, for nearly half the history of software), computer scientist Peter Neumann of SRI International has been collecting reports of failures, first in the newsletter *Software Engineering Notes* and from August 1985 in an online electronic news group, *Risks* Forum, one of the Internet's most popular groups.[11] There is no pretence to comprehensive coverage—Neumann is careful to title his indexes "Illustrative Risks to the Public"—and the cases reported are typically culled from press coverage rather than personal experience, and furthermore primarily from English-language sources. Nevertheless, this body of material offers a useful means of beginning to get a sense of the magnitude of the worst safety failures: computer-related accidental deaths.

In a paper published elsewhere, I attempted to do this for computer-related deaths, world-wide, up to the end of 1992.[12] Wherever possible, I sought to work back from reports in *Software Engineering Notes* and *Risks* to detailed enquiries, seeking further information on causation, discarding cases where the role of computers seemed to be small or negligible, and using other sources to get a sense of the likely magnitude of deaths that were insufficiently newsworthy to be reported in the media, such as industrial accidents. The resulting dataset forms appendix 1 of this paper. I reproduce it in full because I know it must be incomplete, and would be keen to have other cases brought to my attention. Nevertheless, both the overall total numbers and the pattern of causes are of some interest.

I found around 1,100 computer-related accidental deaths up until the end of 1992 (in one of the incidents, a set of failures in radiation therapy in the North Staffordshire Royal Infirmary, a precise number of deaths cannot be determined). The dominant cause (over 90% of deaths) was faults[13] in human-computer interaction. Hardware faults such as electromagnetic perturbation were implicated in some 4% of deaths, and software "bugs" (design faults in software) led to a further 3%, or 30, deaths (from the Therac-25 radiation therapy machine, and from a failure by the Patriot anti-missile system to intercept the Scud attack that led to the single largest losses by Allied Forces in the 1991 Gulf War). Clearly, these conclusions are vulnerable to critique of two different sorts. First, the diagnosis of causation is difficult. For example, the cause of the crashes of the Airbus A320, the first fly-by-wire airliner, was the subject of fierce controversy. While no evi-

---

[10] See Arthur C. Clarke, *2001: A Space Odyssey* (London, 1968).

[11] Current and back issues of *Risk Digest* are accessible at http://catless.ncl.ac.uk/Risks/.

[12] Donald MacKenzie, "Computer-Related Accidental Death: An Empirical Exploration," *Science and Public Policy* 21 (1994): 233-48.

[13] In the context of human-computer interaction, and indeed of software, the terminology of "fault" may seem unusual, but it is a necessary part of systematic use of Laprie's framework.

dence of a software design fault was found by the crash investigators, the possibility is hard to rule out conclusively. Those with a "technical" view of computer system dependability might want to exclude cases caused by faults in human-computer interaction. To my mind, that exclusion would be quite mistaken (see below), but it would obviously reduce the total number of deaths by an order of magnitude. Second, the fact that the dataset is incomplete means that there must be computer-related accidental deaths not in it, and some of those deaths may well have resulted from software design faults. Despite these issues, however, I think one can with some modest confidence conclude that the number of deaths in computer-related accidents, up to 1992, was relatively modest. Underreporting in the sources available to me certainly could push the total up to 2,000, but probably not to more than 10,000, unless one begins to draw in categories that I did not include, such as "collateral" deaths in deliberate military actions.[14] In terms of causation, it seems as if poorly-designed human interfaces have been more important than software design faults. The latter seem so far to have killed considerably fewer people than the view from the Sonnenbichl suggested they might.

The Hoare Paradox

Software, then, has yet to experience its Tay Bridge disaster: a catastrophic accident, unequivocally attributable to a software design fault, in the full public gaze. But, of course, one can write that sentence only with the word "yet" in it. It is hard to find *a priori* grounds on which to argue that such an event cannot happen, and indeed it is surprising that it has not happened. Here, I would suggest, lies the most important problem in the historiography of software dependability. Why has catastrophe not yet happened?

The most interesting reflections on this issue come not from an historian, but from a computer scientist, C. A. R. Hoare. Hoare was not present at the Garmisch meeting, but he took part in the unsuccessful follow-up conference at Rome in 1969, and he was as much a spokesperson for the view from the Sonnenbichl as any of those physically present. He had his own painful experience of the problems that prompted the diagnosis of "software crisis." He had been responsible for a new suite of software, including an ALGOL compiler, for the Elliott 803 computer. Promotion to Assistant Chief Engineer diverted his attention from this project until it failed to meet its March 1965 delivery date. Further delays, and deep problems with the compiler, eventually led to cancellation. At a subsequent meeting with Elliott's customers, the embarrassed Hoare found them unsurprised at the fiasco: "Over lunch our customers were kind to try to comfort me. They had realized long ago that software for the original specification could never have been delivered, and even if it had been, they would not have known how to use its sophisticated features, and anyway many such large projects get cancelled before delivery." Writing in 1969, Hoare pointed out that "two thirds (or more)" of the cost of software projects was typically taken up by detecting and removing pro-

---

[14] I included failures of "defensive" military action (such as anti-missile defences) but not inadvertent civilian deaths resulting from offensive actions. I simply lacked the data plausibly to include the latter.

gramming errors. Furthermore, "the cost of error in certain types of program may be almost incalculable—a lost spacecraft, a collapsed building, a crashed aeroplane, or a world war." He was to comment elsewhere that an "unreliable programming language generating unreliable programs constitutes a far greater risk to our environment and to our society than unsafe cars, toxic pesticides, or accidents at nuclear power stations."[15]

Like the Sonnenbichl participants, Hoare wished not simply to diagnose problems but to provide solutions: in the terminology of the dependability tree, he was concerned not just with "impairments" but also with means of delivering a dependable service and gaining confidence in its dependability. A significant, but not universally shared, component of the view from the Sonnenbichl was that the chief means to achieve dependability was to subject software to formal reasoning. From the 1968 conference, one could see, as it were, not just physical mountain peaks, but what many human cultures take them to symbolize: clear, rigorous thought. Hoare's 1969 article "An Axiomatic Basis for Computer Programming," was the single most important manifesto of this perspective. "Computer programming," Hoare began, "is an exact science in that all the properties of a program and all the consequences of executing it in any given environment can, in principle, be found out from the text of the program itself by means of purely deductive reasoning." If one could produce a formal specification of what a program was intended to achieve, and if the programming language involved were well-designed, then it might be possible to express a program's "correctness" as a theorem, and to prove that theorem. In consequence, "program proving" or "[p]roofs of [p]rogram [c]orrectness" was "not only a theoretical pursuit" but potentially a vital practical technique for preventing program design faults, and for achieving confidence in their absence. The result, it is important to point out, would not be a proof of dependability—the specification itself could be inadequate, as could the compiler, and the implementation of the program on a physical machine could go wrong—but it would be an important contribution to dependability.[16]

A quarter of a century on, in 1994, Hoare returned to the issue of software dependability. He pointed, for example, to the remarkable reliability of modern software-controlled telephone switching systems. Containing tens of millions of lines of program, these operate 24 hours a day, day after day, and the frequency of system "crashes" has gradually been reduced, Hoare reported, from every two hours to around every two years. "[A]ircraft, both civil and military, are now flying with the aid of software measured in millions of lines—though not all of it is safety-critical," said Hoare. "Compilers and operating systems of a similar size now number their satisfied customers in millions."[17]

[15] C. A. R. Hoare and Cliff B. Jones (ed.), *Essays in Computing Science* (New York, 1989), 8, 17; C. A. R. Hoare, "An Axiomatic Basis for Computer Programming," *Communications of the ACM* 12 (1969): 576-83, at 579-80.

[16] C. A. R. Hoare, "An Axiomatic Basis for Computer Programming," at 576, 579-80.

[17] C. A. R. Hoare, "How Did Software Get So Reliable Without Proof?" Presentation to Awareness Club in Computer Assisted Formal Reasoning, Edinburgh, 21 March 1994; Hoare, "How Did Software Get So Reliable Without Proof?" typescript, December 1995, 3.

These dependability successes did not arise from the application of "program proving." Even by the mid 1990s, such proofs were rare in industrial practice.[18] "How did software get so reliable without proof?" asked Hoare. Though one might wish to substitute "dependable" for "reliable," and insert the word "some" before "software," Hoare's question is an important and puzzling one. Even without proof, modern software engineering practice *works*, Hoare suggests. The ever-increasing capacity of computing hardware, and its ever-decreasing relative cost, make it possible to prohibit the most risky practices: "[N]o data packing, no optimal coding, no pointers, no sharing, no dynamic storage allocation. ... no jumps, no interrupts, no multiprogramming, no global variables." Anticipating errors, "defensive programming" is practiced, and in systems like telephone switches where it is permissible occasionally to lose data or to fail to connect a call, "software audits" constantly check "all the records in the global system tables" and remove "suspicious entries" by a "reinitialisation to safe values." Review of designs and programs by team members not directly responsible for them is remarkably effective in detecting errors, and testing is "more effective than it has any right to be:" that is, more effective than its abstract statistical analysis might suggest. Ultimately, said Hoare, what testing checks is not programs, but the people who write them. "Programmers who consistently fail to meet their testing schedules are quickly isolated, and assigned to less intellectually demanding tasks."[19]

Three consequences for historiography seem to me to flow from the puzzling dependability of many software systems. The first is the need for "natural history" of real-world dependable systems, delving deep into the detailed history of systems like digital exchanges and fly-by-wire aircraft. What faults are present in such systems, which of them lead to errors, and how are the errors (largely) prevented from producing failures? How is dependability maintained and improved over the long, evolutionary history of such systems? Why do some systems have an excellent record of dependability, and some a more dubious one?

The second historiographic consequence is that we must take a broad view of the means of achieving dependability. Computer science's formalists and rationalists exercise a strong attraction for historians, myself included. Their work raises profound intellectual questions: I am currently finishing a book on the issues of the "sociology of proof" involved (the question of what kinds of mathematical arguments count for whom, under what circumstances, as proofs).[20] But more mundane contributions to software dependability stand equally in need of historical attention. Where, for example, is the history of defensive programming, software audits and recovery blocks, which are in all probability very important contributors to the dependability of real-world systems? Above all, social-science and historical attention should be devoted to software reviews and to testing. As I have noted, only a limited number of real-world systems have been subject to proof,

---

[18] See, e.g., Donald MacKenzie and M. Tierney, "Safety-Critical and Security-Critical Computing in Britain: An Exploration," *Technology Analysis & Strategic Management* 8 (1996): 355-79.

[19] C. A. R. Hoare, "How Did Software Get So Reliable Without Proof," (1995), 8, 12, and 14; Hoare, "How Did Software Get So Reliable Without Proof," (1994).

[20] Donald MacKenzie, *Mechanizing Proof: Computing, Risk and Trust* (Cambridge, Mass., 2001).

but, despite the well-known limitations of testing and review, their sufficiently systematic use seems in practice often capable of achieving adequate levels of validation. The software in the fly-by-wire Boeing 777, for example, was subject to testing and to review, but not generally to proof; the aircraft has now been in service since 1995 without, to date, a serious mishap. The unsung disciplines of software engineering require their historians as much as do the more prominent ones. Under some circumstances, testing and review can fail catastrophically; under other circumstances they seem to permit adequate validation; but we have little understanding of the social and historical causes of the difference.

Third, the Hoare paradox suggests that the effects on dependability of software's formalists have to be conceived broadly. Proof is still rare, and even formal specification unusual, but this does not mean that the formalist component of the view from the Sonnenbichl has been without influence. The impact of "structured programming" is the most obvious case. At its most basic, pointed out its leading proponent, Edsger W. Dijkstra, structured programming was simply an exemplification of the age-old maxim, *divide et impera*, "divide and rule." A complex mathematical proof, for example, is typically built up out of lemmas: "subtheorems," each with its own proof, which, combined together, give structure to what would otherwise be an over-long, difficult to grasp, proof of a theorem. A complex programming task, argued Dijkstra, similarly had to be divided into subtasks each of which "is implemented independently of how it is going to be used and is used independently of how it has been implemented."[21]

Structured programming is a topic which links the histories of software as science, software as engineering, software dependability, and, perhaps above all, software as labour process. Philip Kraft's 1977 sociological analysis, *Programmers and Managers*, exaggerated the extent of the "routinization of computer programming" that had occurred, but usefully drew attention to the intertwining of the organizational and the technical aspects of programming.[22] Within IBM, for example, Harlan Mills, Director of Software Engineering and Technology in IBM's Federal Systems Division, drew upon theoretical computer science (the Böhm-Jacopini theorem)[23] to undercut opposition to structured programming. He translated the Böhm-Jacopini theorem into a form more "valuable to management" as a structure theorem, "which established the existence of a structured program for any problem that permitted a flowchartable solution."[24] Any programmer

---

[21] Edsger W. Dijkstra, "Programming considered as a Human Activity," *IFIP Congress 65: Proceedings* (London, 1965), 213-7, at 214; Dijkstra, "'Why is Software So Expensive?' An Explanation to the Hardware Designer," in Dijkstra, *Selected Writings on Computing: A Personal Perspective* (New York, 1982), 338-48, at 341-2. See also Dijkstra, "Structured Programming," in Buxton and Randell (n. 6 above), 84-8.

[22] Philip Kraft, *Programmers and Managers: The Routinization of Computer Programming in the United States* (New York, 1977).

[23] The Böhm-Jacopini theorem is that "every Turing machine is reducible into ... a program written in a language which admits as formation rules only composition and iteration." See Corrado Böhm and Giuseppe Jacopini, "Flow Diagrams, Turing Machines and Languages With Only Two Formation Rules," *Communications of the ACM* 9 (1966): 366-71, at 366.

[24] Harlan D. Mills, "Structured Programming: Retrospect and Prospect," *IEEE Software* (November 1986): 58-66, at 60.

claiming to need to use *go to* instructions (famously condemned by Dijkstra),[25] or seeking in other ways to escape the constraints of structured programming, could be met by a manager confident that such violations of good practice were unnecessary. Programmers could not credibly claim that problems were too difficult to be solved with structured programs: the structure theorem could be drawn upon to show such a claim to be false.[26] In other words, we need to attend not just to the (limited) practical adoption of the formalists' technical innovations, but to the broader uses to which their ideas were put. Their rationalist assault—Dijkstra describes himself as "a happy victim of the Enlightenment"[27]—on software's "Middle Ages" had lasting effects on the discipline's culture. That influence has never been uncontested—see, for example, Sherry Turkle's classic descriptions of the differences between structured programming's "hard mastery" and the "soft mastery" of, for instance, MIT's legendary hackers[28]—but in significant areas, including much of safety-critical and security-critical computing, Bauer's Sonnenbichl vision of "software engineering" displacing what he called "software tinkering (bricolage)" has not been without its effects on dependability.[29] Documenting what those effects have been, and understanding what "software engineering" has meant in its different national, sectoral and historical contexts, is a task that has hardly begun, but it is a vital task if we are to understand the history of software dependability.

The Sociology of Software Dependability

Having sketched some historical priorities, let me now turn to the term "sociology" in my subtitle. Why should that discipline have anything to contribute to the understanding of the history of a technical topic such as dependability? Surely, dependability's history is a technical history?

Though dependability is a technical matter, it is not *just* a technical matter. The "phenomenological causes" of faults, in the words of Laprie and his colleagues, divide into the physical ("due to adverse physical phenomena") and the human-

---

[25] Edsger W. Dijkstra, "Go To Statement Considered Harmful," *Communications of the ACM* 11 (1968): 147-8, at 147; see Peláez, *Pandora's Box*, 204-20.

[26] Mills (n. 24 above); Hoare, "How Did Software Get So Reliable Without Proof?" Barry Boehm confirmed to me in a personal communication (Schloss Dagstuhl, 16 August 1996) that Mills did indeed use the Böhm-Jacopini theorem in this way within IBM. The structure theorem is stated in Harlan D. Mills, "The New Math of Computer Programming," *Communications of the ACM* 18 (1975): 43-8, at 45.

[27] Edsger W. Dijkstra, interviewed by A. J. Dale, Austin, Tex., 6 April 1994.

[28] See, e.g., Sherry Turkle, *Life on the Screen: Identity in the Age of the Internet* (London, 1996), 57 and 278-9, note 8.

[29] Friedrich L. Bauer, "Software Engineering" (undated manuscript notes). I am grateful to Professor Bauer for sending me these notes, which are (the word "bricolage" aside) in English. It is interesting that Turkle, quite independently, chooses the term "bricolage" to describe the "bottom-up," concrete, "soft mastery" of the hacker style, as distinct from the "top-down," planned, rule-bound, abstract, "hard mastery" of structured programming: see Turkle, 51, 56. The popularity of "bricolage" as a concept in the social sciences largely derives from Claude Lévi-Strauss, *The Savage Mind* (Chicago, 1968).

made, "which result from human imperfections."[30] In the case of software, it is the latter that are of the greater concern, and this brings us squarely into the realm of the social sciences, though to be sure not just sociology: the economics and the psychology of computer programming are also very important.[31] Furthermore, when one moves from design faults to operational faults "which appear during the system's exploitation,"[32] then in many cases one is again in the realm of the social sciences. To be sure, my estimate of over 90% of deaths resulting from faults in human-computer interaction may not be accurate nor capable of extrapolation to less serious failures and to the other components of dependability (anecdotal evidence suggests that "human factors" are also extremely important in practice in security failures, but the same may not be true of reliability and availability). Ultimately, however, what matters is *system* dependability (not just hardware dependability or software dependability), and in many cases system dependability is a socio-technical, rather than just a technical, achievement. If software dependability is one key problem raised by the growing reliance of our societies on computers, then here, surely is the other: to understand how computer systems can fit into social relations in dependable, equitable, and life-enhancing ways. Plainly, it is a sociological—but not *just* a sociological—problem, one which the now considerable historical record would help us understand, if that record is brought to light systematically. Indeed, I would argue that system dependability, not software dependability, is the correct historical focus: the latter is only one contribution, and not always the crucial one, to the former.

Dependability and the Sociology of Deviance

The sociotechnical nature of system dependability is not the only way in which sociology is potentially relevant. Surprisingly, an area that may provide intellectual resources for the historiography of software dependability is the sociology of deviance, of activities that are taken as breaking a society's rules. Much early sociology of deviance focused, not surprisingly, on understanding who broke the rules and why. In the 1950s and 1960s, however, it was realized that it was also important to study the creation of rules, the decisions as to what acts breach them, and how those involved in such acts are treated. "Deviance," wrote Howard S. Becker, "is *not* a quality of the act the person commits, but rather a consequence of the application by others of rules and sanctions to an 'offender.' The deviant is one to whom that label has successfully been applied; deviant behavior is behavior that people so label."[33] Many white-collar workers, for example, use office stationery, office computers and office telephones for private purposes. Arguably, that use is theft from their employers, but few are prosecuted as thieves, and, indeed, some private use—such as electronic mail to and from friends—is tacitly condoned.

---

[30] Laprie (n. 7 above), 11.
[31] See, for example, Gerald M. Weinberg, *The Psychology of Computer Programming* (New York, 1971).
[32] Laprie (n. 7 above), 11.
[33] Howard S. Becker, *Outsiders: Studies in the Sociology of Deviance* (New York, 1973), 9.

The reaction of the "audience" to an act, as well as the act itself, is therefore important to whether it is taken to be deviant. The same is true in the sphere of computer-system dependability. Dependability is not an absolute matter: the "audiences" for computer systems judge what degree of dependability is adequate, and indeed which events count as "failures." The clearest instance of the importance of audience reaction comes not from the history of software but from that of hardware dependability. In the summer of 1994, a small fault was uncovered in the implementation of floating-point division in the Intel Corporation's new Pentium[TM] processor. Intel detected the fault in its own post-release testing, and, independently, the mathematician Thomas Nicely detected errors in the Pentium's floating-point arithmetic which allowed Tim Coe, an engineer at Vitesse Semiconductor Corporation, to identify the underlying fault. Reactions to the fault differed widely. Intel's internal analysis suggested that it would trigger an error state only once in 9 billion random divisions; the error, furthermore, could at worst affect only the fourth significant decimal digit in a division, and under most circumstances would have even smaller effects. To Intel's president, Andrew Grove, it was a routine event: "After almost 25 years in the microprocessor business, I have come to the conclusion that no microprocessor is ever perfect; they just become closer to perfection with each stepping [new, corrected, set of masks]." The data in Table 1, indeed, is consistent with Grove's viewpoint: design faults in complex microprocessors are commonplace. To others, however, the fault, and what they saw as Intel's complacent reaction to it, seemed scandalous. Key was the Internet news group comp.sys.intel: it was, for example, via this group that Nicely's electronic mail message describing the division errors was circulated, and its circulation led to Coe's involvement. Unlike Nicely, Coe was able to guess the underlying fault, and so could construct a serious instance of the error. The division 4195835/3145727 should have the answer 1.33382044; on the Pentium, the answer was 1.33373906. With the benefit of a simple example, any user could check for the fault's existence in his or her processor, and the story quickly went beyond the internet's hard-core "techies." By the end of November 1994, it had reached the *New York Times* and television news. On December 12, 1994, IBM announced it was halting all shipments of personal computers containing chips with the bug, and Intel's share price on Wall Street fell. Although, to my knowledge, the design fault led to no real-world failure, the reaction to it temporarily damaged both Intel's reputation and its balance-sheet (it set aside U.S. $475 million to cover costs of replacements and stocks that had to be discarded), and had a wider impact on the industry. Proof-based methods rapidly grew in acceptance: in part because of the growing maturity of automated model-checking tools, but in part because the divide bug episode revealed the potential for highly negative "audience" reaction to faults.[34]

A striking feature of the history hitherto of the dependability of mass-market packaged software is that it has not yet encountered an equivalent of the Pentium divide bug. Plainly, this is not because such packaged software is free from design faults! Its dependability is only modest. Even Microsoft, for example, claims only

---

[34] See Donald MacKenzie, *Mechanizing Proof: Computing, Risk, and Trust* (Cambridge, Mass., 2001), chap. 7; Andy Grove, "My Perspective on Pentium," comp.sys.intel, 27 November 1994.

limited reliability for Windows 95, with Bill Gates quoting an estimate of an average 2.1 days of continuous running of Windows 95 before the need to restart.[35] Notoriously, too, packaged software carries with it sweeping waivers of responsibility for failures caused by its faults. These faults and failures are like putatively deviant societal acts: their tolerability is a matter of audience reaction. The response to the divide bug is a warning that even in the absence of real-world failure of any consequence, societal reaction may change dramatically.

Table 1. Reported design faults in 80x86 microprocessors[36]

386 A1 step	28	
386 B0 step	12	
386 B1 step	15	
386 D0 step	3	
386 "some versions"	19	
386 "all versions"	1	
TOTAL for 386 family		78
486 "early versions"	6	
486 "some versions"	8	
486 A-B4 steps	3	
486 A-C0 steps	2	
486 "all versions"	2	
TOTAL for 486 family		21
Pentium 60- and 66-MHz	21	
Pentium 75-, 90- and 100-MHz	42	
TOTAL for Pentium (to February 1995)		56

80x86 microprocessors prior to the 386 are not included, and data for 386 and 486 are not comparable with that for Pentium, since the latter data contains all design faults known to Intel at February 1995, while the former is based upon published reports alone. Totals for Pentium do not add up because 7 design faults were common both to 60-MHz/66-MHz processors and to 75-, 90- and 100-MHz processors. Typically, design faults found in one version of a processor will be corrected in later versions.

---

[35] Christopher Price and Tom Foremski, "Gates Heralds Windows 2000," *Financial Times*, 18 February 2000, 27. For the history of mass-market software, see Martin Campbell-Kelly, "Development and Structure of the International Software Industry, 1950-1990," *Business and Economic History* 24 (1995): 73-110.

[36] *Sources*: Figures for 386 and 486 are taken from Olin Sibert, Phillip A. Porras, and Robert Lindell, "The Intel 80x86 Processor Architecture," paper read to the IEEE Computer Society Symposium on Research in Security and Privacy, Oakland, Calif., May 1995. Figures for Pentium are my calculations based upon Intel Corporation, Pentium Processor Specification Update (Santa Clara, Calif.: Intel, 1995). "Pentium" is a trade-mark of the Intel Corporation.

Moral Entrepreneurship

Though it may change suddenly and dramatically, societal reaction is not a random matter. The sociology of deviance focuses usefully on those who seek to engineer that reaction, whom Becker calls "moral entrepreneurs." As he points out: "rules are not made automatically. Even though a practice may be harmful in an objective sense to the group in which it occurs, the harm needs to be discovered and pointed out. People must be made to feel that something ought to be done about it. Someone must call the public's attention to these matters, supply the push necessary to get things done, and direct such energies as are aroused in the proper direction to get a rule created."[37] The term "moral entrepreneur" is a neutral one: it implies neither approval nor disapproval of such activity.

The history of software dependability is full of moral entrepreneurship in Becker's sense. The warnings issued at the Sonnenbichl are one instance; another is J. C. R. Licklider's 1969 warning of the "potentially hideous folly" of basing software-controlled nuclear anti-missile defenses around American cities;[38] Neumann's collection and dissemination of risks are a third; warnings of the dangers posed by the year 2000 problem, or "Millennium bug," are the most recent prominent example. This moral entrepreneurship has been influential: for example, in its heyday RISKS was said to be Usenet's most popular news group, and those who warned of the year 2000 problem prompted corrective action that may have cost $400 billion globally.[39]

As noted above, the notion of "moral entrepreneurship" is not evaluative in itself. My own judgement is that the activities of software dependability's moral entrepreneurs have been predominantly beneficial. Studying safety-critical and security-critical computing in the U.K. in the early 1990s, my colleague Margaret Tierney and I encountered considerable caution on the part of both engineers and regulators about placing too much dependence upon software. Wherever possible, it appeared, hardware solutions were preferred for the most critical functions. While I am not certain of the situation in other national contexts, it seems possible that this caution could be one cause of the relatively modest number of deaths resulting from software design faults. Knowing of its proneness to such faults, and knowing that regulators would scrutinize critical software components with a special care, system developers have exercised a proper caution, especially in mainstream fields of safety-criticality. (The worst problems seemed to us to have been in areas such as ambulance dispatch and automated industrial equipment where regulation was weak and the safety-criticality of software may have been underestimated.)[40] The worst societal outcome of the year 2000 episode would be if the limited incidence of problems, even in countries where little corrective action was taken, were to lead to a widespread sense that software's moral entrepre-

---

[37] Becker, 162.

[38] J. C. R. Licklider, "Underestimates and Overexpectations," in *ABM: An Evaluation of the Decision to Deploy an Antiballistic Missile System*, eds. Abram Chayes and Jerome B. Wiesner (New York, 1969), 118-29, at 123.

[39] Paul Taylor, "The Beneficial Effects of the Millennium Bug," *Financial Times*, 7 January 2000, 15.

[40] MacKenzie and Tierney (n. 18 above).

neurs are "crying wolf" in respect to dependability. That complacent conclusion would bring its consequences in loss of life. An important public contribution of the historiography of software dependability might well be to demonstrate just how narrow and contingent are the bases upon which the currently adequate dependability of many systems rests, and the consequent potential dangers of straying beyond those bases.

Sociology of Knowledge

The year 2000 problem points us towards another area of the potential relevance of sociology. The episode shows that what matters is not just the procurement of dependability, but also its validation: rightly, many governments and companies were not prepared to tolerate uncertainty as to the consequences of the date problem. They wanted to *know*, and were prepared to incur large expenses to find out (though, in practice, much apparent expenditure on the year 2000 problem may have been replacement and improvement that was desirable on other grounds). In safety-critical and security-critical computing the issue is at its clearest: we want systems not just to be safe and secure, but to be known to be safe and secure. That requirement brings software dependability firmly within the sphere of the sociology of knowledge.[41]

One way of categorizing our knowledge of the properties of artefacts (including computer systems) is a three-fold division:

- authority: people whom we trust tell us what those properties are;
- induction: we learn the properties by testing and using the artefacts or systems;
- deduction: we infer the properties from scientific or other theories.[42]

Authority is plainly a sociological matter; the credibility of induction and deduction, both in general and in particular instances, is also subject to social variation. Software's formalizers, for example, mounted an influential critique of the credibility of inductively-based knowledge of the properties of software systems, a critique famously expressed by Edsger W. Dijkstra in a paper to the 1969 Rome Conference: "program testing can be used to show the presence of bugs, but never to show their absence!"[43] Conversely, the claims of the formalizers have been fiercely contested by computer scientists Richard DeMillo, Richard Lipton and Alan Perlis, as well as by philosopher James H. Fetzer.[44] Dispute over a particular claim of deductive proof, of a hardware design (of VIPER, the Verifiable Integrated Processor for Enhanced Reliability, developed at the U.K. Ministry of De-

[41] The best single introduction to this field, particularly in its application to science, is Barry Barnes, David Bloor, and John Henry, *Scientific Knowledge: A Sociological Analysis* (London and Chicago, 1996).

[42] Donald MacKenzie, "How Do We know the Properties of Artefacts? Applying the Sociology of Knowledge to Technology," in *Technological Change: Methods and Themes in the History of Technology*, ed. Robert Fox (London, 1996), 247-63.

[43] Dijkstra, "Structured Programming"(n. 21 above), 85; emphasis in original deleted.

[44] Richard A. DeMillo, Richard J. Lipton, and Alan J. Perlis, "Social Processes and Proofs of Theorems and Programs," *Communications of the ACM* 22 (1979): 271-80; James H. Fetzer, "Program Verification: The Very Idea," *Communications of the ACM* 31 (1988): 1048-63. For the background to these critiques, see MacKenzie, *Mechanizing Proof* (n. 20 above), chap. 6.

fence's Royal Signal and Radar Establishment in the 1980s) even led to litigation.[45]

The key sociology-of-knowledge point is that knowledge of the properties of things cannot entirely be disentangled from knowledge of the properties of people. In the case of software testing, for example, Hoare's analysis (discussed above) suggests that the quality of testing is intrinsically tied up with the quality of the tester: a skilled tester (presumably because of his or her knowledge of the likely sources of software design faults), seems to be able to achieve better results than would be expected on the basis of the limited proportion of the state space of a program of any complexity that can feasibly be explored by testing. The credibility of the results of testing, therefore, may rest upon a judgement of the trustworthiness of the persons or people doing the testing. Even deduction, which appears to be an entirely individual process, nevertheless leads back to issues of trust. Not only is there a question of the credibility of the application of the theory in question to the particular situation in which it is employed, but in the case of computer-system dependability deductions are often not short chains of reasoning that can readily be comprehended in their entirety by an individual human being. Frequently, the detailed steps in a deduction will be constructed by an automated theorem prover, and so the question arises of the trustworthiness of the prover and of those who designed it.[46]

Sociology of Professions

The conclusion of the sociology of knowledge, then, is that authority or trust is not simply one of the sources of knowledge of the properties of technical artefacts, but is intrinsically interwoven in the other sources: what we believe cannot be entirely separated from whom we believe. In complex societies, of course, trust is not simply an interpersonal matter: particular occupations claim the right, often successfully, to be trusted to perform their tasks dependably, and to have their claims to knowledge believed. In Western societies, these occupations frequently have the form of professions, with formal controls over membership (typically dependent upon passing professional examinations), norms requiring consideration of the public good, not merely self-interest, mechanisms for the disciplining and possible expulsion of incompetent or deviant members, and the capacity to take legal action against outsiders who falsely claim professional status. What is most striking about "software engineering" is the limited extent to which it is a profession. At the meeting on the history of software engineering referred to above, one participant, David Parnas, reported a gathering of his colleagues in which there seemed to be consensus that they could call themselves software engineers if they wished, and his apposite reply: that the key point about being an engineer is that it is something that other people call you, rather than something you call yourself.[47] In 1971, the U.S. Court of Appeal judged that: "... programmers and analysts were better described as 'technical' rather than as 'professional' employees ... [as their work]

---

[45] Donald MacKenzie, "The Fangs of the VIPER," *Nature* 352 (8 August 1991): 467-8.
[46] MacKenzie, *Mechanizing Proof* (n. 20 above), chap. 8.
[47] David Parnas, personal communication.

... did not require a professional measure of skill, knowledge and independent exercise or judgment."[48] Despite much effort to gain professional status, notably by the Association for Computing Machinery by the 1990s it was still illegal, in 48 states of the U.S., to adopt the Sonnenbichl slogan and to describe oneself as a "software engineer."[49] The absence of professional status for many categories of software developers and testers (some, of course, are members of other professional bodies, such as the Institute of Electrical and Electronics Engineers) does not imply an absence of authority and trust: all it means is that the span of trust is likely to be more local, and more dependent upon personal knowledge, than it would be if full professional status had been achieved. Nor does it imply that professionalization is necessarily a desirable goal. A characteristic of Anglo-American societies in the last 20 years has been a decline in the perception that professions deserve respect: the salaries of American lawyers, for example, might be envied, but not their reputations for trustworthiness. Nevertheless, from the point of view of the historian, the fluctuating social status of software's developers is an important question not merely for the fate of "software engineering" but for the perceived dependability of software systems.

Conclusion

The dependability of computing is a problem with which our societies will continue to have to wrestle. There is some justification to Andrew L. Friedman's claim that "The solutions proposed at the Garmisch conference and the techniques developed and diffused [in the subsequent years] did have an effect. The software crisis was not 'solved' but several aspects ... eased. A combination of greater experience with computer systems development in large user organizations, reduced ambitions of systems developers, expanded computer systems core and standardized methods led to the delivery of somewhat more reliable systems within more acceptable cost limitations."[50] But neither that conclusion, nor Hoare's judgement that modern software engineering practice can work tolerably well, even in the absence of proof, means that the problem of software dependability has gone away. A perusal of RISKS or of the computing press is quite sufficient to disabuse one of that notion: problems of dependability are commonplace. One of this paper's conjectures is that the activities of software dependability's moral entrepreneurs have helped keep the problems from costing lives, because of the caution they inspired about making software safety-critical. If that conjecture is right, it is a dangerously narrow basis for confidence in the future, especially if caution is swept away by a wave of post-millennial complacency. Nor, furthermore, do potential safety problems exhaust the importance of computer system dependability. The growing computerization of military logistics, planning and equipment, the increasing computer-dependence of essential services, and, per-

---

[48] Quoted in Wanda J. Orlikowski and Jack J. Baroudi, "The Information Systems Profession: Myth or Reality?" *Office: Technology & People* 4 (1989): 13-30, at 17.

[49] Julia King, "Engineers to IS: Drop that Title!" *Computer World* 28/22 (30 March 1994): 1 and 119; Barry Boehm, "The ACM-IEEE Initiative on Software Engineering as a Profession," *ACM Software Engineering Notes* 19/4 (October 1994): 1-2, at 1.

[50] Friedman (n. 3 above), 174.

haps above all, the rapid growth in electronic commerce all point to the importance of security issues. Even mass-market packaged software developers pay an
economic price for poor dependability, at least if they provide a period of free
telephone help advice (I have been told that a single phonecall to such a help-line
eliminates, when its full costs are properly reckoned, the profit from the sale of the
individual copy of the package that prompted it).[51] They also remain vulnerable to
a sudden switch in "audience reaction" such as was prompted by the Pentium
divide bug.

The historiography of computer-system dependability deals with a crucial issue
facing the societies of high modernity. If it is to realize its promise, it requires
history of computing of a new type: systematic, not merely anecdotal, histories of
faults, errors, and failures; histories of the less glamorous means of achieving
dependability; and so on. This new historiography requires new methods. The
"natural history" of the development and operation of evolving real-world dependable systems has to go beyond the historian's traditional toolbox, and involves a genuine fusion of the approaches of the historian, the social scientist, and
the computer scientist, synthesizing the technical history of systems with their
economic and organizational histories. Issues of culture and gender, the wider
connotations of Turkle's "hard mastery" of the software engineers and "soft mastery" of the bricoleurs, will be encountered. In some contexts, even political history is involved: the history of computer security is not separable from changing
trust in government. In the words of National Security Agency officer George F.
Jelen: "Most of the significant early development of COMSEC [communications
security] devices took place during an era when government was generally trusted.
That of COMPUSEC [computer security] did not. When COMSEC device technology was maturing, the environment was that of a country unified by war
against the common, foreign enemy. The current [1985] political environment
surrounding the government's efforts in computer security is set against the back-
drop of Watergate. ... The 'high politics' factor, then, is that in the minds of many
people today, the enemy most to be feared is government itself."[52]

Computer-system dependability (which is, I have suggested, a more satisfactory
object of research than software dependability) is intrinsically multi-faceted. Dependable hardware is patently of limited value unless accompanied by dependable
software; neither help greatly if human interaction with the hardware and software
system is fault-prone; and the dependable sociotechnical performance of an inappropriate task may cause wider damage. Because dependability has many facets,
its history must be diverse and inter-disciplinary. In the societies of high modernity, computing is becoming both increasingly ubiquitous and increasingly invisible: our dependence upon it may become clear only in its moments of undependa-
bility.[53] The history of a ubiquitous and invisible entity is a hard history to write:
how do you tell the history of something that, increasingly, is everywhere? But

---

[51] Unfortunately, I know no precise reference for this claim, but it seems plausible.
[52] George F. Jelen, *Information Security: An Elusive Goal* (Cambridge, Mass., Harvard University Center for Information Policy Research, June 1985, P-85-8), p. I-11.
[53] I recall my naïveté a few years ago in going a garage to ask for what I took to be simple mechanical adjustments to my car's carburettor and spark plugs, to be told that these were no
longer possible, and the only option was replacement of the computerized engine-management
system!

what makes the history hard also makes it fascinating and important. Because computing is everywhere, the tensions of entire societies run through it.[54] Because we cannot now escape dependence upon computer systems, the history of their dependability is of prime importance.

---

[54] Consider, for example, the place of computerized financial markets and financial transactions in the economic history of high modernity.

Appendix: Cases of Possible Computer-Related Accidental Death (to end of 1992)

Date(s)	Number of deaths	Location	Nature of Incident	Probable Main Cause(s)	Main Reference(s)	Data quality
			PHYSICAL CAUSES			
?	1	US	Accidental reprogramming of cardiac pacemaker	Interference from therapeutic micro-waves	Dennett (1979)	Poor
?	1	US	Accidental reprogramming of cardiac pacemaker	Interference from anti-theft device	SEN 10(2),6 SEN 11(1),9	Poor
1982	20	South Atlantic	Sinking of HMS Sheffield following failure to inter-cept Argentin-ean Exocet missile	Interference from satellite radio transmission	Daily Mirror 15/5/86,1; Han-sard 9/6/86	Fair
1982	1	US	Car accident	Fire may have caused failure of anti-skid braking system	San Francisco Chronicle 5/2/86, 12	Very poor
1986	2	Libya	Crash of US F111 during attack on Trip-oli	Possible electro-magnetic interfer-ence	SEN 14(2),22	Very poor
1982-87	22	?	Crashes of US military heli-copter	Possible electro-magnetic interfer-ence denied by makers, US army	AW&ST 16/11/87, 27-28	Poor, con-tro-ver-sial

Date(s)	Number of deaths	Location	Nature of Incident	Probable Main Cause(s)	Main Reference(s)	Data quality
1988	1	UK	Operator killed by computer-controlled boring machine	Machine restarted unexpectedly due to faulty capacitor	Edwards (n.d.)	Good
				SOFTWARE ERROR		
1986	2	US	Overdoses from radiation therapy machine	Error in relationship between data entry routine and treatment monitor task	Leveson & Turner (1992)	Very good
1991	28	Saudi Arabia	Failure to intercept Iraqi Scud missile	Omitted call to time-conversion subroutine; delayed arrival of corrected software	GAO (1992), Skeel (1992)	Good
				HUMAN-COMPUTER INTERACTION PROBLEMS Medical		
1982-91	"in the tens"	UK	Underdosing by radiation therapy machine	Correction factor for reduced source-skin distance in isocentric therapy applied twice (already present in software).	West Midlands Regional Health Authority (1992), North Staffordshire Health Authority (1993)	Good

Date(s)	Number of deaths	Location	Nature of Incident	Probable Main Cause(s)	Main Reference(s)	Data quality
				Military		
1987	37	Persian Gulf	Failure to intercept attack on USS Stark by Iraqi Exocet missile	Alleged lack of combat-readiness; possible defective friend/foe identification or switching off of audible warning	Sharp (1987), Committee on Armed Services (1987), Adam (1987), Vlahos (1988)	Fair
1988	290	Persian Gulf	Shooting down of Iran Air airliner by USS Vincennes	Stress; need for rapid decision; weapon system human interface not optimal for situation	Fogarty (1988)	Good
				Air		
1979	257	Antarctica	Crash of airliner on sightseeing trip	Communication failure re resetting of navigation system; continuation of flight in dangerous visual conditions	Mahon (1981)	Fair, but aspects controversial
1983	269	USSR	Shooting down of Korean Air Lines airliner following navigational error	Autopilot connected to compass rather than inertial navigation system	AW&ST 21/6/93, 17	Fair
1988	4	UK	Collision of 2 RAF Tornado aircraft	Use of identical navigational cassettes by different aircraft	Sunday Times 11/3/90, A9	Fair

Date(s)	Number of deaths	Location	Nature of Incident	Probable Main Cause(s)	Main Reference(s)	Data quality
1989	12	Brazil	Crash of airliner after running out of fuel	Incorrect input to navigation system?	SEN 15(1), 18	Poor, controversial
1992	87	France	Crash of airliner into mountain during night-time approach	Vertical speed mode may have been selected instead of flight path angle; limited cross-checking between crew; possible distraction; no ground proximity warning system	Sparaco (1994)	Fair
			Robot-related			
1978-87	10	Japan	Workers struck during repair, maintenance, installation or adjustment of robots	Workers entered envelope of powered-up robots; in some cases, deficiencies in training and absence of fences	Nagamachi (1988)	Fair
1984	1	US	Heart failure after being pinned by robot	Worker entered envelope of powered-up robot	Sanderson et al. (1986)	Fair
			Involving other automated plant			
1979	1	US	Worker struck by automated vehicle in computerized storage facility	Absence of audible warning; inadequate training; production pressure	Fuller (1984)	Good

Date(s)	Number of deaths	Location	Nature of Incident	Probable Main Cause(s)	Main Reference(s)	Data quality
1983-88	13	France	Accidents to operators/ installers/ repairers of automated plant	Insufficient individual detail given in source	Vautrim & Dei-Svaldi (1989)	Good but too aggregated for current purpose
1988	1	UK	Maintenance electrician killed by unexpected movement of automatic hoist	Maintenance electrician disconnected proximity switch, which sent signal to controller; machine not isolated.	Edwards (n.d.)	Good
1989	1	UK	Setter/operator killed by palletiser	Machine cycled when boxes interrupting photoelectric beam removed; transfer table not isolated.	Edwards (n.d.)	Good
1991	1	UK	Maintenance fitter killed by hold-down arm of feed unit to log saw	Fitter's body interrupted beam of process sensor; machine not isolated.	Edwards (n.d.)	Good
1991	1	UK	Maintenance fitter killed in automatic brick-making plant	Fitter inside guarding enclosure observing cause of misalignment of bricks.	Edwards (n.d.)	Good
?	3	Netherlands	Explosion at chemical plant	Typing error caused wrong chemical to be added to reactor	SEN 18(2), 7	Fair

Date(s)	Number of deaths	Location	Nature of Incident	Probable Main Cause(s)	Main Reference(s)	Data quality
				INSUFFICIENT DATA		
1986	1	US	Overdose of pain-relieving drugs	Error in medical expert system (?)	Forester & Morrison (1990)	Very poor
1989	1	US	Failure of school-crossing pedestrian signals	Breakdown in radio communications link to computer (?)	Emery (1989)	Poor
1990	1	US	Collision of automated guided vehicle and crane	Unclear	SEN 16(1),10	Very poor
1990	1?	US	Delay in ambulance despatch	Logging program not installed (?) Unclear whether death result of delay	SEN 16(1),10	Poor
c 1983	1	West Germany	Woman killed daughter after erroneous medical diagnosis	"Computer error"	SEN 10(3),8	Very poor
c 1984	1	China	Electrocution	Unclear	SEN 10(1),8	Very poor
c 1989	1	USSR	Electrocution	Unclear	SEN 14(5),7	Very poor
?	2?	?	Sudden unintended car acceleration	Unclear	SEN 12 (1), 8-9 Business Week 29/5/89, 19	Poor, controversial

Acronyms: SEN is the Association for Computing Machinery, *Software Engineering Notes*
             AW&ST is *Aviation Week and Space Technology*
             GAO is the General Accounting Office

For other sources, see D. MacKenzie, "Computer-Related Accidental Death: An Empirical Exploration," *Science and Public Policy* 21 (1994): 233-48. This table appeared originally in that article.

Commentary on Donald MacKenzie, "A View from the Sonnenbichl"

Bernd Mahr

Technische Universität Berlin
Fachbereich Informatik
Franklinstr. 28/29
10587 Berlin
Germany

E-mail: mahr@cs.tu-berlin.de

The 1968 Garmisch Conference not only coined the term 'software engineering,' thus making it clear that the development of software is an engineering task, but it also addressed, for the first time, a profound problem of major concern—the difficulty of achieving dependable software. I can understand well that a historian and sociologist like Donald MacKenzie takes this as a starting point for considering the historical and sociological aspects of software and system dependability. But I believe that this involves the danger of taking too narrow a view, neglecting the commercial aspects of development and maintenance. These factors both inhibit and prohibit software dependability, perhaps to a much greater degree than the skills of the software engineer do. They also force us to distinguish between various types of software and to be more precise about the phenomenon of dependability and ways of achieving it.

Below is a list of software types that differ in terms of their production, commercial deployment and maintenance characteristics, and therefore have different meanings if looked at from the point of view of dependability. The list of types is not exhaustive and it may be difficult to justify the choice made, but it does show that software cannot be judged without taking into account the differences that result from its commercial context and use.

Software may be
- a mass product for all types of users, like Windows,
- embedded in a technical environment, like the brake-control systems in cars,
- dedicated to specialized services, like the post-processing of medical images,
- a tool for software development, like editors, compilers and the like,
- a component for individual customization, like accounting and billing in internet services,
- a single solution, like the control system for a rocket traveling to Mars,
- an experimental prototype, like products in the open source movement.

The term 'dependability' as opposed to reliability is well chosen, as it better reflects the contextual factors resulting from the fact that our everyday life depends on information technology. While in most cases this dependence is harmless and not a matter of serious concern, there are cases and circumstances in which software failure may result in fatalities, in other words there are situations in which dependability is critical. I am unable to go into such situations at length, but I believe that their careful analysis will give us an insight into the situational structure of dependability that can help to reduce risks in the future. While harm and damage due to software failure is certainly an ever-present fact, fatalities may be required to sway public opinion to take such analysis seriously. Donald MacKenzie may therefore be right in drawing our attention to a worst-case scenario.

A term like 'dependability' is certainly a good way to identify the proper place to view the matter from, but, as a model, it is of little value if it stands by itself and is not elaborated into some kind of methodological tool. Laprie's ontology, according to which 'dependability' is overarching 'availability,' 'reliability,' 'safety,' and 'security,' is a good start in the right direction, and the addition of impairments and means with their own terminological structure is certainly a further step. But the tree structure of the resulting ontology does not reveal the methodological substance hidden in the term 'dependability.' I am unable to elaborate here on the impact of this ontology on the lifecycle model of software in its engineering and commercial environment and in its context usage; but I will rearrange the tree structure to show some of the relations between the terms (Fig. 1).

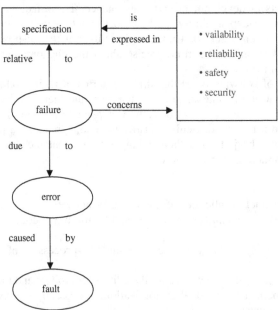

Fig. 1. Relations between terms for classifying failure

Availability, reliability, safety and security form a classification of failure from a users perspective, i.e., from a requirements point of view. Accordingly, failure is failure relative to a specification—a specification seen as a form of contract including the requirements of usage.

From the viewpoint of development, failure is a particular behavior of the system and of user interaction that can only be anticipated during production. What is required here is an understanding of the possible contexts of usage, especially where these are not part of the specification—which is most often the case. The relationship between the specification and the implemented system must be understood and conveyed to the parties involved. Furthermore, cautions have to be taken to avoid errors that might cause the system to fail. Error avoidance can be done in three basic ways: by predicting and removing them in the validation phase, by ensuring fault tolerance in the system's design and architecture, and by quality assurance in the development phase.

Errors occur in the validation and usage phases, but their existence—if not caused by user errors—are part of the delivered system. Their causes lie, then, in faults already existing in the design and production phases. Errors and faults can also be classified in terms of the impact they may have and the steps that can be taken to avoid them.

Understanding dependability in the context of the software life cycle and in relation to various types of software would, if applied to the analysis of failure situations, be extremely useful. The nature of failure is such that this could only be done in retrospect and would naturally lead to a historiography of software as a kind of accompanying research. An analysis of failure situations would not in itself be a way of increasing the dependability of software and systems; we would also need to understand the factors that, in software production, delivery and use, can force actions to be taken to avoid faults, errors and failure. Such actions are not, it would appear, an obvious consequence of our awareness and knowledge of the circumstances that lead to failure, but are dependent on commercial and cultural factors.

The cost of software development and maintenance can both inhibit and prohibit the avoidance of failure. Time to market is, for example, a prohibiting factor, while warrants and other contractual guarantees may inhibit the quality and trustworthiness of software. On the other hand, ethics and competition may force developers and service providers to ensure proper functioning and a high degree of dependability, while public opinion may accept poor performance despite its awareness of potential for improvement, for what ever reasons. Historiography and sociology cannot therefore simply confine their attention to recording failure occurrence and attempting to classify it; they must also discuss the relevant economic and cultural aspects.

Donald MacKenzie is certainly aware of this. His exposition of Hoare's Paradox is an excellent starting point for widening the discussion from a narrow engineering debate about methods, techniques and tools to a view that accepts the sum of factors influencing the software lifecycle: How can we explain that—despite the fact that programming has not become an exact science and a large share of the costs is still accounted for by debugging, and that the programming languages in use are still unreliable and therefore dangerous—how can we explain that, taking Hoare's view expressed, in 1994, as representative of public opinion, software is nevertheless highly dependable today?

An answer to this question will have to be based on cultural, sociological and economic arguments.

The ideas outlined in Donald MacKenzie's paper, which are pertinent to the historiography and sociology of software dependability, are entirely convincing. But he omits a number of points that I consider crucial if we are to understand the importance of dependability in both cases of failure and success.

For historiography, the phases of the software lifecycle should be looked at more carefully. Besides testing, theory and programming style, the software life-cycle is strongly influenced by the development process, the relationship between the contractor, the developer and the user, and by the process of maintenance and usage. Historically, these processes have undergone significant changes. In the past, awareness of the importance of these processes has grown only slowly. Later on, various attempts to organize and control these processes were observable. Styles have changed from strict hierarchies to open cooperation, and tools have been developed to support the management of these processes. Successful projects for commercial applications owe their success to a proper handling of these processes, and not just to the right choice of programming language and testing tool. Lack of success, in the majority of cases, has a similar, though converse, root: projects were unable to cope with the difficulties of managing these processes properly. One can certainly conclude from these findings that dependability of software and systems is influenced by similar factors.

For sociology, aspects of work, organization, economy, market and consumer behavior should be considered more extensively. Deviance, entrepreneurship, knowledge and profession certainly allow a profound insight into the way dependability is dealt with in our society. However, what we accept as a convincing argument for a certain behavior or for success and failure of a certain activity is often of an economic nature. The fact that software has become one of the most important assets in national economies, and is produced and marketed in highly competitive environments, makes arguments about the success or failure of dependability—which are based on macro- and micro-economic observations—very convincing instead. I believe that the sociology of software and system dependability is therefore not at liberty to leave out these additional aspects.

Much of what has been achieved in the science of informatics and in the commercial production of software can fruitfully be looked at from the perspective of avoiding faults, errors and failure.

What is seen from this perspective is a success story, and at the same time a program that failed to live up to expectations. The history of software is therefore well addressed by historiographic and sociological studies on software and systems dependability. They can be a key to an understanding of this field.

Dependability Then and Now: Commentary on Donald MacKenzie, "A View from the Sonnenbichl"

Victoria Stavridou

System Design Laboratory
SRI International
333 Ravenswood Ave
Menlo Park, CA 94025
USA

E-mail: victoria@sdl.sri.com

Introduction

Donald MacKenzie has written an insightful account of the evolution of the term "dependability" and its relationship with the efforts of the software engineering community to produce reliable software artifacts. All I need to do here is underline some of his findings and supply some examples of such efforts that I have encountered in my work as a practitioner of software engineering so far. I will also comment on the still evolving nature of dependability and hazard some predictions about the challenges that future dependability procurement will entail given the rapidly changing computing infrastructure of our time.

What's Dependability Anyway?

When Laprie and his colleagues in IFIP WG 10.4 resolved to create this overarching term of dependability in order to capture the essence of trustworthiness of computing systems,[1] they achieved more than a lexicographer's definition. They in fact captured in a term hours and hours worth of conversations between software engineering practitioners and computer scientists with remarkable brevity and precision. A beautiful term indeed, and one that has saved, in my experience, many hours of protracted debate in workshops and conferences about what we, collectively, were trying to achieve in terms of the trustworthiness of the artifacts we wanted to build. Achieving consensus about the goal has never been easier.

In the last 8 years, like any living idea, Laprie's concept has itself been evolving. First we understood that dependability is not in fact a fixed golden standard. It is itself as variable as it is measurable. Different contexts demand different amounts of it. Put a system in action at wartime and you accept a much higher

---

[1] Jean-Claude Laprie, ed., *Dependability: Basic Concepts and Terminology* (Wien, 1992).

level of risk (and hence reduced dependability) than you would from the same system at peacetime. Deploy a system in a context where it may impact civilians and you will require much higher dependability than what you would ask for were the system to be used where it might affect military personnel only. Make a commodity out of a system so that it is used by many ordinary consumers and the chances are that you will require much higher levels of dependability from individual instances than you would if only a few of these systems ever saw the light of day; much the same way that normal cars have to meet higher safety standards than stock cars.

As MacKenzie points out, Laprie created the "tree of dependability"—a composite definition capturing its attributes, its impairments and its means. In the last 8 years we understood that in fact there are more complex interrelationships between the dependability properties ("attributes" in Laprie's terminology) than the tree of dependability captures. Two examples: First consider the property of noninterference which has been extensively studied in information security.[2] We have come to realize that what is normally considered a security property may in fact be applied very effectively in defining the correctness conditions of safe integration kernels—kernels that allow the provably safe integration of computing functions.[3] Second, consider the traditional dependability techniques of fault tolerance. In the last 3 years or so fault tolerance has migrated into information security where it is creating a powerful body of knowledge on intrusion tolerance—tolerance of computing systems to cyber attacks. In a field where traditionally the only line of defense was the early detection of cyber intrusions which were treated by withdrawing the system from service, we are now creating powerful techniques based on fault tolerance which will allow us to contain intruders, to deny them access to uncompromised parts of the system (and thereby deprive them of the ability to break the entire system) and to, finally, expel them from the system. So, the tree of dependability may yet turn out to be the graph of dependability instead.

The distinctions between the treatment of dependability incidents are also getting increasingly blurred. In his paper, MacKenzie points out that safety failures are always public and high profile whereas security failures are by comparison murky and not well publicized. However, in the age of *n to n* connectivity, security failures are becoming just as notorious as safety failures. Witness the denial of service attacks that plagued the most prominent U.S. E-commerce sites in the spring of 2000. The story commanded as much news media coverage as any safety related disaster. In the era of cyber terrorism, high profile security failures will be just as prominent as safety failures. I will make the case later on that as we move into the post-PC world, where the personal computer is no longer the most prominent form factor, the definition of dependability and its constituency will need not only to evolve, but to drastically change if we are to maintain the levels of trustworthiness that we enjoy today in our computer systems.

---

[2] Joseph A. Goguen and José Meseguer, "Security Policies and Security Models," in *Proceedings of the Symposium on Security and Privacy* (Oakland, Calif., 1982), 11-20.

[3] Bruno Dutertre and Victoria Stavridou, "A Model of Noninterference for Integrating Mixed Criticality Software Components," in *Proceedings of 7th International Conference on Dependable Computing for Critical Applications* (San Jose, Calif., January 1999).

Dependable h/w—Undependable s/w

Reporting on the spirit of the Sonnenbichl meeting, MacKenzie says that

> There was however widespread agreement that the techniques of software production
> were backward by comparison with those of hardware, that delays and cost overruns
> were common, and that the final products were less dependable than they should be.

This was in 1968. Last year a group of US computer scientists, myself included,
formed an alliance in the area of component based design of embedded software,
arguing that software in such devices is much harder to get right than the hardware
itself. So 32 years later, we still believe that software is harder to make dependable
than hardware. After all as MacKenzie points out, one of the reasons that we have
only a modest number of fatalities to attribute to computers, is that we put critical
functions in hardware as opposed to software. So why is software so much harder
to get right, so much harder to get dependable?

First, the stakes have always been much higher for software. We believe that
hardware is easier to get right so we accept a lower standard of proof. Take, for
example, performance statistics for microprocessors. Until not so long ago, one
would buy a processor that came with the claim that it was capable of x millions
of operations per second (MIPs). Even though the claim was based on the performance of the machine on a specific benchmark set of problems, we happily
accepted that it was in fact as fast as the manufacturer claimed for all problems.
Enter software. In order to certify software for use in critical avionics functions,
we demand extreme levels of reliability—of the order of 10^{-9} or 10^{-12} mean time
between failures. A typical desirable design target is that the system experiences a
dangerous failure at most once per million years. As Bob Taylor, amongst others,
has pointed out,[4] whereas achieving these levels of reliability may be possible,
measuring them is not. In other words, you may have a piece of software that will
fail very rarely indeed—say once per billion hours of operation—but you will
never be able to construct a convincing argument that this is indeed the case. Testing for one year, for example, can provide validation for a best estimate of a failure rate of one failure per year. In contrast, even though there is no practical way
of demonstrating conclusively the absolute performance of hardware, we happily
accept the evidence offered by a selection of benchmark tests—which does not
provide the kind of coverage that is necessary to conclusively demonstrate the
performance characteristics of the device across all problems it will be asked to
solve. Benchmark test for software as Dave Patterson, one of the pioneers of modern computer architecture, has suggested? Perhaps.

Second, as any visitor to the Heinz Nixdorf MuseumsForum, the elegant venue
of our conference, will attest, software is the repository of complexity. Look at
any old calculating machine or any early computer exhibit. When you find the
most complex, most involved, most obscure in terms of function piece of the exhibit, chances are you found the "software." By its very purpose, software is
where we put the hard things, the problems that are difficult to solve, which are

[4] J. Robert Taylor, "Very High Reliability Computer Systems," in *Safe and Secure Computing Systems*, ed. Tom Anderson (Oxford, 1989).

changeable and whose nature renders hardware solutions for them impractical. No wonder then that software is hard to get right. Most difficult things are. We need to get over it.

Third, the boundary between what is hardware and what is software has in the past and continues now to shift. What are we to make of ASICs and firmware? What do we do in order to increase their dependability now that, despite their hardware nature, they are also being blessed with the complexity of programming?

So, I do not believe that the software is harder to get right. I believe that it is the complexity of the solutions that software implements that presents us with that challenge. Shift the complexity somewhere else and you will shift the problem somewhere else. For example, I was struck by MacKenzie's conclusion that 90% of computer related deaths are due to poor HCI. Human computer interfaces such as glass cockpits, for example, are arguably very elaborate, complicated artifacts. They are so precisely because they need to give the human operator access to the underlying virtual machine that the computer system implements. And that machine is a complex one. Mastery of that complexity in its software, firmware or HCI form is what our endeavor as computer science practitioners, researchers and teachers is ultimately all about.

The Hoare Paradox Explained

In a particularly candid and thoughtful retrospective in 1994, Tony Hoare pondered the question of how did software get so reliable without proof.[5] For someone who spent a quarter of a century and most of his academic career pursuing the betterment of software through precise methods, weighty words indeed. I would like to take this opportunity to attempt my own explanation of what MacKenzie calls the "Hoare paradox." Undoubtedly others in my field will do so also.

In the early nineties myself and my team collaborated with a team at GEC Marconi Avionics over a period of three years. Our objective was to create a software safety argument for a well known fighter aircraft that had been at that time in operation for near enough 20 years. The safety argument was to be based on formal verification and both teams included highly skilled formal methods practitioners as well as the software engineers who wrote the code that implemented a certain critical function aboard this particular aircraft—the wing sweep function. We had the best technology and the best people. A year into the project, it was time for an early midlife crisis; none of our elegantly stated proofs would work out! It was not that we were novice users of theorem proving tools. It was not that we were not trying hard enough. It was not that we did not know what the code did—we had the original software engineers on our team. So what was going on? Was all I had known about software models and reasoning about them in fact a fallacy? Or was it that this airplane was unsafe? A hard argument to make seen as it had been flying without incident for so many years. I recall how at the end of a particularly fraught meeting we decided it was time to bring in the Systems Engineer (or Architect as we would call him today)—the only person as it turns out

---

[5] C. A. R. Hoare, *How Did Software Get So Reliable Without Proof? Presentation to Awareness Club in Computer Assisted Reasoning*, Edinburgh, 21 March 1994.

who fully understood the system and its context. He came in and joined us and brought with him the longest pieces of drawings I had ever seen. He laid them out on the table, pondered for a few minutes and then he pointed: "There, there's the interlock which you have not included in your assumptions about the environment that the code sits in." Like novices, we had made an elementary mistake: we had failed to capture the context! Software on its own is inert, vaporware and can certainly kill nobody. Put it in the context of a real system with actuators and sensors and interlocks and it comes alive and then—and only then—it acquires safety properties. We had been trying to prove way too strong a theorem—namely put this code in any roughly similar airplane and it will work. So the moral of the story is, as they say in the US, "It's the system, stupid!" Software in itself did not get remarkably reliable. But we observe its behavior in the context of a system which bounds its impact on global properties such as safety.

Table 1. Sequence of events leading to the Ariane 5 accident

Angle of attack greater than 20 degrees caused by full nozzle deflections of the solid boosters and the main engine
Nozzle deflections commanded by the onboard computer on the basis of data transmitted by the active Inertial Reference System (SRI 2)
A software exception caused the SRI 2 to fail-stop thus putting diagnostics in its attitude data
Backup SRI 1 also fail-stopped due to same reason
Internal SRI exception raised by an overflow during conversion from 64-bit floating point to 16-bit signed integer—an operand error
Error occurred in software performing alignment of the strap-down inertial platform, a function which serves no purpose after lift-off
Function continued for 40 secs in Ariane 4 but not required in Ariane 5
The operand error happened because of an unexpectedly high value of a variable BH related to the horizontal velocity sensed by the platform
The value of BH was much higher than expected because the early part of the trajectory of Ariane 5 differs from Ariane 4 and results in considerably higher velocity values ($\times$ 5)

Wow and behold if we forget about the system. Witness the disaster of the maiden flight of the Ariane 5 rocket, flight 501.[6] With the best intentions, the engineers (I would hazard a guess that they were not software engineers) lifted the Inertial Reference System, a piece of code that had served them well in the Ariane 4, their older rocket and installed it in Ariane 5. After all, what better course of action than reuse such a proven piece of code? Minimal changes on something we know works well are likely to yield a system that also works well. The rest is truly history. Forty seconds into its flight Ariane 5 blew up and the world of software reuse would never be the same again. What happened? Table 1 gives some of the detail contained in the report that the European Space Agency commissioned in the aftermath of the accident. The gist of it is that the engineers took the code and put it in a rocket that was 5 times as fast as the one the code came from. This code that

---

[6] Jacques-Louis Lions, *ARIANE 5 Flight 501 Failure, Report by the ESA Enquiry Board*, Paris, 19 July 1996.

had behaved so well in the old rocket had trouble coping with speed measurements five times as high as the ones it had been designed for, it overflowed, raised an exception and put an error code in the data field of the program that calculated the nozzle deflection. "It's the system, stupid!" And it all goes to show that computer science is in fact harder than rocket science.

Hoare's disappointment stems from the lack of uptake of formal methods by the software engineering community. Many other formal methods evangelists would feel the same way. However, what is formal methods for programs about? What's mathematics for the building of bridges? The foundation! Does this mean that every time you cross a bridge you need to do a little mathematical calculation to assure yourself that it will not collapse under your feet? No, you trust that the civil engineers who built the bridge applied the necessary mathematics and built a bridge that can be trusted to withstand your weight. Indeed, do civil engineers go back to first principles and fundamental theories of mechanics when they design the bridge? No, they use an established body of knowledge captured in engineering principles and formulae applicable to the problem in hand. Why do we then expect each and every software engineer to use foundational mathematics every time s/he writes a program? It is as absurd a proposition as the one about the bridge walker. What we need to do is use the foundations in the infrastructure, not from scratch in each specific artifact that the infrastructure supports. What is the purpose of the infrastructure after all if not to remove the onus from each user from revisiting the fundamental principles of its construction? I contend that whenever formal methods has been used to build the infrastructure, it has in fact being outstandingly successful. Consider, for example, programming languages and compilers. They hide the foundations so effectively, most people need to be reminded that they are in fact the most successful manifestations of formal methods ever—formal language theory in practice.

Even so, proof is in fact used on a per artifact basis when necessary. Take, for example, the redundancy management executive of a well known fly-by-wire commercial airliner. The complexity of the RME was hideous. The engineers knew that here they needed to apply extensive analysis—much more than the regular test and debug routine allows. So they used formal methods. Arguably 98% of all currently deployed embedded software is sitting in dumb applications—washing machines, stoves, wristwatches. Do we need formal analysis of these applications? No more than we need to use quantum mechanics to explore the comfort properties of an armchair.

So to summarize: in my opinion, software has not gotten quite as reliable as Hoare supposes. How often do you have to reboot your Windows computer, arguably the world's most widely used operating system? Rumor has it in the order of every two days according to its maker. But people are very conscientious when they build safety critical software. They are also careful to embed it in a system which can bound its effects if necessary. People do use formal reasoning when they are working on hard problems. And people do use formal foundations unwittingly (the best way I would argue) when they use everyday tools like compilers. It is when this infrastructure does not exist that we get into trouble. Areas such as real time design where compilers are not sufficient for the job, we have to use "codesign"—carefully hand crafted solutions that operate within the acceptable envelope. In areas like security we do even worse—there is no such discipline as security codesign with the predictable consequence of a very vulnerable public infrastructure. In the concluding section I will argue that the infrastructure we take for granted today will no longer be able to support our endeavor as we move into the post-PC era.

Dependability in the Post-PC World

The post-PC world is as inevitable as it is exciting. Fuelled by the proliferation of cheap, powerful microprocessors running simple operating systems, the growth of a universal network, unifying multiple technologies and networking scales, whose bandwidth is enormous and whose carrying costs are virtually free and the saturation of existing IT markets forcing companies and investors to look to new markets for growth, pervasive computing will become reality. In this new world, the PC will no longer be the primary form factor through which we access the computing infrastructure. It will be supplanted by dynamic coalitions of devices as diverse as supercomputers, PCs and tiny processors embedded in the every day objects of life. In this world of ubiquitous computing, we will have embedded heterogeneous computing devices that demand massively distributed access to a shared, distributed information base over ad hoc networks. This *will be* the architecture of future computing systems. In order to make such systems work, we will need software to create, task and manage these coalitions, to engineer coherent perception and behavior out of aggregations of noisy and fallible components and to do so in a dependable manner so as not to compromise security, safety and privacy. The plain fact is that we cannot today build software for this world. The "software crisis" will hit us yet again. What is the likely impact of this? Software is no longer an option, nor is it conveniently "contained" by the system. Software is the glue that will hold the platform together and thus "create" the system. This is a tremendous challenge for the computer science field. Our community is actively pursuing solutions, amongst the most promising of which are the ones that strive to build "frameworks." Frameworks that embody foundational solutions to hard problems that are likely to be encountered often in this new world. Ideal places for the application of formal methods.

Let me conclude by asserting that dependability has been achieved todate largely at the expense of innovation. Do something well and stick to it. I believe that innovation is now inevitable. With it will come the demand for commodity software to be just as reliable as other consumer products such as cars and hairdryers. The oxymoron of having the world's most popular software also be the world's least regulated software will no longer be sustainable or acceptable to the general public.

Discussion following "Software as Reliable Artefact"

Mary Croarken

National Maritime Museum
Centre for Maritime Research
Greenwich, London, SE10 9NF
UK

E-mail: mcroarken@nmm.ac.uk

&

David Grier

George Washington University
Department of Statistics
2138 G Street NW
Washington, DC 20052
USA

E-mail: grier@gwu.edu

Several discussants felt the paper lacked historical consideration of specific times and places involved with the notion of software dependability. In particular it did not pay attention to different groups interested in the idea of dependability or frame this interest within a broader historical context. Other issues not addressed were changing ideas on acceptable dependability, software strategies to improve dependability and what causes dependability. MacKenzie was also asked why he had selected human safety as his case study, from the much broader range of dependability issues sketched in the very useful taxonomy he had presented.

In reply MacKenzie acknowledged that these were very important questions and that one paper could not deal with so many issues adequately. MacKenzie had chosen to focus on human safety because it appeared to have an inherent social importance and interest that more monetary loss could not match. It also allowed for comparison with the Hoare Paradox. The question of what kind of history historians were trying to write was put forward because this choice affected the aspects on which one focused. That said MacKenzie argued that security was a very interesting kind of dependability so far ignored in historical work.

Most of the remainder of the discussion centered on the question of "trust". The issue was raised by the question how has our experience of software dependability changed our notions of software reliability? It was stated that at the 1968 Garmisch conference reliability meant mean time to failure. Mean time to failure had changed over time from an average of once every two hours to once every two years and with this had come a change in what we perceive as dependability. It was the users' perception of the dependability of software than engendered trust. A participant asked if a reputation for poor reliability could be overcome. It was suggested that today packaged software vendors try very hard to produce dependable software but that while companies did work on the problem of reliability, they also had to consider functionality and backwards compatibility—factors which in turn affected reliability.

The issue of trust was further explored along with the idea that trust in an object depended on trust in the person selling it. A connection was made between the public trust engendered by different technologies. MacKenzie found the public bizarrely willing to trust software. Software is more trusted than technologies such as nuclear fuels or genetic modification which have lost public trust. Stavridou suggested three elements that effected trust: the element of loss, the element of risk, and the element of choice. How much was there to lose?—a great deal in the case of nuclear reactor reliability. If people can make a choice on what risk to take there is more trust than if a decision is forced upon people.

The question of trust based on previous good experiences was put forward, as was trust in software systems, such as railway signaling, in which the question of trusting software had not entered the public consciousness. MacKenzie felt that public trust in safety critical systems must exist despite of, not because of, their personal experiences with shrink-wrapped software.

The final topic discussed was the use of formal methods in increasing dependability. MacKenzie and Stavridou agreed that some mathematical techniques to check correctness had been useful to practitioners, although mostly in the hardware area where model checking was easy to apply. On the whole, software practitioners found formal methods difficult to apply and therefore did so only rarely.

Part 4
Software as Labor Process

Software as Labor Process

Nathan Ensmenger

William Aspray

University of Pennsylvania
Department of the History and
Sociology of Science &
303 Logan Hall
Philadelphia, PA 19104-6304
USA

Computing Research Association
1100 17th St. NW # 507
Washington, D.C. 20036
USA

E-mail: aspray@cra.org

E-mail: nathanen@sas.upenn.edu

The Software Crisis and the "Labor Problem" in Programming ...

For almost as long as there has been software, there has been a software crisis.[1] Laments about the inability of software developers to produce products on time, within budget, and of acceptable quality and reliability have been a staple of industry literature from the early decades of commercial computing to the present. In an industry characterized by rapid change and innovation, the rhetoric of the crisis has proven remarkably persistent. The acute shortage of programmers that caused "software turmoil" in the early 1960s has reappeared as a "world-wide shortage of information technology workers"[2] in the 1990s. Thirty years after the first NATO Conference on Software Engineering, advocates of an industrial approach to software development still complain that the "vast majority of computer code is still handcrafted from raw programming languages by artisans using techniques they neither measure nor are able to repeat consistently."[3] Corporate managers and government officials release ominous warnings about the desperate state of the software industry with almost ritualistic regularity. The Y2K crisis is only the most recent manifestation of the software industry's apparent predilection for apocalyptic rhetoric.

References to the chronic "software crisis" are so ubiquitous that it is possible to lose sight of their historical origins and significance. Specific claims about the

---

[1] The *Oxford English Dictionary* identifies the first use of the word "software" in a 1960 article in the *Communications of the ACM*. By early 1962 Daniel McCracken was already lamenting the "software turmoil" that threatened to "set the software art back several years." ("The Software Turmoil: Nine Predictions for '62," *Datamation* 8/1 (1962)). References to the "Gap in Programming Support" appear even earlier (Robert Patrick, "The Gap in Programming Support," *Datamation* 7/5 (1961)).

[2] United States Department of Commerce, Office of Technology Policy, "America's New Deficit: The Shortage of Information Technology Workers" (1997).

[3] W. Wayt Gibbs, "Software's Chronic Crisis," *Scientific American*, September 1994.

nature and extent of the crisis can be used, however, as a lens through which to examine broader issues in the history of software. In this paper we discuss the historical construction of the software crisis as a crisis of programming labor. We argue that many of the crucial innovations in modern software development—high-level programming languages, structured programming techniques, and software engineering methodologies, for example—reflect corporate concerns about the supply, training, and management of programmers. We suggest that the labor crisis in software threatened the viability of software as an economic activity; that it originated in the failure of software as a reliable artifact; that it stimulated efforts to establish the discipline of software engineering; and that it undermined the legitimacy of software as scientific and engineering practice.

Because the labor crisis in programming has been so widely referred to and written about, it serves as an ideal launching pad for an exploration of other, less familiar issues in the labor history of software. In our paper, for example, we re-examine the perennial debate about programming training and management in terms of contemporary debates about socially constructed notions of "skill," "knowledge," and "productivity." We argue that the changing role of women in software reflects larger developments in the professional fortunes and occupational identity of programmers. We describe the role of institutions such as unions, professional associations, and the government in the shaping of software development practices. Our goal is to suggest some directions for further scholarship in what we regard as an essential element of the history of computing.

It should be noted, however, that the study of labor processes presents serious methodological challenges to historians. Conventional interpretations of the software crisis are often based on the software management literature, which is typically biased towards the perspective of employers and managers. This literature also tends to reflect an ideal rather than reality. The voice of the worker is rarely represented in the types of sources that we as historians are accustomed to dealing with. We know very little about the experiences and attitudes of the typical software developer, or about the craft practices and "shop floor" activities of programmers.[4] There is almost no secondary literature available on this subject. Our discussion of software as labor process is therefore more historical than historiographical, to exemplify some of the historical issues that deserve further attention. To repeat, we try to show some of the historical questions mainly by sketching some of the history. In an attempt to counter the traditional bias towards management perspectives, we deliberately chose to construct our narrative around an eclectic sampling of sources and perspectives. The ongoing debate about the software labor crisis has been passionate, contentious, and replete with ambiguities and self-contradictions. The fact that the community of software workers included both former theoretical physicists and Helen Gurley Brown's "Cosmo Girls" is not an incidental curiosity; it is an essential element of the labor history of software.[5] In this paper we hope to convey the sense of excitement and drama experienced by

---

[4] Michael S. Mahoney has more fully described these difficulties in his "The History of Computing in the History of Technology," *Annals of the History of Computing* 10/2 (1988): 113-25.
[5] Helen Gurley Brown was the controversial editor of *Cosmopolitan Magazine* and the author of the 1962 *Sex and the Single Woman*. Her "Cosmo Girls" were modern, hard working, and sexuality aggressive.

early software workers. Our hope is that in doing so we will encourage historians to explore the rich history of software labor, and perhaps to make use of some previously undiscovered resources. We understand that the story we are telling is an entirely American story, and that when one looks at the international scene, the relevant issues may be different.

The Acute Shortage of Programmers ...

Historically, the software crisis has often been portrayed explicitly as a problem of programming labor. In 1962 the industry journal *Datamation* warned of a "gap in programming support" that threatened to "get worse in the next several years before it gets better."[6] Several decades later Bruce Webster declared that the "heart of the real software crisis ... [is that] there is more software to be developed than there are capable developers to do it. Demand will continue to outstrip supply for the foreseeable future. Hence, more and more software will be behind schedule, over budget, underpowered, and of poor quality—and there's nothing we can do about it."[7] The problem was not so much a lack of programmers *per se*; what the industry was really worried about was a shortage of experienced, *capable* developers. That there was little agreement within the software community about who exactly qualified as an experienced, capable developer only served to emphasize their real or perceived rarity.

The potential shortage of programmers materialized as early as 1954, when the first-ever Conference on Training Personnel for the Computing Machine Field was held at Wayne University.[8] At the time it was generally felt that mathematical knowledge was an essential component of programming expertise. Several speakers noted that although in 1951 there were only 2,000 Ph.D. mathematicians in the nation, there were already 2,000-4,000 jobs available in computing, and the annual demand for programmers was expected to double.[9] E. P. Little of Wayne University warned that "estimates of manpower needs for computer applications ... [are] astounding compared to the facilities for training people for this work."[10] W. H. Wilson of General Motors observed "a universal feeling that there is a definite shortage of technically trained people in the computer field."[11] There was little hope current production could meet expected demand.

The largest employer of programmers in this period was the System Development Corporation (SDC), the RAND Corporation spin-off responsible for devel-

---

[6] Robert Patrick, "The Gap in Programming Support," *Datamation* 7/5 (1961).

[7] Bruce Webster, "The Real Software Crisis," *Byte Magazine* 21/1 (1996).

[8] Wayne University had an active, early university computing program, strengthened by its partnerships with the local Detroit industries; thus it was a logical choice to host this training conference. The conference provides a good snapshot of the supply of computing workers at the time.

[9] *Manpower Resources in Mathematics*. National Science Foundation and the Department of Labor, Bureau of Labor Statistics, 1951.

[10] Arvid W. Jacobson, ed., *Proceedings of the First Conference on Training Personnel for the Computing Machine Field*, held at Wayne University, Detroit, Michigan, June 22 and 23, 1954 (Detroit, 1955), 79.

[11] Arvid W. Jacobson, 21.

oping the SAGE missile defense system. SDC employed seven hundred programmers in the late 1950s, and several thousand by the early 1960s. Like many large software development companies in this period, SDC was forced to train most of its own programmers. One manager at SDC noted proudly that, although it was estimated in 1954 that all of the computer manufacturers *combined* could only provide 2,500 student weeks of instruction annually, three years later "during a comparable period, SDC devoted more than 10,000 student weeks to instructing its own personnel to program."[12] Between 1956 and 1961 the company trained 7,000 programmers and systems analysts.

Not only did SDC train more programmers than anyone else in this period ("We trained the industry!")[13], it also propagated its own systems-oriented approach to software development. The SAGE project was unusual in that it was a large, monolithic effort involving thousands of programmers and mission-critical systems. The only other projects of comparable size and complexity at this time were being undertaken at IBM. Most other commercial software developers were working on smaller, more self-contained efforts requiring far fewer programmers. Programmers at these installations worked on multiple projects involving a diverse range of business problems. They often participated in every aspect of system development, from requirements gathering to system design to implementation; consequently they experienced more intellectual stimulation and satisfaction from their work.[14] Large government-oriented employers like SDC and IBM may have trained the majority of programmers in the 1950s, but they had difficulty keeping them around.

As the market for commercial computers expanded in the 1960s, the demand for experienced programmers increased rapidly. In 1962 the editors of *Datamation* declared that "first on anyone's checklist of professional problems is the manpower shortage of both trained and even untrained programmers, operators, logical designers and engineers in a variety of flavors."[15] Five years later, "one of the prime areas of concern" to electronic data processing (edp) managers was still "the shortage of capable programmers," a shortage which had "profound implications, not only for the computer industry as it is now, but for how it can be in the future."[16] A widely quoted AFIPS study from 1967 noted that although there were already 100,000 programmers, there was an immediate need for at least 50,000 more.[17] "Competition for programmers has driven salaries up so fast," warned a contemporary article in *Fortune* magazine, "that programming has become probably the country's highest paid technological occupation. ... Even so, some companies can't find experienced programmers at any price."[18] At one point the so-called "population problem" in software became so desperate that service bureaus in

---

[12] T. C. Rowan, "The Recruiting and Training of Programmers," *Datamation* 4/3 (1958).

[13] Claude Baum, *The Systems Builders: The Story of SDC* (Santa Monica, 1981), 47.

[14] B. Conway, J. Gibbons, and D. E. Watts, *Business Experience with Electronic Computers, a Synthesis of What has been Learned from Electronic Data Processing Installations* (New - York, 1959), 89.

[15] Editorial, "Editor's Readout: A Long View of a Myopic Problem," *Datamation* 8/5 (1962).

[16] Richard Tanaka, "Fee or Free Software," *Datamation* 13/10 (1967).

[17] Quoted in Edward Markham, "Selecting a Private EDP School," *Datamation* 14/5 (1968).

[18] Gene Bylinsky, "Help Wanted: 50,000 Programmers," *Fortune* (March 1967), 141.

New York farmed out programming work to inmates at the nearby Sing-Sing prison, promising them permanent positions pending their release![19]

The acute shortage of programming labor was not entirely alleviated by the increased production of programmers. In fact, a 1968 study by the ACM SIGCPR (Special Interest Group on Computer Personnel Research) warned of a growing *oversupply* of a certain undesirable species of software specialist: "The ranks of the computer world are being swelled by growing hordes of programmers, systems analysts and related personnel. Educational, performance and professional standards are virtually nonexistent and confusion growths rampant in selecting, training, and assigning people to do jobs."[20] It quickly became apparent that certain programmers were much more productive than others. An early study at IBM suggested that exceptional programmers were ten times more efficient than their merely average colleagues.[21] The alleged 10:1 performance ratio quickly became firmly embedded in the cultural wisdom of the industry. And so the fundamental question facing employers was not so much "where can I hire a programmer" as "where can I hire an exceptional programmer." This of course begs the question of what exactly constituted exceptional programming ability, but we will return to that issue. For the time being it is enough to point out that, like it or not, many large software corporations in this period were forced to underwrite "full scale training efforts, not because they want to do it, but because they have found it to be an absolute necessary adjunct to the operation of their business."[22]

Many employers were anxious to produce better standards for training and curriculum, but it was unclear to whom they should turn for guidance. In the late 1940s and early 1950s, computers were generally used as mathematical instruments. It was not inappropriate, therefore, to require of programmers formal mathematical training and a university education. By the middle of the 1950s, as commercial computing emerged, it was increasingly business-oriented. The results of a survey presented at the 1954 Wayne University conference reflect this fundamental shift: although only 5% of the computers in operation at that time were used in business, when the machines on order were considered the number rose to 16%.[23] The university computer training programs that focused on formal logic and numerical analysis became increasingly out-of-touch with the needs of business. The authors of a 1959 Price-Waterhouse study on "Business Experience with Electronic Computing" suggested that mathematics training had little to do with programming ability:

> Because the background of the early programmers was acquired mainly in mathematics or other scientific fields, they were used to dealing with well-formulated problems and they delighted in a sophisticated approach to coding their solutions. ... When they ap-

[19] News Brief, "First Programmer Class at Sing-Sing Graduates," *Datamation* 14/6 (1968).

[20] H. Sackman, "Conference on Personnel Research," *Datamation* 14/7 (1968).

[21] H. Sackman, W. J. Erikson, and E. E. Grant, "Exploratory Experimental Studies Comparing Online and Offline Programming Performance," *Communications of the ACM* 11/1 (1968): 3-11.

[22] James Saxon, "Programming Training: A Workable Approach," *Datamation* 9/12 (1963): 48.

[23] William Aspray, "The Supply of Information Technology Workers, Higher Education, and Computing Research: A History of Policy and Practice in the United States," in *The International History of Information Technology Policy*, ed. Richard Coopey (Oxford, forthcoming).

plied their talents to the more sprawling problems of business, they often tended to underestimate the complexities and many of their solutions turned out to be oversimplifications. Most people connected with electronic computers in the early days will remember the one or two page flow charts which were supposed to cover the intricacies of the accounting aspects of a company's operations.[24]

The mismatch between university training and the needs of the corporation was in part a function of the institutional history of university computing centers. Most of these were originally housed in engineering departments—and were therefore more machine-oriented than programming proficient—or functioned as service bureaus for traditional academic departments. These service bureaus generally focused on scientific applications, heavily dependent on mathematics and generally coded in a scientific programming language such as FORTRAN. Students educated in this environment tended to absorb the academicians' traditional disdain for practical application—an attitude probably not often well received by potential corporate employers. As Richard Hamming pointed out in his 1968 Turing Award Lecture, "Their experience is that graduates in our programs seem to be mainly interested in playing games, making fancy programs that really do not work, writing trick programs, etc., and are unable to discipline their own efforts so that what they say they will do gets done on time and in practical form."[25] The tension between the theoretical orientation of academic computer specialists and the practical demands of industry employers served to exacerbate the perceived shortage of experienced business programmers.[26]

The relatively small number of colleges and universities that did offer some form of practical programming experience were unable to provide trained programmers in anywhere near the quantities required by industry. As a result, aspiring software personnel often pursued alternative forms of vocational training. Some were recruited for in-house instruction programs provided by their employers. IBM provided programming training services to many of its clients. Others enrolled in the numerous private edp training schools that began to appear in the mid-1960s. These schools were generally profit-oriented enterprises more interested in quantity than quality. For many of them the "only meaningful entrance requirements are a high school diploma, 18 years of age ... and the ability to pay."[27] The more legitimate schools oriented their curricula towards the requirements of industry. The vocational schools suffered from many of the same problems that plagued the universities: a shortage of experienced instructors, the lack of established standards and curricula, and general uncertainty about what skills and aptitudes made for a qualified programmer. "Could you answer for me the question as to what in the eyes of industry constitutes a 'qualified' programmer?" pleaded one *Datamation* reader: "What education, experience, etc. are considered to satisfy the 'qualified' status?"[28] The problem was not only that the universities

[24] Conway (n. 14 above), 82.
[25] Richard Hamming, "One Man's View of Computer Science," in *ACM Turing Award Lectures: The First Twenty Years, 1966-1985* (New York, 1987), 207-18.
[26] This seems to be as true in the 1990s as it was in the 1960s. See Gibbs (n. 3 above).
[27] Edward Markham, "EDP Schools—An Inside View," *Datamation* 14/4 (1968): 22.
[28] John Callahan, "Letter to the editor," *Datamation* 7/3 (1961).

and vocational schools could not provide the type of educational experience that interested corporate employers; the real issue was that most corporations were simply not at all sure what they were looking for.

Wrapped up in all of the debates about the labor shortage in software are a series of fascinating questions about the essential nature of programming expertise. Is programming aptitude an innate ability or can it be acquired? What skills and abilities distinguish the exceptional programmer from his merely average colleagues? Is it more important for the programmer and analyst to understand the business or the technology? Questions like these inspired a series of psychological and personnel studies aimed at understanding the minds and motivations of programmers.

In the late 1950s and early 1960s it was not uncommon for programmers to refer to what they did as more of an art than a science. Many would have agreed with Carl Reynolds, the president of the Computer Usage Development Corporation, when he declared that "There isn't an ideal programmer any more than there is an ideal writer. All sorts of people, from divinity to mathematics students to music and romance-language majors have gravitated to programming."[29] Employers were frustrated by the inability of standard selection mechanisms to tangibly assist in the recruitment and training of programmers.[30] What they wanted was a litmus test for programming aptitude. Anecdotal evidence suggested that there must be some psychological or intelligence factors that correlated with programming ability. When this turned out not to be related to mathematics (or chess or musical ability, the other popular candidates[31]), employers turned to industrial psychologists for alternative measures. The IBM Programmer Aptitude Test (PAT), developed in 1955, correlated performance in training programs with subsequent performance ratings by project managers and served for many years as a *de facto* industry standard. Although many personnel departments used the IBM PAT as a sort of primitive filtering method, for the most part these early attempts at empirical research proved remarkably inconclusive. A review of the 1950s literature on the selection of computer programmers identified only those skills and characteristics that would have been assets in any white-collar occupation: the ability to think logically, to work under pressure, and to get along with people; a retentive memory, the desire to see a problem through to completion; careful attention to detail. The only surprising result was that "majoring in mathematics was not found to be significantly related to performance as a programmer!"[32] Gerald Weinberg, the outspoken author of *The Psychology of Computer Programming*, spoke for many when he argued that "nobody has ever been able to demonstrate that any of the various 'programmer's aptitude' tests was worth the money it cost

[29] Carl Reynolds, quoted in Bylinsky (n. 18 above), 143.
[30] John Hanke, William Boast, and John Fellers, "Education and Training of a Business Programmer," *Journal of Data Management* 3/6 (1965).
[31] Joseph O'Shields, "Selection of EDP Personnel," *Personnel Journal* 44/9 (1965); Dean Dauw, "Vocational Interests of Highly Creative Computer Personnel," *Personnel Journal* 46/10 (1967).
[32] W. J. McNamara and J. L. Hughes, "A Review of Research on the Selection of Computer Programmers," *Personnel Psychology* 14/1 (Spring 1961), 41-2.

for printing."[33] More than four decades after the first Conference on Training Personnel for the Computing Machine Field, one project manager confessed that "The conclusion I have reluctantly come to after more than 20 years of software development is this: Excellent developers, like excellent musicians and artists, are born, not made."[34] Although at this point we know very little about the historical construction of notions of programmer skill and ability, it seems clear that these are issues of interest not only to historians, but also to contemporary observers and participants.

Programmers as Professionals ...

Many software personnel were keenly aware of the crisis of labor and the tension it was producing for their industry and profession, as well as for their own individual careers. Calling computer programmers the "Cosa Nostra" of data processing, industry pundit Herbert Grosch accused software professionals (himself included) of being "at once the most unmanageable and the most poorly managed specialism in our society. Actors and artists pale by comparison. Only pure mathematicians are as cantankerous, and it's a calamity that so many of them get recruited [as programmers] by simplistic personnel men."[35] Although computer specialists in general were appreciative of the short-term benefits of the software labor shortage (in terms of above average salaries and plentiful opportunities for occupational mobility), many believed that a continued crisis threatened the long-term stability and reputation of their industry and profession. "With a mounting tide of inexperienced programmers, new-born consultants, and the untutored outer circle of controllers and accountants all assuming greater technical responsibility, a need for qualification of competence is clearly apparent."[36] The inability of the software community to provide its own solution to certification problem within edp, warned some observers, "will result in a solution imposed from without. In several fields, the lack of professional and industrial standards has prompted the government to establish standards."[37]

Computer programmers in particular were worried that an influx of the kind of "narrow, semi-literate technicians"[38] put out by vocational schools and junior colleges would undermine their claims to professional legitimacy. The lack of established certification standards rankled some aspiring software professionals. "As long as anyone with ten dollars can join the ACM (Association for Computing Machinery) and proclaim himself a professional computer expert," it would be impossible to "guarantee the public a minimum level of competence in anyone who is permitted to claim membership in the profession."[39] Others worried about

---

[33] Gerald Weinberg, *The Psychology of Computer Programming* (New York, 1971); William Ledbetter, "Programming Aptitude: How Significant is It?" *Personnel Journal* 54/3 (1975).

[34] Bruce Webster, "The Real Software Crisis," *Byte Magazine* 21/1 (1996).

[35] Herb Grosch, "Programmers: The Industry's Cosa Nostra," *Datamation* 12/10 (1966).

[36] Editorial, "Editor's Readout: The Certified Public Programmer," *Datamation* 8/3 (1962).

[37] David Ross, "Certification and Accreditation," *Datamation* 14/9 (1968).

[38] L. Fulkerson, "Should there be a CS Undergraduate Program? (letter to editor)," *Communications of the ACM* 10/3 (1967).

[39] Daniel McCracken, "The Human Side of Computing," *Datamation* 7/1 (1961): 10.

incursions by other, more established professions into what software workers regarded as their own proprietary occupational territory: "We can wait for the CPA types to find out the tricks of our trade, train a substantial number of their younger sub-alterns in machines and programming languages, and take over the task. Or we can establish a parallel license, team up with the CPA's for accounting and auditing tasks, and work in other directions independently."[40] In the sociological literature of the era, jurisdictional control over training and certification was presented as the *sine qua non* of professionalism.[41] Like many white-collar workers in this period, software personnel self-consciously attempted to replicate the institutional structures of the established professions.

One of the obstacles faced by the various certification committees that were established in the 1960s, however, was the general lack of agreement about what made for a good programmer: "At present, there is no established mechanism to qualify even the qualifiers."[42] A second obstacle was the great diversity of background within the existing software community. "Professional programming is fortunately wide open. In what other field are you likely to find a Ph.D. and a person whose education stopped at the high school level working as equals on the same difficult technical problem?"[43] No single certification program seemed able to reflect the diverse needs of the software community. When the National Machine Accountants Association announced its first business data processing certificate program in 1962, its efforts were greeted with deafening silence by more academically oriented groups such as the ACM.[44] In a similar manner, programs that required college-level degrees or formal mathematical training were rejected by the thousands of otherwise qualified and experienced programmers who would thereby be disqualified from working in their chosen profession. For whatever reason, despite numerous attempts by various groups to impose standard criteria for the education and certification of programmers, software specialists were never able to establish effective control over entry into their profession. In the words of one cynical observer, the lack of established certification standards unfortunately indicated that none of the "industry's widely publicized upcoming incompetents would find their accession to financial stardom impeded by the need for specific qualification such as the passing of a reasonable test of competency."[45]

Concerns about the future of their occupation weighed heavily on the minds of many programmers. What was the appropriate career path for a software worker? "There is a tendency," suggested the ACM SIGCPR, "for programming to be a 'dead-end' profession for many individuals, who, no matter how good they are as programmers, will never make the transition into a supervisory slot. And, in too many instances this is the only road to advancement."[46] Whereas traditional engineers were often able (and in fact expected) to climb the corporate ladder into

[40] Herb Grosch, "Computer People and their Culture," *Datamation* 7/10 (1961): 51.

[41] Harold Wilensky, "The Professionalization of Everyone?" *American Journal of Sociology* 70/2 (1964).

[42] *Datamation* Editorial (n. 36 above).

[43] Alex Orden, "The Emergence of a Profession," *Communications of the ACM* 10/3 (1967): 146.

[44] Datamation Report, "DP Certification Program Announced by NMAA," *Datamation* 8/3 (1962); David Ross, "Certification and Accreditation," *Datamation* 14/9 (1968).

[45] Editorial, "Editor's Readout: The Certified Public Programmer," *Datamation* 8/3 (1962).

[46] Datamation Report, "The Computer Personnel Research Group," *Datamation* 9/1 (1963): 38.

management positions, programmers were often denied this opportunity.[47] It was not clear to many corporate employers how the skills possessed by programmers would map onto the skills required for management. Part of the problem was the lack of a uniform programmer "profile." There was no "typical" programmer. The educational and occupational experience of programmers varied dramatically from individual to individual and workplace to workplace. There was a vast gulf, for example, "between the systems programmers—who must tame the beast the computer designers build—and the applications programmers—who must then train the tamed beast to perform for the users."[48] It was possible for two programmers sitting side by side—and managed by the same data processing manager and hired by the same personnel administrator—to be working on entirely different types of project each requiring distinctly different sets of skills and experience.

In the 1950s many programming recruits were migrants from other more traditional scientific and engineering disciplines. For many of these well educated "converts," the move to a new career posed personal and professional challenges. They were fascinated by computers but were wary of abandoning established careers for an uncertain and immature industry. Edsger Dikjstra, in his 1972 ACM Turing Award Lecture entitled "The Humble Programmer," described the dilemmas he faced while deciding on transition from theoretical physics to professional programming:

> ... I had to make up my mind, either to stop programming and become a real, respectable theoretical physicist, or to carry my study of physics to formal completion only, with a minimum of effort, and to become ... what? A programmer? But was that a respectable profession? After all what was programming? Where was the sound body of knowledge that could support it as an intellectually respectable discipline? I remember quite vividly how I envied my hardware colleagues, who, when asked about their professional competence, could at least point out that they knew everything about vacuum tubes, amplifiers and the rest, whereas I felt that, when faced with that question, I would stand empty-handed.[49]

Dijkstra and his fellow erstwhile engineers and scientists formed the vanguard of the nascent programming profession. They possessed many of the skills and credentials required for corporate advancement. It was not difficult for these men to imagine themselves following a career path similar to that of their more traditional colleagues. It was this first generation of university-trained programmers who felt particularly threatened by the hordes of new software personnel who entered the profession in the 1960s. The composition of the programming workforce was changing, and was becoming more specialized and diverse. Gone were the days "when programmers taken as a group were overpaid ... programming in general, and for a user company in particular, is a dead-end proposition, unless there is true incentive and genuine advancement to be had in other areas upon completion of the dp [data processing] requirement."[50] A hierarchy developed within the software

---

[47] Louis Kaufman and Richard Smith, "Let's Get Computer Personnel on the Management Team," *Training and Development Journal* (December 1966).

[48] Christopher Shaw, "Programming Schisms," *Datamation* 8/9 (1962).

[49] Edsger Dijkstra, "The Humble Programmer," in *ACM Turing Award Lectures: The First Twenty Years, 1966-1985* (New York, 1987), 17-32.

[50] N. Rings, "Programmers and Longevity," *Datamation* 12/12 (1965).

professions, as the more broadly educated "systems analysts" attempted to distinguish themselves from the narrowly technical "coders" and keypunch operators.
The programmers sat somewhere in between these two extremes. Systems analysis
was portrayed as a more abstract and transferable form of problem solving than
mere programming, and therefore suggested wider applicability.[51] "To rise to the
ranks of the systems analysts, the elite of the profession, a man not only has to
master the technique of translating detailed instructions into a machine code, he
must also be able to grasp concepts and to define the over-all, organized, systemic
approach to the solution of a problem, or series of problems. And if he's to work
with scientific or technical problems, he has to have the background to cope with
the subject matter. ... Men with such qualifications aren't easy to come by."[52]
Systems analysts were more likely than programmers to rise to the level of upper
management.[53]

Many of the job advertisements in the late 1960s and early 1970s reflected the
concerns that programmers had regarding their occupational future and longevity.
"At Xerox, we look at programmers ... and see managers."[54] "Working your way
towards obsolescence? At MITRE professional growth is limited only by your
ability."[55] "Is your programming career in a closed loop? Create a loop exit for
yourself at [the Bendix Corporation]."[56] Like their counterparts in the 1990s, programmers in this period were worried about burning out by age forty. Corporations struggled to retain the employees that they had invested so much time and
money in recruiting and training. The average annual turnover rate in the industry
approached 25%, and at one edp installation turnover reached more than 10% *per
month.* Poor management, long hours, and easy mobility "too often made an already mobile workforce absolutely liquid."[57] One problem was a labor market that
provided plentiful opportunities for experienced developers: "Once a man is
taught the skills, he may be hard to keep. Companies that use their computers for
unromantic commercial purposes risk losing their programmers to more glamorous fields such as space exploration."[58] Managers attributed excessive employee
turnover to the tight labor market, unscrupulous "body snatchers and other recruiting vultures,"[59] and the inherent fickleness of over-paid, prima donna program-

---

[51] Scott Overton, "Programmer/Analyst: The Merger of Diverse Skills," *Personnel Journal* 52/7 (1972).

[52] Bylinsky (n. 18 above), 168.

[53] Frank Greenwood, "Education for Systems Analysis: Part One," *Systems & Procedures Journal* (January/February 1966).

[54] Xerox Corp., "At Xerox, We Look at Programmers ... and See Managers (ad)," *Datamation* 14/4 (1968).

[55] Mitre Corp., "Are You Working Your Way Towards Obsolescence (ad)," *Datamation* 12/6 (1966).

[56] Bendix Computers, "Is Your Programming Career in a Closed Loop (ad)?" *Datamation* 8/9 (1962).

[57] "EDP's Wailing Wall," *Datamation* 13/7 (1967). While this high level of turnover was no doubt disruptive, it hardly compares to that experienced in certain traditional manufacturing industries. During the Ford Motor Company's 'labor crisis' of 1914, annual employee turnover reached 380%. Turnover in the contemporary software industry still averages 19% (based on the 11th Annual Salary Survey, *Computerworld*, 1 September 1997).

[58] Bylinsky (n. 18 above), 168.

[59] John Fike, "Vultures Indeed," *Datamation* 13/5 (1967).

mers. Interestingly enough, however, a 1971 study of job satisfaction and computer specialists suggested that the majority of programmers valued the psychological benefits of their work—in terms of self-development, recognition, and responsibility—over its financial rewards.[60] What programmers disliked was the imposition of the "ultra-strict industrial engineering and accounting type controls"[61] aimed at limiting their professional autonomy.

Despite their concerns about the status and future of their profession, software developers in this period seemed to hold the position of power in the labor/management relationship. Programmers were able to vote with their feet on many crucial aspects of the terms and conditions of their employment. Large government projects had difficulty attracting qualified programmers, in part because of salary considerations but mostly because they were seen as being boring and rigid. As one contemporary organizational sociologist suggested, programmers appeared to be "one group of specialists whose work seems ideally structured to provide job satisfaction."[62] What is curious, however, is that programmers on the whole do not seem to have translated their monopoly of the software labor market into stable long-term career prospects. They were unable to establish many of the institutional structures and supports traditionally associated with the professions. Although starting salaries were high and individual programmers were able to move with relative ease horizontally throughout the industry, there were precious few opportunities for vertical advancement.[63] Many programmers worried about becoming obsolete, and felt pressure to constantly upgrade their technical skills.[64] Most significantly, however, they faced the open hostility of managers. It was no secret that many corporate managers in this period were only too eager to impose new technologies and development methodologies that promised to eliminate what they saw as a dangerous dependency on programmer labor.[65]

Programmers and Managers: the Routinization of Labor ...

The labor crisis in software has always been about much more than a mere disparity between supply and demand. By the end of the 1960s software development costs dominated the budget of most computer installations, and labor costs dominated the production of software. Managers quickly turned their sights on the programmers. Only the proper management of software personnel could save the software projects from a descent into "unprogrammed and devastating chaos."[66] Computer programmers often served as the symbolic representation of all that was wrong with the industry. They soon developed a reputation, deserved or otherwise,

[60] Enid Mumford, Job Satisfaction: A Study of Computer Specialists (London, 1972), 93.
[61] Robert Head, "Controlling Programming Costs," *Datamation* 13/7 (1967).
[62] Mumford, 175.
[63] James Jenks, "Starting Salaries of Engineers are Deceptively High," *Datamation* 13/1 (1967).
[64] "Learning a Trade," *Datamation* 12/10 (1966).
[65] Avner Porat and James Vaughan, "Computer Personnel: The New Theocracy—or Industrial Carpetbaggers," *Personnel Journal* 48/6 (1968).
[66] Robert Boguslaw and Warren Pelton, "Steps: A Management Game for Programming Supervisors," *Datamation* 5/6 (1959).

for being careless, unprofessional, and difficult to manage. As one senior vice-president of a Fortune 50 company, speaking of edp personnel, expressed it, "They don't exercise enough initiative in identifying problems and designing solutions for them. ... They are impatient with my lack of knowledge of their tools, techniques, and methodology—their mystique; and sometimes their impatience settles into arrogance. ... These technologists just don't seem to understand what I need to make decisions."[67] Many of the technological, managerial, and economic woes of the software industry became wrapped up in the crisis of software management.

Even when the software crisis was not explicitly articulated as a problem of programmer management, the relationship was often implied in the recommended "silver bullet" solution. When a prominent adherent of object-oriented programming spoke of "transforming programming from a solitary cut-to-fit craft, like the cottage industries of colonial America, into an organizational enterprise like manufacturing is today,"[68] he was referring not so much to the adoption of a specific technology, but rather to the imposition of established and traditional forms of labor organization and workplace relationships. The solutions to the "software crisis" that most frequently recommended—among them the elimination of rule-of-thumb methods (i.e., the "black art" of programming), the scientific selection and training of programmers, the development of new forms of management, and the efficient division of labor—are not fundamentally different from the four principles of scientific management espoused by Frederick Taylor in an earlier era.[69]

In his 1977 book *Programmers and Managers*, the labor historian Philip Kraft described what he called the "routinization of programming."[70] Building on the work of Karl Marx and Harry Braverman, Kraft situated the history of programming in one of the grand conceptual structures of labor history: the ongoing struggle between labor and the forces of capital. In his *Labor and Monopoly Capital: The Degradation of Work in the Twentieth Century*, Braverman argued that the basic social function of engineers and managers was to oversee the fragmentation, routinization, and mechanization of labor. Cloaked in the language of progress and efficiency, the process of routinization was envisioned primarily as a means of disciplining and controlling a recalcitrant work force. The ultimate result was the deskilling and degradation of the worker. David Noble described the institutional foundations of the deskilling process in *America By Design* (1977) and its specific application in the numerically controlled machine tool industry in *Forces of Pro-*

---

[67] Editorial, "The Thoughtless Information Technologist," *Datamation* 12/8 (1966).

[68] Brad Cox, "There is a Silver Bullet," *Byte Magazine* 15/10 (1990).

[69] Taylor's four principles of scientific management can easily be mapped on the software management literature of this and other periods. In brief, his four principles were: 1) develop a science for each element of work to replace traditional rule-of-thumb methods; 2) scientifically select, train, and develop the workers, rather than let them define their own work practices; 3) cooperate with the workers to insure adherence to the new scientific principles; 4) establish an equal division of the work and the responsibility between management and labor, with management taking over all the tasks for which they are better suited.

[70] Philip Kraft, Programmers and Managers: The Routinization of Computer Programming in the United States (New York, 1977).

duction (1984).[71] His fellow Braverman disciple Philip Kraft applied the argument to computer programmers and the software industry:

> Programmers, systems analysts, and other software workers are experiencing efforts to break down, simplify, routinize, and standardize their own work so that it, too, can be done by machines rather than people. ... Elaborate efforts are being made to develop ways of gradually eliminating programmers, or at least reduce their average skill levels, required training, experience, and so on. ... Most of the people that we call programmers, in short, have been relegated largely to subsidiary and subordinate roles in the production process. ... While a few of them sit at the side of managers, counseling and providing expert's advice, most simply carry out what someone else has assigned them.[72]

Kraft suggests that managers have generally been successful in imposing structures on programmers that have eliminated their creativity and autonomy. His analysis is remarkably comprehensive, covering such issues as training and education, structured programming techniques ("the software manager's answer to the conveyor belt"), the social organization of the workplace (aimed at reinforcing the fragmentation between "head" planning and "hand" labor), and careers, pay, and professionalism (encouraged by managers as a means of discouraging unions). Although Kraft's conclusions may be controversial, his research addresses an essential aspect of the history of software as labor: attempts by corporate managers to address the software crisis by developing new methodologies of project management and process control.

There is no lack of evidence of pervasive management dissatisfaction with both programmers and the programming process. We have already described the enormous expenses incurred in the training, recruitment, and retention of software specialists. And since labor costs comprised almost the entire cost of any software development project, any increases in programmer efficiency or reductions in personnel immediately impacted the bottom line. In addition, software specialists had acquired a negative reputation in the eyes of corporate managers as being intractable and individualistic. According to one unflattering depiction, a programmer "doesn't want to be questioned, doesn't want to account accurately and in detail for his time. ... He doesn't want to be supervised ... doesn't want to supervise. Says he wants responsibilities, but gripes if they're assigned to him. ... The computer was acquired for him, not for operating results. ... It's not a pretty profile ..."[73] A widely quoted psychological study that identified as a "striking characteristic of programmers ... their disinterest in people,"[74] reinforced the managers' contention that programmers were insufficiently concerned with the larger interests of the company. The apparent unwillingness of programmers to abandon the "black art of programming" for the "science" of software engineering was interpreted as a deliberate affront to managerial authority: "The technologists more closely identified with the digital computer have been the most arrogant in

---

[71] David Noble, America by Design: Science, Technology, and the Rise of Corporate Capitalism (New York, 1977); David Noble, Forces of Production: A Social History of Industrial Automation (New York, 1984).

[72] Kraft, 26-8.

[73] Editorial, "Checklist for Oblivion," *Datamation* 10/9 (1964).

[74] Dallis Perry and William Cannon, "Vocational Interests of Computer Programmers," *Journal of Applied Psychology* 51/1 (1967).

their willful disregard of the nature of the manager's job. These technicians have clothed themselves in the garb of the arcane wherever they could do so, thus alienating those whom they would serve."[75] The reinterpretation of the software crisis as a product of poor programming technique and insufficient managerial controls suggested that the software industry, like the more traditional manufacturing industries of the early twentieth century, was drastically in need of a managerial overhaul.[76]

The 1968 NATO Conference on Software Engineering is perhaps the earliest and best-known attempt to rationalize the production of software development along the lines of traditional industrial manufacturing. Comparing software writers unfavorably to hardware developers ("they are the industrialists and we are the crofters"), one speaker criticized the software industry for appearing "in the scale of industrialization somewhere below the more backward construction agencies."[77] Other conference participants echoed this call for the adoption of "mass-production techniques" of software production. The NATO conference stimulated further interest in the software engineering approach to system development, and was succeeded by a lengthy series of conferences, proposals, methodologies, and technological innovations aimed at eliminating corporate dependence on the craft knowledge of individual programmers. It would not be inaccurate to characterize much of the history of software as an ongoing and determined effort to develop what Frederick Brooks referred to as a "silver bullet" capable of slaying the werewolf monster of "missed schedules, blown budgets, and flawed products."[78] These efforts have typically belonged to one of three general categories: *procedural structures* aimed at disciplining both the labor force and the process of software development; *professional structures* intended to assure standard levels of programmer ability and product; and *technological structures* meant to reduce the number and required skill level of software personnel.

Procedural Structures for Managing Programmers

In the late 1950s, computer programming was often considered to be a uniquely creative activity—genuine "'brain business,' often an agonizingly difficult intellectual effort"[79]—and therefore almost impossible to manage using conventional methods. The limitations of early computers often demanded the development of creative innovations and work-arounds. For example, many of these machines did not have floating-pointing hardware, so the programmers had to do complicated calculations to ensure that the values of the variables would stay within the machine's fixed range throughout the course of the calculation. Little was known about the best algorithms and numerical methods to use for this purpose, so a programming problem could often turn into a research excursion in numerical

---

[75] Editorial, "The Thoughtless Information Technologist," *Datamation* 12/8 (1966).
[76] H. V. Reid, "Problems in Managing the Data Processing Department," *Journal of Systems Management* (May 1970).
[77] M. D. McIlroy, quoted in Peter Naur, Brian Randall, and J. N. Buxton, *Software Engineering: Proceedings of the NATO Conferences* (New York, 1976), 5.
[78] Frederick P. Brooks, "No Silver Bullet: Essence and Accidents of Software Engineering," *IEEE Computer*, April 1987.
[79] Bylinsky (n. 18 above), 141.

analysis. Memory devices had very little capacity, and programmers had to develop great skill and craft knowledge to fit their programs into the available memory space. Devices were also slow, so tricks and intricate calculations were required to make sure to get every bit of speed out of the machines, such as carefully placing an instruction at a particular location on the drum memory so that the read head would be passing by that very location on the drum at the time when it came time to execute that instruction. As John Backus would later describe the situation, "programming in the 1950s was a black art, a private arcane matter ... each problem required a unique beginning at square one, and the success of a program depended primarily on the programmer's private techniques and inventions."[80]

By the middle of the 1960s, a perceptible shift in the relative costs of hardware and software had occurred. The falling cost of hardware allowed computers to be used for more and larger applications, which in turn required larger and more complex software. As the scale of software projects expanded, they became increasingly difficult to supervise and control. The pressing problems for software developers were now more managerial than technical. New perspectives on these problems began to appear in the industry literature. "There is a vast amount of evidence to indicate that writing—a large part of programming is writing after all, albeit in a special language for a very restricted audience—can be planned, scheduled and controlled, nearly all of which has been flagrantly ignored by both programmers and their managers," argued Robert Gordon in his review of Charles Lecht's *The Management of Computer Programmers*.[81] Numerous potential solutions to the problem of programming management were suggested over the next several decades. In a presentation to the Fall Eastern Joint Computer Conference in 1965, J. Presper Eckert argued that programming would become manageable only when it could be referred to as "software engineering."[82] A few years later structured programming was advocated as the ideal tool for reducing the "vagaries of individual personality and 'style'."[83] In 1973 Terry Baker and Harlan Mills outlined their "chief programmer team" system, which they claimed would redefine software development as a "true professional discipline with a recognized, standard methodology."[84] Others recommended the virtues of rapid-prototyping and the iterative-spiral system of project management. In the late 1980s object-oriented programming (OOP) took over as the methodology *du jour*. "There is a silver bullet," claimed OOP advocate Brad Cox, suggesting that the adoption of OOP methods would finally bring about the long-awaited "software industrial revolution ... that will alter the software universe as surely as the industrial revolution changed manufacturing."[85] The point is that although the particular management methodologies changed over time, the underlying message remained the same: "This time it will be different. This time it will work. This time we will be

---

[80] Nick Metropolis, J. Howlett, and Gian-Carlo Rota, eds., *A History of Computing in the Twentieth Century: a Collection of Essays* (New York, 1980), 126.

[81] Robert Gordon, "Review of Charles Lecht, The Management of Computer Programmers," *Datamation* 14/4 (1968).

[82] Eckert quote reprinted in Gordon.

[83] Libellator, "Programming Personalities in Europe," *Datamation* 12/9 (1966): 28.

[84] Terry Baker and Harlan Mills, "Chief Programmer Teams," *Datamation* 19/12 (1973): 58.

[85] Brad Cox, "There is a Silver Bullet," *Byte Magazine* 15/10 (1990).

able to successfully impose the methods of 'scientific' management on an unruly and intractable workforce."

Professional Structures for Managing Programmers

In addition to these procedural solutions to the problem of programmer management, corporate employers also encouraged software specialists to pursue their own professional development. "Professionalism instead of expertise can wipe out idealistic schedules and platitudinous projections and allow the data processing system group to do a realistic, efficient job."[86] If the programmers could regulate themselves and certify standard levels of education and competence, then companies would need to spend less money on training and oversight.[87] They would also have a more reliable basis for making hiring decisions and evaluating productivity and performance. Codes of professional ethics were suggested as a means of encouraging high standards of performance and behavior.[88] Although the literature is replete with calls for the establishment of such codes, historians know little about how the various professions' associations responded or to what effect. In any case, it appears that many companies honestly believed that enabling programmers to think of themselves as professionals "would be highly beneficial in the eventual progression of the industry toward well-ordered maturity."[89] Several scholars have studied the role of the corporation in the development of the engineering professions; there is a great need for similar work in the history of the software.[90]

Technological Structures for Managing Programmers

Perhaps the most clearly aggressive attempts to eliminate corporate dependence on expensive and unreliable labor involved the adoption of new "automatic programming" devices. These are the technologies that Philip Kraft accuses managers of using to "break down, simplify, routinize, and standardize ... work so that it, too, can be done by machines rather than people."[91] We are using the term "automatic programming" to refer not to any one specific technology but rather the managerial ideal of ordered, assembly line software development. A number of computer manufacturers did produce "automatic programming" systems intended to reduce that need for experienced programmers. The G-WIZ compiler from General Electric, for example, claimed that it would eliminate the need for programmers by allowing managers to do their own programming.[92] Similar claims

---

[86] Jay Wesoff, "The Systems People Blues," *Datamation* 14/6 (1968).

[87] Editorial, "Professionalism Termed Key to Computer Personnel Situation," *Personnel Journal* 51/2 (February 1971).

[88] RAND Symposium, "Defining the Problem, Part II," *Datamation* 11/9 (1965).

[89] Editorial, "Editor's Readout: The Certified Public Programmer," *Datamation* 8/3 (1962).

[90] For example, see David Noble, Forces of Production (n. 71 above); Edwin Layton, The Revolt of the Engineers: Social Responsibility and the American Engineering Profession (Baltimore, 1971); Robert Zussman, Mechanics of the Middle Class: Work and Politics Among American Engineers (Los Angeles, 1985).

[91] Kraft (n. 70 above), 26.

[92] The G-WIZ compiler is described in the RAND Symposium, "On Programming Languages: Part II," *Datamation* 8/11 (1962).

were made for FORTRAN and COBOL. More recently the Department of De-
fense-sponsored ADA programming language has been trumpeted as "a means of
replacing the idiosyncratic 'artistic' ethos that has long governed software writing
with a more efficient, cost-effective engineering mind-set."[93] The effectiveness of
these systems, both past and present, was over-sold in the marketing literature.[94]
What is important is the obvious appeal that these systems and languages held for
corporate employers. In its "Meet Susie Meyers" advertisements for its PL/1 programming language, the IBM Corporation asked its users an obviously rhetorical
question: "Can a young girl with no previous programming experience find happi-
ness handling both commercial and scientific applications, without resorting to an
assembler language?" The answer, of course, was an enthusiastic "yes!" Although
the advertisement promised a "brighter future for your programmers," (who would
be free to "concentrate more on the job, less on the language") it also implied a
low-cost solution to the labor crisis in software. If pretty little Susie Meyers, with
her spunky miniskirt and utter lack of programming experience, could develop
software effectively in PL/1, so could just about anyone.

How should we then understand the claims of Kraft and others that the history
of programming in the recent decades has been one of continual discipline, deskilling, and degradation? An uncritical reading of the management literature on
software development, with its confident claims about the value and efficacy of
various performance metrics, development methodologies, and programming
languages, would suggest that Kraft and his associates were correct. In fact, many
of these methodologies do indeed represent "Elaborate efforts" that "are being
made to develop ways of gradually eliminating programmers, or at least reduce
their average skill levels, required training, experience, and so on."[95] Their authors
would be the first to admit it. By taking these claims at face value, Kraft is able to
provide a comprehensive interpretation of a wide variety of developments and
phenomena: the fragmentation of the workforce, the appeal of structured programming, rising levels of job turnover and employee dissatisfaction, the increased use of foreign laborers. Joan Greenbaum, a contemporary of Kraft and
intellectual "fellow traveler," has recently reaffirmed her belief in the Braverman
deskilling hypothesis: "If we strip away the spin words used today like 'knowledge' worker, 'flexible' work, and 'high tech' work, and if we insert the word
'information system' for 'machinery,' we are still talking about management attempts to control and coordinate labor processes."[96]

A more critical reading suggests that the claims of the management literature
represent imagined ideals more than current reality. Writing in 1971, the occupational sociologist Enid Mumford actually lauded data processing as an "area
where the philosophy of job reducers and job simplifiers—the followers of Taylor—has not been accepted."[97] The fact that the software crisis has survived a half-
century of supposed 'silver bullet' solutions suggests that Kraft may have over-

[93] David Morrison, "Software Crisis," *Defense* 21/2 (1989).

[94] RAND Symposium, "On Programming Languages: Part II," *Datamation* 8,11 (1962).

[95] Kraft (n. 70 above), 26.

[96] Joan Greenbaum, "On Twenty-five Years with Braverman's 'Labor and Monopoly Capital.'
(Or, How did Control and Coordination of Labor get into the Software so Quickly?)," *Monthly
Review* 50/8 (1999).

[97] Mumford (n. 60 above), 175.

looked a crucial component of this history. What is missing from his analysis is the perspective on the software labor process provided by the many companies who recognized that computer programming was, at least to a certain extent, a creative and intellectual demanding occupation, and who, in their management of software personnel stressed "the importance of a judicious balance between control and individual freedom."[98] In the words of an astute contemporary observer:

> We lament the cost of programming; we regret the time it takes. What we really are unhappy with is the total programming process, not programming (i.e. writing routines) per se. ... All the programming language improvement in the world will not shorten the intellectual activity, the thinking, the analysis, that is inherent in the programming process.[99]

Although Kraft accurately describes the features of a specific managerial response to the software crisis, he misses its larger historical significance. Attempts to 'resolve' the crisis, by either pronouncing it over or suggesting particular solutions, are typically either a historical or just plain uninteresting. It is the persistence of the crisis that makes it so fascinating to the historian. In what ways have popular perceptions of the software crisis been politically influenced and socially constructed? What does the perpetual crisis of programming labor tell us about the unique characteristics of the software industry and the complex and controversial relationship between the "art of programming" and the "science" of software engineering? How can we explain the failure of traditional labor market mechanisms to alleviate the ongoing shortage of programmers? How can we relate the history of software to larger themes in social and labor history? We have only hinted at some possibilities—the opportunities for further significant research are enormous.

Women in Software

In recent years labor historians have devoted considerable attention to issues of race and gender in the history of labor-management relations and the dynamics of the workplace environment. The conventional wisdom argues that corporate managers often use women and minorities as low-wage, low-skill replacements for skilled white male laborers. Occupations tend to become sex-typed as being either male or female, depending on their relative position in the wage and status hierarchy. An influx of women and/or minorities into an occupation is usually considered to indicate that routinization, degradation, and deskilling has occurred. Women have rarely held high positions within the scientific or engineering community in significant numbers, at least until fairly recently.

There is evidence that the story of gender and software labor is a little less clear-cut. As a number of scholars have suggested, women have played an important role in the history of software development. The first ENIAC programmers were women, and Jennifer Light has argued that these women significantly influ-

---

[98] Robert Head, "Controlling Programming Costs," *Datamation* 13/7 (1967): 141.
[99] Willis Ware, "As I See It: A Guest Editorial," *Datamation* 11/5 (1965): 27.

enced early computing and programming practice.[100] The Association for Computing Machinery's first "Man of the Year" was a woman.[101] Women have not only held a greater percentage of jobs in software than might otherwise have been expected, they were also able to advance farther and faster than their peers in other high-tech industries. Clearly there is something interesting going on in the history of the software professions that deserves further scholarly examination.

What do we know about women and software? Women were the very first programmers, or 'coders' as they were called in the earliest years of computing. The intended role of these women was clearly articulated in the three volumes on "Planning and Coding of Problems for an Electronic Computing Instrument," written by Herman Goldstine and John von Neumann in the years between 1947 and 1949.[102] These three volumes served as the principal textbooks on the programming process at least until the early 1950s. The Goldstine/von Neumann method assumed that the computer would be used for complex scientific computation, and the division of labor in the programming task seems to have been based on the practices used in programming the ENIAC.

Goldstine and von Neumann spelled out a six-step programming process: (1) conceptualize the problem mathematically and physically, (2) select a numerical algorithm, (3) do a numerical analysis to determine precision requirements and evaluate potential problems with approximation errors, (4) determine scale factors so that the mathematical expressions stay within the fixed range of the computer throughout the computation, (5) do the dynamic analysis to understand how the machine will execute jumps and substitutions during the course of a computation, and (6) do the static coding. The first five of these tasks were to be done by the "planner" who was typically the scientific user and overwhelmingly often was male; the sixth task was to be carried out by "coders"—almost always female (on the ENIAC project). Coding was regarded as a "static" process by Goldstine and von Neumann, one that involved writing out steps of a computation in a form that could be read by the machine, such as punching cards, or in the case of ENIAC in plugging cables and setting switches. Thus there was a division of labor envisioned that gave the most skilled work to the high-status male scientists and the lowest skilled work to the low-status female coders.

It turns out that the coders on the ENIAC project ended up doing many more tasks than envisioned. Programming was a very imperfectly understood activity in these early days, and much more of the work devolved on the coders than anticipated. To complete their coding, the coders would often have to revisit the dynamic analysis; and with their growing skills, some scientific users left many or all six of the programming stages to the coders. In order to debug their programs and to distinguish hardware glitches from software errors, they developed an intimate knowledge of the ENIAC machinery. "Since we knew both the application and the machine," claimed ENIAC programmer Betty Jean Jennings, "we learned to diag-

---

[100] Jennifer Light, "When Computers Were Women," *Technology & Culture* 40/3 (1999).

[101] Admiral Grace Hopper received her "Man of the Year" award in 1962. Needless to say, it was extremely unusual for an association of technical professionals to grant its highest honor to a woman, especially in the early 1960s!

[102] These technical reports are most easily found today in reprint form in William Aspray and Arthur Burks, eds., *The Papers of John von Neumann on Computing and Computer Theory* (Cambridge, Mass. and Los Angeles, 1987).

nose troubles as well as, if not better than, the engineers."[103] Thus what was supposed to have been a low-skill, "static" activity prepared these women coders well for careers as programmers—and indeed, those who did pursue professional careers in computing often became programmers and did well at it. A few women, Grace Hopper and Betty Holberton of UNIVAC and Ida Rhodes and Gertrude Blanche of the National Bureau of Standards in particular, continued to serve as leaders in the programming profession.[104]

However, during the 1950s, business applications began to surpass scientific applications; a computer manufacturing industry grew up to service the rapidly expanding need for computers for business applications; and a tremendous demand grew up for programmers. The number of new programmers, most of whom were male at first, swamped the number of female coders who had become programmers. Programming quickly became primarily a man's job.

If the Braverman/Kraft thesis about the deskilling of programming labor were correct, we would expect to see the employment of women in software increase as the occupation became less skilled and more routine. In a 1964 survey, 76 percent of the respondents expected to see the ratio of women in programming increase: "The only limitation is the number of qualified applicants," stated one manufacturer.[105] There are indications that certain types of female employees were seen, at least in the 1960s, as being more stable and reliable than their male counterparts, based upon some typical sexual stereotyping: "Women are less aggressive and more content in one position ... Women ... are more prone to stay on the job if they are content, regardless of a lack of advancement. They also ... are less willing to travel or change job locations, particularly if they are married or engaged. For these reasons there is a considerably lower turnover rate in women programmers and as a result, the initial investment in training pays a greater dividend for their employees."[106] Employers were warned away, however, from hiring "the most undesirable category of programmer," the female "about 21 years old and unmarried," who was likely to marry, become pregnant, or waste precious energy worrying about her social commitments for the weekend.[107]

There is no doubt that some male programmers were threatened by a perceived incursion of females into their profession. For many of these men, women were associated with low-skill clerical labor, even though many of the ENIAC 'girls' had actually possessed college degrees in mathematics. The new generation of female programmers was being recruited from the ranks of keypunch operators or 'coders.' In an era when programmers were anxious to distinguish programming as a creative intellectual activity from coding as manual and narrowly technical

[103] W. Barkley Fritz, "The Women of ENIAC," *Annals of the History of Computing* 18/3 (1996): 20.

[104] Frances Elizabeth ("Betty") Snyder Holberton was awarded the Association for Women in Computing's Ada Lovelace Award in 1997. Grace Hopper described her as being "the best programmer that she had known during her long career." (Fritz, 20).

[105] Report, "Advanced Programmers, Women Employment Seen Rising," *Datamation* 10/2 (1964).

[106] Valerie Rockmael, "The Woman Programmer," *Datamation* 9/1 (1963): 41.

[107] William Paschell, Automation and employment opportunities for office workers; a report on the effect of electronic computers on employment of clerical workers (Washington, D.C., 1958); also Rockmael, 41.

labor, these women represented the lowest rungs of the occupational hierarchy ("There's nothing lower than a coder"[108]). An influx of low-skill, low-wage labor threatened both the professional self-identify of the programmers and their superior bargaining position in the labor market for software workers. It is hard to imagine, therefore, that they would have been pleased or flattered by Helen Gurley Brown's exhortation to the readers of *Cosmopolitan* that they go out and get jobs as programmers making U.S. $15,000 after five years.[109] Many of the advertisements for "automatic programming" languages and systems used women as a proxy for less expensive, more tractable labor. If you could teach your secretary to program in COBOL, there was no need to pay for expensive programming talent.

There are other historical questions to be asked about gender and software labor. Recent statistics on computer science enrollments and software industry employment indicate that the number of women in computing has been dropping since the early 1980s. Why? It has been argued that many women perceive computer careers as being overly competitive, incompatible with a well-rounded family oriented lifestyle, and solitary rather than social.[110] Writers such as Sherry Turkle and Tracy Kidder have described the various ways in which the programmer subculture emphasizes culturally masculine traits such as competitiveness, practical joke playing, and aggressive hacking and cracking.[111] How and why did this masculine subculture develop? How does it relate to the perpetual software labor crisis? Anecdotal evidence suggests that women are attracted to programs in information systems, rather than computer science or computer engineering, because "information systems is perceived as more people-oriented and more attuned to the uses of information technology."[112] What does this tell us about the historical and social construction of computer knowledge and specialties? In what ways has the absence of women from the programming profession been used to emphasize its rational, "scientific" qualities? Labor historians have developed an extensive literature on work and gender; historians of software should make use of their expertise and experience.

Other Major Players ...

The bulk of this paper has focused on specific issues in the history of software as a labor process. It seems appropriate at this point to step back and briefly situate these issues in the larger context of post-war social and technological developments. Let us begin with a discussion of other major players in late-twentieth century labor and technology: labor unions, the defense community, and other government agencies.

---

[108] "Checklist for Oblivion," *Datamation* 10/9 (1964).

[109] The quote from Helen Gurley Brown appears in an advertisement for the Computer Sciences Corporation, "In Case You Missed Our First Test," *Datamation* 13/9 (1967).

[110] Peter Freeman and William Aspray, *The Supply of Information Technology Workers in the United States* (Washington, D.C., 1999), 113.

[111] Sherry Turkle, *The Second Self: Computers and the Human Spirit* (New York, 1984); Tracy Kidder, *The Soul of a New Machine* (New York, 1984).

[112] Freeman and Aspray, 111.

Labor Unions

Formal labor organizations have played almost no role in the history of the software industry. In one respect this is not entirely unexpected, since white-collar professionals have traditionally resisted unionization. Employers tend to encourage their software workers to think of themselves as professionals, at least in regard to this particular issue. There is recent evidence to suggest that this situation may be changing, however. The Washington Alliance of Technology recently won important concessions from Microsoft over its treatment of so-called "permatemp" employees.[113] Although these high-tech consultants are often paid relatively high hourly wages, they typically do not receive health-care benefits, vacation time, stock options, pension plans, or overtime. Whereas so-called "free agents" like these make up only 10 percent of the overall workforce in the United States, they comprise almost half of all software employees.[114] Like many high-tech workers in the late twentieth-century, software specialists straddle the border between the professional and the technician. In the past, programmers resisted association with hourly workers and other wage laborers. They prided themselves on being salaried professionals on par with other engineers and managers. It may be that changes in the labor market, the rise of overseas competition, and an influx of foreign laborers may foreshadow an increased presence of organized labor in the software industry.

Defense Community

There are few technology industries in the late twentieth century that have been unaffected by Cold War politics and the imperatives of the military-industrial complex. The software industry is presumably no exception to this general rule. It is unfortunate, therefore, that historians know so little about the influence of the Cold War and the military on the production of software. James Tomayko, who has written widely about both history of computing in aerospace and the historical development of software engineering, has argued that the NASA software development efforts, like the SAGE System and the IBM OS/360 operating system, were "major software projects that directly contributed to the evolution of software engineering."[115] Philip Kraft argues that it was the Korean War that "provided the incentive to organize the training of programmers in the same manner as other engineering occupations," and, not surprisingly, "the military which provided both the means and the setting to do so."[116] He suggests that a Cold War mentality entered the programming profession through the RAND Corporation and its association with the SAGE project. Paul Edwards' more recent argument that the highly centralized SAGE system "provided the technical underpinnings for an emerging dominance of military managers over a traditional experience- and responsibility-

---

[113] "Microsoft Moves to End Permatemping," *The Washington Alliance of Technology Workers,* September 2, 1999 (http://www.washtech.org/roundup/contract/ms_conversion.html).

[114] Austin Bunn, "No-Collar Workers: Is There Room for Unions in the New Media World?" *The Village Voice,* January 13, 1999.

[115] James Tomayko, *Computers in Spaceflight: The NASA Experience* (Linthicum Heights, MD, 1998).

[116] Kraft (n. 70 above), 37.

based authority system" perhaps applies equally well to the software as well as the military professions.[117] There is some evidence to support this opinion. In the late 1950s the SAGE project did indeed serve as "the training ground for an industry." Many SAGE veterans went on to hold prominent positions in the software community. The sheer size and complexity of the SAGE project, along with its particularly sensitive nature, did encourage a modular, hierarchical approach to software production. It may be that this did have a strong influence on later developments. The truth is that we just do not know. There is a strong need for further research in this area.

Other Government Agencies

Generally, the federal government has not established direct labor policy for information technology workers, including software workers. Instead, this policy in the postwar period has been embedded in policies for science, education, public welfare, economics, and business. Through the 1970s, IT labor policy was mainly the result of legislation related to science and education policy concerning the National Science Foundation. Some unknown number of programmers were trained in the formal higher educational system under the provisions of the National Defense Education Act, which was stimulated by the Russian launch of Sputnik. NSF provided an important computer facilities program from 1957 to 1973, which helped some 500 U.S. universities acquire their first computers. These computers were used to train a generation of computer professionals, including many programmers. DARPA opened its computer science program in 1962, and NSF opened an Office for Computing Activities in 1967. Although funding from these programs often went to support research projects, these projects were the training ground and means of financial support for many graduate students, some of whom became software professionals. White papers written by the National Academy of Science and the NSF led to substantially increased support for campus computing programs for both research and education.[118]

Federal budget trimming to pay for the Vietnam War and the Mansfield Amendment to the 1972 Military Procurement Authorization, which narrowed the scope of research that the military could support, significantly harmed academic computer science. Support for computer facilities was suspended, research and education funds for computer science dwindled, and universities turned increasingly to theoretical research projects rather than large-team, empirical studies. The universities were becoming progressively less interesting places for computing research, and faculty members and graduate students took flight to industry. Undergraduate enrollments in computer science were burgeoning at the same time,

---

[117] Paul Edwards, *The Closed World: Computers and the Politics of Discourse in Cold War America* (Cambridge, 1996), 104.

[118] For further information on the role of the federal government on United States information technology policy see William Aspray, "The Early History of IT Worker Policy," *Computing Research News*, September 1999; "The Recent History of IT Worker Policy," *Computing Research News*, November 1999; "The Supply of Information Technology Workers, Higher Education, and Computing Research: A History of Policy and Practice in the United States," in *The International History of Information Technology Policy*, ed. Richard Coopey (Oxford, forthcoming).

and there was widespread concern that industry pull was eating the seed corn of potential faculty available to train the next generation of students. Moreover, the people coming out of university programs were not all that attractive to industry. A response that involved NSF, the universities, the information technology (IT) industry, and the professional societies slowly overcame these problems in the 1980s.

Computing had first hit the federal radar screen in the 1960s. During the 1980s it became of serious policy interest for the first time. NSF and the National Research Council formed major organizations to deal with computer science. Computing was seen as having an important role in national economic competitiveness. This was one of the reasons behind 1991 legislation that established the High Performance Computing and Communications Initiative, funded in the billion dollars range. Academic research and educational programs received strong financial support under this legislation.

The Immigration Act of 1990 shifted the balanced of immigration somewhat away from family-based immigration and more towards career-based education. This enabled the number of IT workers on permanent visas to increase, but the numbers remained small. Even with the legislative change, fewer than 2,000 permanent visas were awarded per year to mathematicians and computer scientists. Under pressure from industry who needed more IT workers, the H-1B temporary visa program was implemented; and new legislation was passed in 1998 to greatly increase the number of these visas awarded annually. The issue of foreign workers and temporary visas remains a hot political topic today. Other recent issues that have been subject to federal policy are another round of seed-corn problems in university computer science programs, the under-representation of women and minorities in the computing field, and industry demand for tax credits to companies to provide training for their workers. The increasingly important role of the computer and the Internet in the economy and everyday life has been noticed in Washington, and interventionist policies directed at computing technologies are now more common and likely to increase in the future. Unlike some of the general education and science legislation of past decades, which had only indirect bearing on software labor, issues concerning the number and training of programmers are of direct policy interest today.

Conclusions

In the previous sections of this paper, we have identified issues in the labor history of software by briefing telling aspects of the history. In this section, we stand back from the history and identify several key areas deserving further historical attention. So we simply close by asking a list of questions. Work in these areas will support the scholarship of historians of computing aiming to get a more complete picture of their subject, as well as labor historians who want to draw examples from this important technical area. These are questions for studying the U.S. software labor situation; perhaps the international situation will require a different set of questions.

Training, Education, and Identification of High-Quality Workers

The general understanding of what a computer is, and what it is for, has changed significantly over time. As the computer transitioned from a scientific instrument to an information processor to a communications device, how has the software industry met the ever-increasing demand for programmers (or perhaps more specifically, a certain *type* of programmer)? What qualifications and character traits did managers seek in their software laborers? How have the skills required to do programming work effectively, as well as the aspirations and background of the workers, evolved over time? Who was attracted to these jobs? How were they educated, recruited, and trained? What made for the big differences in the productivity levels across individual programmers?

Professionalization, Certification, Career Development, and Occupational Identity

Labor historians have shown that many workers are concerned not only with the material conditions of their work (such as safety, pay, hours, etc.), but also with less tangible issues of status, personal development, and identity. Programmers have long had an interest being perceived as professionals, rather than technicians. How have the role and occupational identity of software personnel changed over time? To what extent has professionalism been encouraged through the creation of barriers to entry such as certification, accreditation, and standardized curricula? How have programmers worked to establish an occupational or professional identity through the construction of programming as an engineering or scientific discipline, or through the elevation of the status and visibility of programming within the corporation? Have programmers managed to successfully establish themselves as professionals? In what ways is this profession like and unlike those that have traditionally been studied by labor historians?

Structures Imposed by Management on Labor, and by Labor on Management

The "Taylorization" of work in the twentieth century is a (and perhaps *the*) major theme in contemporary labor history. To what degree has there been an attempt to apply to programming the scientific management techniques that seemed to have worked so well in the traditional manufacturing industries? To what degree has management been able to define programming skill and practice and therefore assure themselves of a standardized worker and product? How has management attempted to fragment, routinize, and deskill software work? Have these attempts generally been successful? Given that labor seems to have the upper hand over management today and for much of the past because of the laws of supply and demand, in what ways and to what extent has labor been able to shape the work environment?

Gender, Race, and the Culture of the Workplace

Why has the participation of women and minorities been so low in this field, especially in the last two decades during which other science and engineering groups have experienced improvements in the participation of such underrepresented groups? To what degree has there been deskilling and gender typing in the software field, and how has this varied over time? What has been the effect of under representation of these groups on those seeking to produce software products?

Government Regulation and Government Programs that Affect Software Labor

In what ways, if at all, have government programs in the United States to provide support for research and education in the universities shaped the development of software workers? In what ways has defense needs for computing technology shaped either the demand for software labor or the way that it is organized and managed? How has immigration law affected the supply for software labor and the ways in which software workers are employed and relate to their employers? Have tax training and other corporate incentives from government changed the nature of the people who have been hired to do software work or the career path of software workers?

As we begin to answer some of these questions, we will enrich our understanding both of software history and of the history of labor.

Are Programmers Oppressed by Monopoly Capital, or Shall the Geeks Inherit the Earth? Commentary on Nathan Ensmenger & William Aspray, "Software as Labor Process"

David A. Hounshell

Carnegie Mellon University
Henry R. Luce Professor of Technology and Social Change
Pittsburgh, PA 15213
USA

E-mail: Hounshell@cmu.edu

In their bold, provocative paper, "Software as Labor Process," Nathan Ensmenger and William Aspray examine the history of software production through the lens of labor history. They do so to make sense of the ever-present "software crisis" that has attended society almost from the outset of the electronic digital computer. They do so employing principally the framework of the now-OLD "new labor history"—i.e., "labor process" study in which what takes place "on the shop floor" becomes central and how struggle for control of the shop floor takes priority over other parts of the story such as the union organizing campaigns and politics of the old labor history. Their deployment of the old new labor history in writing the history of software distinguishes this paper as a pioneering effort, though like most pioneering enterprises, it is not without problems. Ensmenger and Aspray also employ some of the framework of the NEW "new labor history" in which attention is focused on how matters of gender and race, not just class, play out on the shop floor. Here, again, their effort is bold but not without problems. In what follows, I critique this paper by addressing the paper's discussion of early software workers, the relevance of the deskilling framework for software history, and the relevance of the NEW new labor history for software history. I will conclude by suggesting what the labor history of software should include were one to be executed fully.

The authors' first major section is entitled "The Acute Shortage of Programmers ..." Both this title and the section raise the question of where "programmers" or what we might call "early software workers"—or even early "software engineers"—came from. The authors hardly treat this question. I would suggest that the origins of computer programming and thus of computer programmers constitute the mid-twentieth-century equivalent of what became known as "the Eric Canal School" of American civil engineering in the first quarter or third of the nineteenth century. Absent formal schools of engineering, the American civil engineer (as distinct from the *military* engineer[1]) learned the art and science of engineering through working on projects, the most fecund of which was the state-funded construction of the Eric Canal between 1817 and 1825. Here would-be engineers began working on chain gangs surveying the run of the canal and worked their way up, in some cases from common laborers to positions in which they had engineering responsibility for whole sections of the Eric Canal. As Daniel Hovey Calhoun documented so well in his seminal book, *The American Civil Engineer: Origins and Conflict*, large-scale projects like the Eric Canal served to create a supply of engineers who went on to work on—often to be in charge of—other major civil engineering projects in the United States, including other state-funded canals, railroads, harbors, and bridges.[2] In turn, they trained other engineers in the methods they had learned on the Eric Canal and developed in their subsequent projects.

With the history of computer programming in the United States, one can see quite clearly the parallel. Programming and hence, computer programmers, got their start in projects—in the great scientific and technological projects of World War II and the Cold War, beginning with ENIAC in 1945 and continuing through SAGE and beyond. Just as one can construct a genealogy of American civil engineers firmly rooted in the Eric Canal project, one can construct a genealogy of computer programmers (and programs) that have roots in ENIAC and its successors and Whirlwind and its successors. To take but a single example, consider the lineage of programming and programmers emerging from ENIAC, moving to the Institute for Advanced Study Computer at Princeton, then to the Johnniac at RAND, and finally to SAGE (by which I allude to the Systems Development Corporation, RAND's spin-off, and the Whirlwind computer and its IBM successors). Branching, of course, occurred at each step of the way, and these branches yielded other branches, and so forth. The point is simple. Early programmers got their start on big, important, and often formative state-funded projects. They learned on the job. Like civil engineering in America, programming eventually grew to the point where knowledge could be codified and then formally taught in educational institutions, yielding specialists who began to distinguish their activities (i.e., programmers) from those of others (e.g., project engineers). So much for the parallels between the "origins" of civil engineering and computer programming in America. But what about the "conflict" part?

As Calhoun shows so brilliantly, almost from the moment when civil engineers emerged from large-scale projects such as the Eric Canal, conflict also emerged, centered on engineers' identity and role. This conflict became all the more pressing as large-scale projects were increasingly funded with private capital. Specifically, were civil engineers to be regarded as professionals who possessed autonomy comparable to that of doctors, attorneys, or ministers, or were they "hired hands"? If the latter, were they to be treated like an everyday worker, whose

---

[1] The eighteenth-century British engineer John Smeaton coined the term "civil engineering" to distinguish the activities he and a growing number of engineers in England were engaged in (building roads, canals, bridges, lighthouses, harbor facilities, etc.) from military engineering. Later, as new areas of civil engineering activity opened up, such as machine design ("mechanical engineering") and laying out electric light and power systems (electrical engineering), "civil engineering" took on its present-day connotations.

[2] Daniel Hovey Calhoun, *The American Civil Engineer: Origins and Conflict* (Boston, 1960).

autonomy was kept as restricted as possible, or were they to be treated as a manager possessing some authority as an intermediary between everyday workers and owners? Conflict in engineering centered precisely on this question of autonomy. Studies in the history of engineering published subsequent to Calhoun's book, from Monte Calvert's book, *The Mechanical Engineer in America*, and Edwin Layton's *Revolt of the Engineers*, to David F. Noble's *America by Design* and Bruce Sinclair's *Centennial History of the American Society of Mechanical Engineers* all noted—and elaborated upon—this inherent conflict *vis-à-vis* engineering and organizations.[3]

Ensmenger and Aspray's paper points toward definite parallels in the emergence of computer programming, where conflicts arose immediately upon the emergence of computer programming as a "profession." On the one hand, computer programmers held high professional aspirations and sought autonomy. On the other hand, those who hired them or managed them often treated them as they would any other "hired hand," dismissing any notions they might have had about autonomy. Hence conflict.

This clear parallel points to a major weakness in Ensmenger and Aspray's paper: their failure to pay attention to the what might be termed the "professionalization issue." There is a rich body of literature in the history and sociology of professions and the process of professionalization, which the authors have largely ignored.[4] I would suggest that the history of programming as a "profession" can be understood—if not predicted—by the chief findings of this literature. To my mind, probably the most significant aspect of this literature on professionalization deals with the very basis of professions. That basis is the possession by some group of a body of esoteric knowledge that others in society both value highly and cannot easily duplicate or access. This group's possession of a body of esoteric knowledge allows it to assert its autonomy. As long as this group is willing to police itself and prevent individuals who have mastered this body of knowledge from unfairly or unscrupulously exploiting this knowledge, society is willing to sanction the group as a profession and to grant the group a good deal of autonomy. Self-policing usually means not only maintaining standards of performance, conduct, and service in the profession but also controlling entry into the profession through licensing, accreditation, or some other means. Here is where true professions are made or broken.

Of course, the history and sociology of professions has corollaries in the history and sociology of guilds and trades. Treating programming as a trade rather than a profession may, in some instances, be beneficial. Here, too, Ensmenger and

---

[3] Monte A. Calvert, *The Mechanical Engineer in America, 1830-1910* (Baltimore, 1967); Edwin Layton, Jr., *The Revolt of the Engineers: Social Responsibility and the American Engineering Profession* (Cleveland, 1971); David F. Noble, *America by Design: Science, Technology, and the Rise of Corporate Capitalism* (New York, 1977); Bruce Sinclair, *A Centennial History of the American Society of Mechanical Engineers* (Toronto, 1980).

[4] Layton's bibliographic essay identifies some of the pre-1970 landmarks in the literature; see Layton, 259-63. See also Burton J. Bledstein, *The Culture of Professionalism: The Middle Class and the Development of Higher Education in America* (New York, 1976); Andrew D. Abbott, *The System of Professions: An Essay on the Division of Expert Labor* (Chicago, 1988); and Michael Burrage and Rolf Torstendahl, eds., *Professions in Theory and History: Rethinking the Study of the Professions* (London, 1990).

Aspray's paper pays no attention to the general process by which some workers cohere into well-established trades or crafts. I won't belabor the processes by which trades emerge and maintain their autonomy, but certainly one of the key factors in the long-run sustainability of trades has been control of entry.

In seeking to understand the history of programming as a profession or as a trade, one must ask the question, how was entry controlled? The short answer to this question—and indeed the factor that explains so much about the "software crisis" around which Ensmenger and Aspray center their paper—is that at no time since the first electronic digital computer was first programmed has entry into programming been effectively controlled. Computer programming is neither a strong profession nor a strong trade; it is a pseudo profession and a pseudo trade. Even when and where barriers have arisen, they have proven to be highly permeable. I suspect the major reason lies in the fundamentals of programming in that it does not rest on too deep a body of esoteric knowledge (hence precluding professionalization) and that its "secrets" are not easily kept (hence precluding a strong guild, craft, or trade tradition).[5]

Calhoun's book on the origins of the civil engineer in America also showed—and the subsequent work in the history of engineering has confirmed in spades—that within an organization, whether a capitalist firm or a state bureaucracy—an engineer's career reached definite limits unless that engineer moved into management. Thus, the forces of organizational hierarchy and job stratification were at work in the engineering profession, also serving to undermine the "strong autonomy" position of engineers within organizations. Career advancement via management served to produce a hierarchy within engineering itself, and this has been one of the thorniest problems in the engineering profession. When does an engineer-manager cease being an engineer and become merely a manager? When does such a person give up loyalties to engineering ideals and act solely on the basis of bureaucratic or capitalistic ideals?[6] These are questions that are highly relevant for the labor history of computer programming.

The career advancement of an engineer or a programmer through pursuit of the management track has historically proven to be a double-edge sword for organizations. In any organization, be it a large technology-driven corporation with a formal research and development department or a government regulatory body in which scientific, technological, and organizational knowledge is critical, managers know that some scientists, engineers, or computer programmers are far more productive as research scientists, design engineers, or software designers than the average employee. This productivity differential might be anywhere from five to ten—and even as high as twenty—times that of the average employee. To "lose" such an employee to management is costly. This was a huge problem in industrial research and development organizations that was finally—and reasonably—

---

[5] Ensmenger and Aspray briefly treat attempts at certification in their paper. Most recently, in response to the "software crisis" and as part of its attempt to overcome this problem, the United States Department of Defense (DoD), through the Software Engineering Institute (SEI) at Carnegie Mellon University, has mandated that firms producing software for DoD become certified within what SEI has developed as the Capabilities Maturity Model. Although the Capabilities Maturity Model seeks to certify firms in the production of software, it has the effect of pushing elements of certification down to the level of individual programmers.

[6] Layton, *Revolt of the Engineers*, deals with this issue quite thoroughly.

addressed in the immediate post-World War II years by large, research-intensive firms such as E. I. du Pont de Nemours & Company. Du Pont created a dual ladder system in which a select number of scientists and engineers were named "research associates" (later called "research fellows") and put on a career track comparable to the professorial ranks in a university (i.e., assistant professor, associate professor, and professor). Scientists and engineers in this track were given a tremendous amount of autonomy to establish their own research programs, to publish freely, etc., and they were also essentially granted "tenure" in the company.[7]

I would suggest that if probed deeply enough, the histories of firms that employed a large number of programmers created dual ladder systems for truly talented programmers. We know that IBM adopted dual ladder career systems in its R&D organization early in its electronic digital computer days, and we also know that Microsoft, the much-studied, much-maligned software giant of today, employs something like the dual ladder scheme in that its job category of "Developer" has a lot of features similar to Du Pont's Research Associate.[8] But for ambitious programmers of average programming capability, advancement often meant movement into management. Those who were left faced a career perhaps fraught with the problems that Ensmenger and Aspray articulate in their paper, in which software production and maintenance was part of the routinization of labor.

Here is where Ensmenger and Aspray invoke the deskilling hypothesis and focus on the labor process à la Harry Braverman's classic 1974 book, *Labor and Monopoly Capital*. For their analysis, the authors rely almost exclusively on Philip Kraft's little book, *Programmers and Managers: The Routinization of Computer Programming in the United States*.[9] This is a curious book. It stands virtually alone in addressing the subject of computer programmers. Written by a sociologist whose previous work was focused on planning, class, and the state in India, the book grew out of a project of the American Sociological Association to study "issues raised by the study of white collar workers."[10] Kraft had studied with Robert Boguslaw, who is best known for his 1965 book, *The New Utopians: A Study of System Design and Social Change*, which was among a handful of books issued in the 1960s critical of systems analysis, system theory, and the new social sciences in general. *The New Utopians* was one of the "must read" books of the mildly anti-technology intellectuals of the late 1960s, not as shrill as Theodore Roszak's *The Making of a Counter Culture* and *Where the Wasteland Ends* or as observant as Ida Hoos's *Systems Analysis in Public Policy*.[11] Boguslaw had once

---

[7] On the history of dual ladders within R&D organizations, see David A. Hounshell and John Kenly Smith, Jr., *Science and Corporate Strategy: Du Pont R&D, 1902-1980* (New York, 1988), 371-2.

[8] On Developers at Microsoft, see Michael A. Cusumano and Richard W. Selby, *Microsoft Secrets: How the World's Most Powerful Software Company Creates Technology, Shapes Markets, and Manages People* (New York, 1998).

[9] Philip Kraft, *Programmers and Managers: The Routinization of Computer Programming in the United States* (New York, 1977).

[10] Philip Kraft, "The Development of Planning: Class and State in India," Ph.D. diss., Washington University, 1971. The quotation appears in Kraft, *Programmers and Managers*, vii.

[11] Theodore Roszak, *The Making of a Counter Culture: Reflections on the Technocratic Society and Its Youthful Opposition* (Garden City, N.Y., 1969) and idem., *Where the Wasteland Ends: Politics and Transcendence in Postindustrial Society* (Garden City, N.Y., 1972); Ida R. Hoos,

been an enthusiastic insider in what he called "the first heady and frantic years of software development," who had become increasingly critical of, though not disenchanted with, the promise of the new technology of computer-aided decision making and computer simulation of social processes.[12] Perhaps to lend legitimacy to Kraft's book, Boguslaw wrote a forward to *Programmers and Managers*, which I found as interesting as the text itself. "So today I marvel," Boguslaw exclaimed of his former student, "at the boundless audacity of a rank outsider in writing a book like *Programmers and Managers*."[13]

Indeed, Kraft was an outsider. *Programmers and Managers* was the work of a relative novice who had only recently happened upon the question of who computer programmers were, what they did, and what issues surrounded their work. One thing becomes very clear in reading the Introduction to *Programmers and Managers*. That is how limited were both Kraft's set of questions he sought to answer and the empirical data on which he ostensibly based his analysis. Two books formed the principal set of questions that Kraft explored: Harry Braverman's *Labor and Monopoly Capital*, which owed its inspiration to Karl Marx, and David F. Noble's *America by Design*, which owed its inspiration to both Braverman and Marx, as well as to Edwin Layton. Using a non-scientifically derived sample of one hundred programmers, Kraft interviewed some, surveyed some, and followed the career paths of still others to draw his conclusions about computer programmers. The empirical basis of his study was incredibly thin. He supplemented information derived from his sample with articles from *Datamation* and *Infosystems*, the principal trade journals of the field. I would argue that Kraft wanted to see deskilling and the degradation of work, even where and when there might not have been any. Kraft was looking for the separation of head and hand, and he found it.

Inspired by Kraft, the authors of this paper have also found the separation of head and hand.[14] In their text and then in footnote number sixty-nine, they have specifically drawn the parallel between Frederick W. Taylor's *Principles of Scientific Management*, which Braverman had deconstructed into capital's separation of head and hand as the basis for the deskilling of labor, and management's solution to the software crisis, the Taylorization of programming. The question that neither Kraft nor the paper's authors have answered is this: Where is computer programming's Frederick W. Taylor? When did he or she emerge? I suggest one clear parallel to Taylor's *Principles of Scientific Management*. That is T. Capers Jones's 1981 *Tutorial, Programming Productivity: Issues for the Eighties*, which tried to get at the programming productivity measurement problem that had begun to be

---

Systems Analysis in Public Policy: A Critique (Berkeley, 1972). Interestingly, Langdon Winner saw Boguslaw as a Taylor-like technocrat and *The New Utopians* as a "panegyric" for systems analysis "Although under the guise of warning the public about the possible dangers of such people." Langdon Winner, *Autonomous Technology: Technics-out-of-Control as a Theme in Political Thought* (Cambridge, 1977), 143.

[12] The quotation appears in Robert Boguslaw, "Foreword to Kraft", *Programmers and Managers*, v.

[13] Ibid.

[14] Kraft discusses the separation of head and hand in his first chapter in a section entitled "Programmers as Engineers," 18-22.

addressed in the 1970s (including by one of the distinguished Paderborn Software History Conference participants, Albert Endres).[15]

By the time this work appeared, however, a revolution in computer hardware had been unleashed that rendered obsolete, if it existed at all, a condition in which programming had become routinized (and thus programming as work degraded). Here I refer to the movement away from stand-alone mainframe computers to minis to desktops. This hardware revolution saw a dramatic shift in the capabilities of systems from being fairly "stable" to being bound (or, really, "unbound") by Moore's law. Attendant with these dramatic changes in hardware was a move from bundled to unbundled software and then from unbundled to packaged software and from machine language to higher level languages to very high-level languages. Attendant with both the hardware and software developments was a movement in which computer use in Western societies went from being comparatively limited to being almost universal. The development of the Internet and the World Wide Web have served to transform this revolution into one in which, if he or she ever existed, the proletarian programmer has been liberated into the free agent programmer, able to command unprecedented respect, wages, and autonomy in the marketplace of software and "dot-com" start-up firms. Simply put, I do not see the same dynamics at work in the history of the computer industry, vis-à-vis programming, that one sees, say, in the history of steel making (in the change from puddling to Bessemer or open-hearth steelmaking) or in the automobile industry (in the change from hand-assembled automobiles to manufacture using the moving assembly line). It just is not there. In this respect, I would simply underscore the statement that appears in a 1987 dissertation on software engineers and computer programmers by Bernadette Tarallo entitled "The Production of Information":

> The results [of this dissertation] also demonstrate that the deskilling argument is inadequate for understanding the employment relations found in the high tech sector of the economy.[16]

This conclusion is also consistent with the findings of a more recent dissertation that studies employment decisions of software programmers in two software companies.[17]

---

[15] Capers Jones, ed., *Tutorial, Programming Productivity: Issues for the Eighties* (Los Angeles, 1981). See Endres's 1975 paper, "An Analysis of Errors and Their Causes in Systems Programs," in ibid., 86-95. In the discussion following the oral delivery of my remarks at the Paderborn Conference, Michael S. Mahoney, a scholar who has been thinking and writing deeply on the history of software, offered what he believes is the best candidate for the "Taylor of software": Robert W. Bemer, "Position Paper for [the] Panel Discussion [on] the Economics of Program Production," *Information Processing 68*, vol. II (Amsterdam, 1969), 1626-27. Bemer was employed at the time by the General Electric Company. Mahoney's nomination seems sound to me, and he is working on a paper that will show more clearly the parallels between Bemer's thinking and that of Taylor.

[16] Bernadette Mary Tarallo, "The Production of Information: An Examination of the Employment Relations of Software Engineers and Computer Programmers," Ph.D. diss., University of California, Davis, 1987.

[17] Nathan David Ainspan, "'The Geek Shall Inherit' or Leave the Money and Run? Role Identities and Turnover Decisions among Software Programmers and the High-Technology Employ-

Ensmenger and Aspray's paper breaks ground in exploring the history of software through the lens of the NEW new labor history by considering the role of gender in the production of software. Their section on "Women in software" is built principally on the work and implications of Jennifer Light's important *Technology and Culture* article on the programmers of ENIAC, "When Computers Were Women," which in turn builds on much of the conceptual framework being developed in the terrific new work on gender and technology.[18] The authors suggest that women dropped out of computer programming some time in the 1960s and that a "masculine subculture develop[ed]." They ask the extremely important question of why this occurred. Finally, Ensmenger and Aspray conclude that "labor historians have an extensive literature on work and gender; historians of software should make use of their expertise and experience." I can only second this statement, but I would add "let's get some empirical data to work with." Moreover, I would push the authors and those who follow their trail into asking questions about race in the labor history of software. Where are the African Americans, the Latinos and Latinas, and the non-native-born immigrants in the history of software? Race has become a central part of the NEW new labor history, and it should not be ignored in any labor history of software.

The authors touch on a large set of questions and ideas near the end of their paper that should be considered in a labor-process history of software production. In fact, their paper becomes something of a potboiler near the end. But the broth is very thin and will continue to under-nourish the hungry reader until the labor history of software is constructed on a more solid empirical basis.

A labor history of software that would meet Ensmenger and Aspray's expectations would not only address the criticism, questions, and approaches I have offered above but would also include both quantitative and qualitative data on the following:

* the number of programmers over time,
* the number of programming employers,
* the concentration of the industry and its implications for labor,
* data on the formal education of programmers over time,
* breakdown of programmers by sex and race, over time,
* consistent data on the advancement of programmers in corporate ranks and the extent of job segmentation in programming (a central concern of many of the followers of Braverman in labor history during the 1970s and early 1980s),
* labor union organizing attempts from the perspective of both programmers inside firms and the professionals in various unions that have considered or attempted organizing software production workers,
* a mapping of the variety and pecking order of computer programming education, from vocational education programs in high schools, to post-secondary trade schools, to university training, and to in-house corporate educational

---

ees," Ph.D. diss., Cornell University, 1999. Obviously, the title of my comment derives inspiration from the title of this dissertation.

[18] Jennifer Light, "When Computers Were Women," *Technology and Culture* 40 (July 1999): 455-83.

programs, and the career paths and ceilings resulting from these different modes of education.

A robust labor history of software production would also demonstrate a keen knowledge of and appreciation for the changing environment in computer hardware, the patterns of use of computers, and the varieties of programming cultures (from corporatist models to free agents). Appreciation for the changing environment would also include a understanding of business trends and fads over time, from the "organization man" models of the 1950s to the downsizing and re-engineering of the 1990s. Finally, such a history would also seek to trace and understand the power dynamics and the economics of shifting software production—or parts of the process—offshore to countries such as Ireland and India, both from the vantage point of corporate managers and decision makers and from the point of view of the offshore programmers. Right now, the dynamics involved in software production in India, as well as the American importation (green-carding) of software writers from India, are fascinating and deserve careful study.

In summary, Ensmenger and Aspray have written an important, provocative paper that opens up a new world in the history of software. We can only hope that the trails that they have sometimes hastily blazed for historians to follow will be both clear enough and attractive enough for adventuresome scholars to follow, exploit, and enlarge.

A Commentary on David A. Hounshell's Commentary on "Software as Labor Process"

Nathan Ensmenger

University of Pennsylvania
Department of the History and
Sociology of Science   &
303 Logan Hall
Philadelphia, PA 19104-6304
USA

E-mail: nathanen@sas.upenn.edu

William Aspray

Computing Research Association
1100 17th St. NW # 507
Washington, D.C. 20036
USA

E-mail: aspray@cra.org

We particularly value David Hounshell's commentary for the way in which it situates our work in relation to both the old "new" and new "new" labor historiography. We endorse his suggestion to draw a connection between the recent professionalization efforts of "software engineers" and the larger histories of the established engineering disciplines. Hounshell challenges us to engage further with the professionalization literature. In retrospect we could have been more explicit, but it had been our intention to pose provocative questions rather than provide definitive analysis. We expect that our readers will have no difficulty recognizing our description of the historical controversy over "what is programming?" and "what makes for an exceptional programmer?" as attempts to establish autonomous control over what sociologists of professions refer to as "socially valuable body of esoteric knowledge." The psychological profiles and programming aptitude tests of the early 1950s, the certification debates of the mid-1960s, and the persistent tension between the "art" of programming and the "science" of software engineering are expressions of an ongoing struggle by computer programmers to establish professional and intellectual legitimacy.

On several occasions Hounshell reminds us of the severe need for further empirical research on software labor markets past and present. On this point we agree with him wholeheartedly. The recent debates over the alleged shortage of skilled American information technology workers have exposed how remarkably little we know even about contemporary software workers, much less the laborers of previous decades. A few of Hounshell's criticisms seem misplaced, however—as though we were actually writing the labor history of software, rather than setting a research agenda for writing this history. But even in our agenda-setting task, we were hampered by the lack of secondary literature and accurate empirical data. For example, Hounshell suggests that "dual ladder" programs provided substantial career paths for programming professionals. We did not find evidence to suggest that such programs were either widespread or effective, but this is indeed an open and interesting empirical question. Our brief sketch of this history attempts to make creative use of some well-worn traditional sources, but we agree that there is a great deal of research, both quantitative and otherwise, that needs to be accomplished before the comprehensive history of software workers can be accurately established.

One issue on which we do not entirely agree with Hounshell's assessment is his reading of our treatment of the Kraft/Braverman deskilling hypothesis. The "routinization of labor" is a traditional theme in labor history that deserves to be taken seriously, and Kraft represents one extremely common perspective on management/labor relationships in the software industry. It is clear that the rhetoric of scientific management, if not necessarily the substance, has often been applied to the process of software development. The historical record is full of calls for the establishment of "mass production techniques" of program assembly. We would never suggest, however, that this deskilling process had occurred in the software industry to the extent Kraft has described it; in fact, at several points we suggest that Kraft's interpretation is wholly inadequate. In this we are very much in agreement with Hounshell. We are bothered by the simplicity of Kraft's "routinization" hypothesis, and we look forward to an interpretation of the software crisis that fully addresses the complex interactions between the software worker's professional aspirations, the needs and desires of managers, and unique history of the information technology industry. Whereas Hounshell sees the Internet era as exceptional, we see a remarkable parallel between the "software turmoil" of the early 1960s and the "software crisis" of the 1990s. We believe that it is the similarities between these two periods—the emphasis on the rhetoric of crisis, the perceived imbalance between the supply and demand of skilled programmers, and the widespread call for a legitimately "scientific" approach to software engineering—that are the key to understanding the history of the programming professions.

Discussion following
"Software as Labor Process"

Mary Croarken

National Maritime Museum
Centre for Maritime Research
Greenwich, London, SE10 9NF
UK

E-mail: mcroarken@nmm.ac.uk

The discussion following the Software as Labor Process workshop generally applauded both the paper and the commentaries presented and the authors were complemented on their thought provoking presentation. The paper had illustrated that there were big gaps in our knowledge of software as labor process and many of the comments and questions addressed areas for possible consideration.

The discussion began with Aspray replying to remarks made by Denert in his commentary on the need for more computer science graduates. Aspray stated that many more IT workers were hired than there were computer science graduates. He observed that Germany was actually producing more computer science graduates than the US but that the patterns of growth were similar. Aspray had found it very difficult to get accurate empirical data concerning the actual numbers of professional IT workers companies needed.

The issue of professionalization of IT workers was then raised. One discussant raised parallels with the Netherlands, in which two professional societies, one academically oriented and one vocationally based, had unhappily split the computing field. It was claimed that these two cultures of computing could be traced within the internal hierarchies of companies. The discussant used this example to challenge Hounshell's endorsement of the current sociology of professions as an unproblematic basis for historical analysis. It was suggested that this approach was itself in crisis, because traditional hallmarks of professionalism had broken down in recent decades. Ironically, IT workers themselves have provided one of the most problematic cases for sociologists seeking to demarcate professional status. In addition, attempting to periodize the development of software labor would show major shifts as computer use itself moved from the centralized computer centers of the 1960s into ever wider circles. What might be more useful was to do periodization marking and track changes such as the point at which software stopped being exclusively written by experts and engineers were expected to do their own programming.

It was then suggested that history might be a rare source of empirical insights into a highly charged topic: the skill and qualification profile of successful IT workers. Companies had done little work to establish the qualification profile of IT workers but a lack of IT worker education was often cited as a labor process issue. It was one of the main reasons behind Germany's recent policy of increasing the permitted number of IT worker immigrants. Companies working to deadlines had their own ideas of how many IT workers were needed and this was not always accurate. In "boom" times the pressure of projects behind schedule created a demand for more "bodies." When jobs were scarcer, there was no reliable way of matching applicants to opportunities. It was suggested that the profile of IT workers, and changes to that profile, was an interesting way to look at software as labor process.

During the presentation it had been noted that software appeared to lack its own Frederick W. Taylor. It was suggested that this role could be filled by Watts Humphrey, creator of the capability maturity model, the personal software process and pioneer of stopwatch measurement of the program cycle. He also shared Taylor's unenthusiastic reception by the established engineering community. Humphrey was not the only candidate—another was Licklider, who had turned the stopwatch on himself to demonstrate that most programmer time was spent performing clerical duties that could easily be automated.

The discussion moved on to discuss ideas concerning the nature of skill and the deskilling process based on the work of Braverman and others. What is the skill that the programmer possesses? Has there been a skill change over time in IT workers? The situation of older IT workers not being hired because their knowledge was outdated was also raised. The skills of programmers were tightly bound to access to machines that they did not themselves control. In a sense, every user of a spreadsheet has now become a programmer, just as every user of a telephone is now an operator. Human experience of work has shifted along with the technology.

Aspray had concluded the Software as Labor Process paper with a brief overview of how US government policies had affected software labor. This theme was taken up during the discussion and the influence of defense contracting in the training of IT workers was agreed upon. But what real effect did recent US government policies really have? Had initiatives in areas such as high performance computing involved little more than a reclassification of funds that had already been committed? In reply Aspray acknowledged that in many cases "new" money had gone into existing projects but argued that keeping projects going did help to maintain the numbers of IT workers. Such projects were also a vehicle for education programs. One of the biggest influences on IT education was the fact that the US NSF stopped specifically funding computer equipment in universities in 1973 and did not restart until the 1990s.

Ensmenger concluded the discussion by acknowledging that both authors were acutely aware of the lack of empirical quantitative data in the paper. He stated that while the paper had concentrated on the 1960s and 1970s it was also very difficult to obtain data for the 1990s as Aspray's recent investigations into contemporary IT labor markets had shown. Ensmenger was particularly interested in developing ideas about IT worker skills and productivity and how their profile changed over time. Ensmenger agreed with Hounshell that professionalization was another vital topic but was concerned that the necessary data needed to do this successfully would never be available to us. Another problem has been the lack of agreement amoung IT workers on the kind of profession they are. During the 1960s and 1970s the Data Processing Managers Association promoted an accounting model of profession building while the Association of Computing Machinery favored the model of a scientific profession and the IEEE tried to extend its engineering approaches. Another problem highlighted by Ensmenger was giving a definition of "programmer"—a task that the Ensmenger/Aspray paper had not attempted to do. Ensmenger felt that it was important for historians to examine all of these themes in context.

Part 5
Software as Economic Activity

Software as an Economic Activity

Martin Campbell-Kelly[1]

University of Warwick
Department of Computer Science
Coventry, CV4 7AL
UK

E-mail: mck@dcs.warwick.ac.uk

Introduction

In the history of software, we have perhaps just gone through what Thomas Kuhn called the pre-paradigmatic stage of knowledge development, when we could do little more than report the phenomena we observed.[2] The next stage of development will be to develop frameworks and unifying theories to categorize and make sense of what we observe. We have not got very far along this path yet, but we have made a start.

Rationale: Why do We Need an Economic History of Software?

To date, the history of software has been very much focussed on particular artifacts such as operating systems or programming languages. Some excellent work has been done, but I believe that most efforts have been handicapped by the lack of an economic context to inform the historical narrative. Let me give two examples.

The first example is Peter Salus's *A Quarter Century of Unix*. The tone of the book is set out in the blurb, which reads:

> UNIX is a software system that is simple, elegant, portable, and powerful. It grew in popularity without the benefit of a large marketing organization. Programmers kept using it; big companies kept fighting it. After a decade, it was clear that the user had won.[3]

The thesis of the author is that Unix won out largely because of its intrinsic technological merits—which were undoubtedly very great. However, the history of computing is littered with the corpses of meritorious developments that failed in the market place, so there must surely be a deeper story to tell. I would argue that

---

[1] The author's work on the history of the software industry has been supported by the Economic and Social Research Council (award number R000237065). My thanks to my research associates at Warwick University, Dr. Mary G. Croarken and Dr. Ross Hamilton.
[2] Thomas Kuhn, *The Structure of Scientific Revolutions* (Chicago, 1962).
[3] Peter H. Salus, *A Quarter Century of Unix* (Reading, Mass., 1994).

the economic environment was Unix's silent helper. Thus, the low-cost of Unix enabled it to get an initial toe-hold in the market; it then benefited from the network effect of a community of academic users and developers; and finally it gained widespread acceptance by being the incumbent non-proprietary operating system when the workstation market took off in the early 1980s. None of this is intended to slight Salus's work, which is well contextualized and rates high on my personal scale of works in the history of software. But it would undoubtedly be stronger for a deeper economic analysis.[4]

My second example concerns the rise of Microsoft. Most of the literature on Microsoft is written by journalists, and they usually account for the rise of the company by some variant of the "evil genius theory." By far the most cited history of Microsoft is James Wallace and Jim Erickson's *Hard Drive* whose tone is established in the blurb:

> Part entrepreneur, part salesmen, Gates is a brilliant—some say manipulative—businessman, an *enfant terrible* who, according to friends and foes alike, "simply must win."[5]

Wallace and Erickson published their book in 1992, when Microsoft's turnover was a mere $1.8 billion. Since the author's most dramatic projections for Microsoft have been fully borne out in the years since publication, it is hard to make the charge stick that their analysis is naive. Nonetheless, there is another view. A much more measured account of Microsoft is given by Randall Stross, an academic economist, in his book *The Microsoft Way*.[6] Without discounting Gates's remarkable business instincts, Stross argues that Microsoft has benefited from an economic environment that causes IT products to converge towards a single platform. According to Stross, Gates's genius (or instinct) was to recognize these forces and take advantage of them. I find this a much more satisfactory explanation of the Microsoft phenomenon.

The Literature

Let me begin with the bad news: the biggest single topic in the economic and business literature of software is Microsoft. There have been published at least twenty monographs on Microsoft and biographies of Bill Gates, and I personally have lost any sense of urgency in keeping up with the flow of books and articles about Microsoft. The vast majority of accounts are heroic in tone, focusing on Gates as a personality. Many seem to be written by journalists looking for an easy buck. My hard-won conclusion is that three books, Wallace and Erickson's *Hard Drive*, Stross's *Microsoft Way*, and Ichbiah and Knepper's *The Making of Microsoft* cover essentially all of the ground.[7]

---

[4] See, for example, Ed Dunphy, *The Unix Industry*, 2nd ed. (New York, 1994).

[5] James Wallace and J. Erickson, *Hard Drive: Bill Gates and the Making of the Microsoft Empire* (New York, 1992).

[6] Randall E. Stross, *The Microsoft Way* (Reading, Mass., 1996).

[7] Daniel Ichbiah and Susan Knepper's *The Making of Microsoft* (Rocklin, Calif., 1991) is a pleasantly traditional history, giving a factual and exhaustive discussion of the firm and its

Set against the torrent of Microsoft histories, there are less than a dozen worthwhile histories of other software companies. Some of the more useful include Claude Baum's history of SDC *The System Builders*, Sandra Kurtzig's personal account of ASK Inc. *CEO*, W.E. Petersen's personal history of the WordPerfect Corporation *AlmostPerfect*, John Walker's *The Autodesk File*, and Mike Wilson's journalistic account of Oracle *The Difference between God and Larry Ellison*.[8] Other books on the software industry, such as Hesh Kestin's account of Computer Associates *Twenty-First Century Management* and John P. Imlay's reflections on his role in MSA *Jungle Rules* are disappointing—at least for their insights into the history of the software industry.[9] By far the best account of any individual company is Richard Forman's *Fulfilling the Computer's Promise*, a commissioned history of Informatics.[10] This exists only as an unpublished typescript and I know of no copies in the public domain. There are also a few article length reminiscences by industry pioneers—such as Elmer Kubie's recollections of the early years of the Computer Usage Company and J. Lesourne and R. Armand's description of the first decade of SEMA; although lacking in detail, these are useful because they do at least add to the volume of the literature.[11]

Inevitably the history of individual firms focuses on the largest companies—those with hundreds or thousands of employees, and revenues of a billion dollars or more. Since the average software company has less than 30 employees, this is very unrepresentative. Hence, for me, one of the hidden gems of software history is the little known privately-published *The MacNeal-Schwendler Corporation: The First Twenty Years*, written by its founding President Richard MacNeal in 1988, when the firm numbered only a couple of hundred workers.[12]

The biographies of individual firms, however many they number, are not truly representative of the software industry, any more than a random collection of biographies—of say Mozart, Marconi, and Kissinger—are representative of the human race. The best sources for the broader industrial scene are the reports of

products, rather than a rhetorical account of Gates's machiavellian persona. One should also note Michael Cusumano and Richard Selby's *Microsoft Secrets* (New York, 1995). This is a book in an entirely different class to the journalistic literature, and is one of the most significant books on software in recent years. However the book is primarily about Microsoft's internal organization rather than its broad business strategy.

[8] Claude Baum, *The System Builders: The Story of SDC* (Santa Monica, Calif., 1981). Sandra L. Kurtzig, *CEO: Building a $400 million Company from the Ground Up* (New York, 1991). W. E. (Pete) Petersen, *AlmostPerfect: How a Bunch of Regular Guys Built WordPerfect Corporation* (Rocklin, Calif., 1994). John Walker, ed., *The Autodesk File: Bits of History, Words of Experience,* 3rd ed. (Thousand Oaks, Calif., 1989); the latest edition can be downloaded from http://www.fourmilab.to/autofile/. Mike Wilson, *The Difference between God and Larry Ellison: Inside Oracle Corporation* (New York, 1996).

[9] Hesh Kestin, *Twenty-First-Century Management: The Revolutionary Strategies that Have Made Computer Associates a Multi-Billion Software Giant* (New York, 1992). John P. Imlay with Dennis Hamilton, *Jungle Rules: How to be a Tiger in Business* (New York, 1994).

[10] Richard L. Forman, "Fulfilling the Computer's Promise: The History of Informatics, 1962-1982," unpublished typescript (Woodland-Hills, Calif., 1985).

[11] Elmer C. Kubie, "Recollection of the First Software Company," *Annals of the History of Computing* 16 (1994): 65-71. J. Lesourne and R. Armand, "A Brief History of the First Decade of SEMA," *Annals of the History of Computing* 13 (1991): 341-9.

[12] Richard H. MacNeal, *The MacNeal-Schwendler Corporation: The First Twenty Years* (Los Angeles, 1988).

government-sponsored software policy studies, a few academic monographs, and the publications of market research organizations. Three major national software policy reports were written in the mid-1980s, when the software industry experienced its most dramatic growth spurt. These reports were published by the U.S. Department of Commerce, the OECD, and the UK Government's Advisory Council for Applied Research and Development (ACARD). The reports are all in the public domain, accessible, and give an excellent 1980s view of the software industry.[13]

During the 1990s, the software industry has had some attention from mainstream economists and business analysts. Publications include David Mowery's edited book *The International Computer Software Industry*, Salvatore Torrisi's *Industrial Organisation and Innovation: An International Study of the Software Industry*, and Detlev Hoch et al.'s *Secrets of Software Success*.[14] Although these works are not primarily historical, they are all informed by history, and will in time become important historical sources in their own right.

Market research reports for the computer software and services industry are by far the richest source of solid quantitative data. Such reports date from the late 1960s and early 1970s, and were produced by organizations such Auerbach, ICP, Frost & Sullivan, IDC, Input, Business Communications, Communication Trends, and numerous others. Reports were produced for subscribers only, who were primarily software firms and large scale users, and rarely migrated to the public domain. In the last thirty years there must have been several hundred reports published, of which perhaps fifty survive in the Library of Congress.[15] Examples of the kind of reports that I found useful include a 1971 report by Frost & Sullivan *The Computer Software and Services Market*, a 1980 report by Business Communications *Software Packages: An Emerging Market*, a 1984 report by Efrem Sigel and the staff of Communication Trends *The Business/Professional Microcomputer Software Market*, and Burt Grad Associates 1992 report *Evolution of the U.S. Packaged Software Industry*.[16] Clearly, the reports that survive in the Library of

[13] U.S. Department of Commerce, *A Competitive Assessment of the United States Software Industry* (Washington, D.C., 1984). OECD, *Software, an Emerging Industry* (Paris, 1985). Advisory Council for Applied Research and Development (ACARD), *Software: A Vital Key to UK Competitiveness* (London, 1986). The U.S. report was summarized in Ware Myers, "An Assessment of the Competitiveness of the United States Software Industry," *IEEE Computer*, March 1985, 81-92.

[14] David C. Mowery, ed., *The International Computer Software Industry* (New York, 1996). Salvatore Torrisi, *Industrial Organisation and Innovation: An International Study of the Software Industry* (Cheltenham, 1998). Detlev J. Hoch et al., *Secrets of Software Success: Management Insights from 100 Software Firms Around the World* (Cambridge, Mass., 1999).

[15] There may be other public-access libraries with significant holdings of market research reports, but if so I do not know of them. Market research reports were very costly and supplied with confidentiality agreements that prohibited their use by persons other than the subscriber. One bright spot is that the Charles Babbage Institute has recently acquired the records of International Computer Programs Inc.

[16] Frost & Sullivan, *The Computer Software and Services Market* (New York, 1971). Business Communications Corp., *Software Packages: An Emerging Market* (Stamford, Conn. 1980). Efrem Sigel, and the staff of Communications Trends, *The Business/Professional Microcomputer Software Market, 1984-86* (White Plains, N.Y., 1984). Burt Grad and Associates Inc., *Evolution of U.S. packaged Software Industry* (Tarrytown, N.Y., 1992).

Congress are the tip of a vanished iceberg. My approaches to market research firms, and to trade associations such as ADAPSO and BSA, indicate that few of them hold materials going back further than ten years, and that they are not in general anxious to co-operate with academic researchers.

Measuring Software as an Economic Activity

Up to about 1975 we have a relatively clear picture of the scale of software activity, but in the last twenty-five years, as software development has diffused from the air-conditioned mainframe environment into the wider economy, the picture becomes progressively less clear.

The Scene up to 1975

Up to about 1975, computing activity was dominated by the mainframe, and almost all software activity took place within a data processing "department." We know how many mainframes there were, year to year, and there are reliable estimates of how much of the data processing budget was spent on programming. Using this data it would be possible to estimate total software investments, and indeed this was presumably the basis on which the OECD computed that the world's software stock in 1982 was $500 billion—which was more than four times the stock of mainframe and minicomputers at the time.[17]

As an example of the quality of evidence available, Fig. 1, adapted from *Datamation* in 1973, shows the data processing budget of U.S. corporate users, derived primarily from a market research survey conducted by the magazine.[18] Although I know of no complete systematic run of such pie-charts, they are common enough to infer that computer software was user-produced to an overwhelming extent during this period. Thus in the data processing budget of 1973, staff costs (predominantly systems analysis, programming, operations, and data entry) accounted for 44.6 percent of the total, while purchases of computer software (packages and custom programming) accounted for just 1.5 percent.

Expenditure on programming did not vary very much in the first quarter century of mainframe computing, a fact which is borne out by the Montgomery Phister's *Data Processing Technology and Economics*, which provides a time-series for data processing expenditures.[19] This shows systems analysis and programming costs rising very slowly from 20 percent of the budget in 1955 to 30 percent by 1975. Incidentally, Phister's data tends to refute one of the most pervasive pieces of rhetoric in software history, the changing ratio of hardware to software costs, of which Werner Frank of Informatics and Barry Boehm of TRW were the most

---

[17] OECD (n. 13 above), 21 and 44.
[18] Richard A. McLaughlin, "A Survey of DP Budgets for 1973," *Datamation*, January 1973, 61-63.
[19] Montgomery Phister Jr., *Data Processing: Technology and Economics,* 2nd ed. (Bedford, Mass. and Santa Monica, Calif., 1979), 151.

influential advocates.[20] These authors claimed, perhaps unconsciously appealing to Pareto's Law, that while the ratio of costs had been 80 percent hardware to 20 percent software in 1955, by the mid-1980s, it would be the other way about. Phister's data suggests that there was not nearly such a dramatic transformation. This is a software myth that Frank later corrected, suggesting that the ratio of software to hardware costs might be as low as 2 to 3 rather than the 4 to 1 claimed by Boehm.[21] For at least the period up to the mid-1980s, the veracity or otherwise of the changing ratio of hardware and software costs is a tractable, but as yet unanswered, research question.

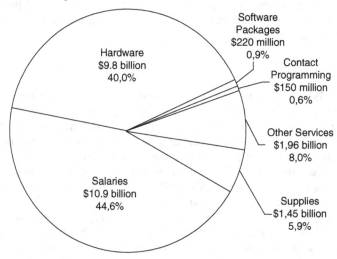

Fig.1. U.S. EDP expenditure, 1973 (adapted from McLaughlin [n. 18], Fig. 1, p. 62)

Post-1975 Confusion

After 1975, software activity multiplied and fragmented. We have a good measure of the software spend in the corporate data processing department—increasingly termed the information systems or IS department. During the last 25 years, journals such as *Datamation* and privately published reports such as the *PriceWaterhouse Survey* have continued to track the corporate IS budget. The picture has changed surprisingly little. Thus in 1987 a *Datamation* survey estimated that the average salary spend in corporate IS departments was 47 percent—only marginally more than in 1973.[22] At the same time, spending on hardware and software had changed in an interesting way. In 1973, 40 percent of the data processing budget went on hardware, with only 1.5 percent on software; in 1987 hardware

---

[20] Werner L. Frank, "Software for Terminal Oriented Systems," *Datamation*, June 1968. Barry Boehm, "Software and Its Impact: A Quantitative Assessment," *Datamation*, May 1973, 48-59.

[21] Werner L. Frank, "The History of Myth No. 1," *Datamation*, May 1983, 252-6.

[22] "Industry by Industry IS Survey," *Datamation*, 1 September 1987, 46ff.

took up 34 percent of the budget and software 11 percent. Thus the combined hardware-software spend was little changed, the different proportions spent on hardware and software really only reflecting the effect of the unbundling of software.

Beyond the corporate IS department, however, the extent of software economy is very difficult to estimate, and I know of no useful guides. The problem began in the early 1970s with the deployment of minicomputers in contexts such as process control, instrumentation, and communications switching. The number of engineers who programmed these computers and the value of the software they produced cannot be estimated from the available data. Engineers may have been programmers in practice, but from an occupational census viewpoint they were counted as engineers; and the software they produced was simply an operating cost. It might be possible to estimate the extent of this hidden software activity, given knowledge of the size of the minicomputer population and typical user expenditures on programming, but it would be a considerable challenge and would at best give us a only a partial picture of total software activity after 1975.

After the early 1980s, with the widespread diffusion of the microprocessor, the extent of the hidden software economy was even greater. Apart from the ubiquitous personal computer, many capital goods and consumer products—from automobiles to telephone handsets—were produced that contained vast amounts of embedded software. Such software development costs were not captured in any systematic way, but they were clearly immense. For example, I have been told, anecdotally, that for products such as laser printers, software is the principal development cost. Yet another realm of activity not captured by any software census is computer games and recreational software; and to add to the difficulty, in this industry the boundaries of software and content, or programming and graphic design, are very difficult to draw.

Probably the best tangible measure we could get for software activity is the number of people employed as IT workers. But as Freeman and Aspray have shown in their recent *The Supply of Information Technology Workers in the United States*, the available measures are of poor quality, and there is hardly any reliable data prior to 1980.[23] Moreover the available data leaves entirely out of account the many workers who wrote software but were not called programmers. This is a very different situation compared with, say, the construction industry. There, besides having reliable measures of the number of workers employed, we also have gross measures of physical inputs—such as timber or bricks—that give us further meaningful measures of activity. With software, not only do we have no reliable measure of IT workers, we have no tangible inputs either.[24]

To summarize, I think that we may never know the extent of software activity in the post-1975 period. We may be able to answer the question for some industries or government sectors, but it would be a monumental task to get anything like a comprehensive global picture over an extended time frame. In fact, I am not

---

[23] Peter Freeman and William Aspray, *The Supply of Information Technology Workers in the United States* (Washington, D.C., 1999).
[24] One could make a case for counting as inputs capital software goods such as programming tools or SAP licenses, but it would be difficult to make a direct relationship between these inputs and total software activity because software development costs are so variable.

quite sure that the question is entirely meaningful. It is perhaps akin to asking the question: What is the extent and value of *writing* as an economic activity? Writing is simply too diffused in the economy for the question to be meaningful. For this reason the rest of this paper will focus on the traded software industry, which is more amenable to measurement.

Periodization and Sectorization of the Software Industry

There is a consensus among the three most recent historical overviews of the software industry on its periodization and sectorization.[25] These authors all divide the industry into three sectors: software contracting; corporate software products; and personal computer software products. The terminology to describe the sectors is somewhat problematical—or at least ahistorical—since all three sectors continued to flourish and adopt the preferred terminology of the day. For example, "software contracting" which began in 1955 pre-dated the invention of the word "software," and originally went under such terms as "custom programming" or "programming services." Similarly the first pre-packaged programs were simply called "software products," no further distinction being necessary. However with the rise of the personal computer software industry it became necessary to distinguish between the corporate and PC software markets by introducing terms such as "enterprise software" or "shrink-wrapped software," respectively.

The division of the software industry into the three sectors is natural both in market terms and in terms of the distinctive business models that the firms have evolved. The firms' competencies and knowledge of their specialized markets have enabled the more successful to maintain dominant positions in their own sector, but at the same time have made it difficult for them to cross over into either of the other sectors. In this respect software firms fit very well the economic models discussed by Nelson and Winter in their classic *An Evolutionary Theory of Economic Change.*[26]

Software Contractors

All writers agree that the defining event in the software contracting industry was the creation of the Systems Development Corporation (SDC) in 1956 to develop the programs for the massive SAGE project. At about the same time small start-up firms such as the Computer Usage Company (CUC), C-E-I-R, and the Computer Sciences Corporation (CSC), also began to undertake custom programming for computer manufacturers and computer users. The business model consciously or unconsciously adopted by custom-programming firms was that of an engineering or construction contractor. They existed by bidding for, and winning, contracts executed on a time-and-materials or fixed-price basis.

[25] Martin Campbell-Kelly, "Development and Structure of the International Software Industry, 1950-1990," *Business and Economic History* 24, No. 2 (1995): 73-110. W. Edward Steinmueller, "The U.S. Software Industry: An Analysis and Interpretive History," in Mowery, (n. 14 above), 15-52. Hoch et al. (n. 14 above), chap. 1.
[26] Richard Nelson and Sidney G. Winter, *An Evolutionary Theory of Economic Change* (Cambridge, Mass., 1982).

The critical capabilities the software contracting firm developed were:

1. The exploitation of scope
2. Cost estimation and project management skills

The successful software contractor exploited the economies of scope by specializing in particular sub-markets. For example, SDC specialized in real time defense projects, while CSC specialized in systems software for computer manufacturers. By specializing in these narrow markets, firms could reduce costs by reusing software from one project in the next, and could develop specialized human resources by working in a consistent application domain. In the case of non-American firms, specialized domestic knowledge has enabled them to survive against multi-national competitors.

The profits on software contracting were surprisingly low, typically 7-15 percent of sales, so that cost estimation and project management skills were essential. Accurate cost estimation was necessary to prepare a price-competitive bid, and project management skills were needed to ensure completion within time and cost constraints. By contrast, marketing was a relatively unimportant competence, with most selling being done through the personal contacts of senior staff or by responding to openly published requests for quotation.

Corporate Software Products

Two software products, ADR's *Autoflow* and Informatics *Mark IV*, announced in 1966 and 1967 respectively, are generally agreed to be the first software products. These products, and a handful of others, had already proved themselves viable in the marketplace when IBM announced its unbundling decision in June 1969. However, the unbundling announcement had the effect of firmly establishing a vibrant market place for software products, which previously had been merely embryonic. As JoAnne Yates has put it, the unbundling announcement was "the crucial inflexion point" in the development of the software-products industry.[27]

At first the software-products business was likened to "the record industry," because of the analogy between the low incremental costs of reproducing programs and recorded music. In fact, this turned out to be an illusion. Because of the high marketing costs and the need for sales support, corporate software products were classic capital goods. Thus the business model adopted by the software-products firms, often quite consciously, was that of capital goods producer—and the firms often looked to computer manufacturers, particularly IBM, as role models. The key capabilities that the firm's developed included:

1. The exploitation of scale
2. Corporate marketing
3. Quality assurance
4. Pre- and after-sales support

---

[27] JoAnne Yates, "Application Software for Insurance in the 1960s and Early 1970s," *Business and Economic History* 24, No. 1 (1995): 123-34 [124].

Exploiting scale was the most critical capability, because selling in volume was the only way to recover the high initial development costs of a generalized software product—which were much higher than for custom software. Software products typically sold in hundreds or occasionally thousands of units. Because volume sales were so important, it was necessary to develop quota based sales operations, typically on the IBM model—firms often recruiting ex-IBM sales people. Software products, such as database programs or industrial applications, were usually "mission critical" and for this reason product reliability was paramount. The software-products firms develop skills in quality assurance—using such techniques as beta testing—to ensure that products were ruggedly productized and reliable in use. Finally, as with all capital goods, pre- and after-sales support was vital to establish a long-term relationship with the client. In the case of software products, this took the form of product customization, user training, and regular upgrades. These services turned out to be unexpected sources of income that the pioneers of the industry had not initially planned for.

PC Software Products

The origin of the personal computer software industry is widely attributed to VisiCalc being the "killer app." for the Apple II computer in 1979. The phenomenon of the killer app. has been heavily used in the journalistic literature, but has not been taken up by academic theorists (see section "Economic and Innovation Theory" below). My own view is that the killer app. thesis probably confuses cause and effect, putting the cart before the horse. Thus, I would argue, that the Apple II created a platform on which many software products could exist, of which VisiCalc was simply a prominent example. If VisiCalc had not existed, then some other software product would have earned the epithet killer app.

The personal computer software products industry was completely disjoint from the corporate software products industry: the essential difference between the two was the size of their markets, which differed by two orders of magnitude. For example, in 1984 the world's top-selling corporate software product was Informatics *Mark IV* with 3000 installations, while the top-selling PC software product was *WordStar*, which had 700,000 sales.

When analysts observed that the PC software industry was like the recorded-music business, the analogy held good, and the business model adopted by the industry was that of an information goods producer, sometimes known as the "Hollywood model." Another industry parallel was drawn with the pharmaceutical industry, which had a similar cost structure based on very high R&D inputs, low production costs, and high marketing expenses.

The key capabilities developed by the PC software firms included:

1. The exploitation of scale
2. Mass marketing
3. Ease-of-use technologies

Exploiting scale through very high volumes was the defining characteristic of the PC software industry, and its product cost structure was entirely different to the corporate software products industry. For example, the cost of a *Mark IV* installation was about $100,000, while *WordStar* cost about $500. In terms of marketing, the PC software firms targeted their products at the end user, rather than the corporate information systems manager, making use of low cost distribution channels such as retail outlets and mail-order. This required the development of a very different set a marketing competencies compared with the corporate software products firms, with their IBM-type sales forces. So that PC software products could be used without any after sales support by many thousands of customers, programs had to have intuitive interfaces and require no customization. This again required the development of a different set of skills to corporate software products makers, who could rely on training courses and third parties to install and customize software.

After 1995– What?

As historians we do not need to concern ourselves directly with events more recent than five years ago, but our view of today's software industry inevitably shapes our view of its past. The three sector model explains very adequately the evolution of the industry to mid-1990s, and its structure at that time. For example, the different competencies developed by firms in the three sectors explains why they found it so difficult to make the transition from one sector to another.

However, there is a contemporary view that the convergence produced by the Internet will change everything. For example, the delivery of software by the Internet has undermined the metaphor of shrink-wrapped software for personal computers, while the integration of the personal computer into the corporate information system—rather than existing as an isolated desktop—is currently reshaping industry strategy. Thus while Microsoft is relentlessly moving into enterprise computing, Oracle is migrating from the world of the mainframe and departmental computer to the world of PCs and networked computing.

In their *Secrets of Software Success* Detlev Hoch and his co-authors have projected a new period in the development of the software industry that they call the "Internet Era," and suggest boundary dates 1994-2008.[28] My expectation is that we will indeed, as historians, moved towards such a periodization in due time. For the present we just need to be assured that the history we are writing today is robust enough to make sense 10 or 15 years from now.

Taxonomy as an Historical Handle

In 1968 there were estimated to be between 1,500 and 3,000 firms in the computer software and services industry, mostly in the United States. Today, one source estimates that there are, world-wide, 35,000 software firms with more than five employees, while another estimates that there are 150,000 firms world-wide regardless of size.[29] These widely varying estimates of the industry's size have existed throughout its history, and are symptomatic of its wildly fragmented structure. Hence, getting to grips with this bewildering number of firms, and an even

---

[28] Hoch et al. (n. 14 above), 269-70.
[29] Ibid., 38.

larger number of products, has been a long-term concern of both industry analysts and historians. Analysts have adopted the taxonomic methods used by genealogists, information scientists, zoologists, and others to "understand" the industry structure by locating firms and products on taxonomic trees. These trees effectively represent views of the industry and the market, respectively.

Taxonomy of Firms

Software producers have almost always been conflated with computer service providers, as the computer software and services industry (CSSI). Four distinct sectors of the CSSI had emerged by the end of the 1960s:

1. Processing services
2. Programming services
3. Facilities management
4. Software products

Processing services firms, which performed data processing for a client organization, evolved from punch-card service bureaux in the late 1940s and 1950s—ADP, for example, was formed in 1949 as a punched card bureau, and acquired its first computer in 1953. Programming services firms, which undertook custom programming for clients, emerged in the mid-1950s, with organizations such as SDC and CUC. Facilities management firms, which ran the computer operations of client organizations, emerged in the early 1960s with companies such as EDS (formed in 1962). Finally, software products firms emerged in the second half of the 1960s, with firms such as ADR and Informatics.

The four sectors of the computer software and services industry have been treated as one industry because there were relatively few pure plays in any one sector, and it was very difficult to disaggregate these activities in the individual firms. Historically, start-up firms often began in one sector and horizontally integrated into another. For example, CSC began as a software contractor in 1959, but had become a major processing services firm by the mid-1970s. Likewise, Informatics was established in 1962 as a software contractor, but was active in all four sectors by the late 1960s. And of course, the computer manufacturers, particularly IBM, were active in all sectors. In the 1970s systems integrators such as TRW and MITRE, consultancies such as A. D. Little and SRI, and accounting firms such as Arthur Andersen, had also become significant players in computer services. Another class of firm that entered the CSSI in the 1970s was the value added reseller (VAR) or "turnkey" supplier, such as Wang or Computer Vision. These firms integrated hardware and software into a single product. All these developments confused the picture still further.

When one tries to analyze the software industry, it is necessary to consider firms whose dominant activities were not actually software. For example, although firms such as IBM, CSC, EDS, and Fujitsu, were (and still are) major programming services organizations, for all of them custom-software writing contributed less than 10 percent of their total revenues. The situation in software products is generally clearer, with firms such as Oracle and Microsoft deriving 80 percent or more of their revenues from software products. One industry analyst, incidentally, has defined software firms as ones that derive at least 50 percent of their revenues from software.[30] This makes for a clean separation, but it excludes important players such as IBM and CSC whose software activities are greater than those of medium-sized producers.

To summarize, attempts at organizing software producers in a systematic way have had limited success. Getting a more effective handle on producers of both traded and non-traded software remains a major historical challenge, and I can offer no insights.

Classification of Packages

The classification of software products has been much more successful than the classification of software producers. All taxonomies are similar in structure, and are historically grounded (although not all taxonomists are probably aware of their debt to history).

The different taxonomies have varied in detail and have evolved over time as the market has constantly reshaped. However, there have been two invariants in all the taxonomies. First, products have been divided into systems programs and applications packages. This was a very natural division, which IBM had adopted semi-formally in the 1950s and used in its System/360 Type I and Type II software classifications prior to unbundling. The second invariant has been to divide applications software into industry-specific and cross-industry applications. Industry-specific packages were those designed for a particular industry, such as banking, manufacturing, or health care, and which would only be sold to a member firm of that industry. Cross-industry packages were generic programs that could be sold to many different industries: examples included payroll programs, word-processing systems, and linear programming packages.

The most widely known taxonomy was that used by the U.S. Department of Commerce in its influential *Competitive Assessment of the U.S. Software Industry* published in 1984. This taxonomy was effectively a consensus view of industry analysts such as Input and IDC, and the trade association ADAPSO. The Department of Commerce report was a key source for the OECD and UK inquiries into the software industry in 1985 and 1986, and so the taxonomic view is well embedded in policy circles and market research firms.

The taxonomic view of software products has proved remarkably adaptable and expandable over time. For example, while in 1975 payroll programs were one of the principal cross-industry applications (accounting for 93 out of a total of 777 packages), by the late 1980s they were subsumed as a minor division of "human resources" software. Again, the taxonomic structure was readily able to accommodate the emergence of the microcomputer software market in the 1980s. Thus MS-DOS, WordPerfect and Lotus 1-2-3 could be readily attached to the taxonomic tree.

There is, however, a major limitation of the existing software product taxonomy in that it only catches packaged software, mostly in the form of traded products, and fails to capture most forms of embedded software. Thus within the tax-

---

[30] "CBR Worldwide Software Top 50," *Computer Business Review*, special report, 1996.

onomy of software there is a place for word processing packages, but none for the embedded software in an electronic typewriter. I believe that the reason for this limitation is that the taxonomy represents a market view of software, rather than a "content" view. This is perhaps an inevitable outcome of the process by which the taxonomies evolved historically in industry analyst's reports. But this is a limitation that historians should seek to overcome by establishing a more inclusive taxonomy. To draw an analogy, almost all printed matter can be accommodated within the Dewey Decimal or the LC cataloging systems—whether formally published books, or internal communications used within industry. It is this kind of organizational power that we need to classify software artifacts.

Economic and Innovation Theory

Much of the literature on the software industry focuses on winners and losers, but mainly the winners. The rise of successful firms and product's are explained—particularly in the journalistic literature—by the interplay of technological excellence, heroic individuals, industry sharp practice, and serendipity.

Hence, a major problem for the history of software is for it to become more connected with the wider business, economic, and innovation literature in order to draw parallels with other industries and to explain market phenomena in well grounded academic terms, rather than by hyperbole. Two examples of relevant recent research are the economic theory of increasing returns and the innovation theory of disruptive technologies.

Theory of Increasing Returns

The best-known writer on the theory of increasing returns, and probably the most accessible, is Brian Arthur of the Santa Fe Institute, whose work dates from the late 1970s—although the phenomena he describes long pre-dated his interest.

The economics of increasing returns applies to industries that exist by "crafting knowledge into products" and whose products include "pharmaceuticals, computer hardware and software, aircraft and missiles, telecommunications equipment, bioengineered drugs, and suchlike." [31] All of these industries exhibit characteristics of very high development costs and relatively low manufacturing costs. Of course mass-market software, with its uniquely low manufacturing costs exhibits increasing returns to the greatest degree, and has popularly become known as "Microsoft economics."

The theory of increasing returns explains a number of phenomena that help us to understand the emergence of dominant platforms, such as operating systems, programming languages, and databases. The theory tells us that a particular platform comes to dominate not primarily because of its technological superiority, but because of *network effects* and *lock-in*. Successful platforms attract a network of users; more users beget more software products which in turn generate more platform sales; additional sales of the platform enables the producer to invest in fur-

---

[31] W. Brian Arthur, "Increasing Returns and the New World of Business," *Harvard Business Review*, July-August 1996.

ther product refinement which enhances sales; and so on in a virtuous circle. The theory argues that this inevitably leads to a very small number of platforms, typically only one. One can see this effect at work in such classic examples as VHS versus Betamax, and Windows versus MacOS.[32]

Once a platform has become established, users become locked-in to the platform because the *switching costs* to an alternative are too high. Making a change would involve abandoning investments in the old platform, in the form of hardware, software, and training. Once a user has adopted a platform, the advantages of a rival platform to have to be economically compelling to make the user change, or else the switching costs of a change have to be made tolerable—for example by easing file conversion or by having some form of backwards compatibility with the previous platform.

Arthur has argued that given a number of competing but unestablished platforms, the one that eventually becomes dominant—other things being equal—is essentially a matter of chance. Once a platform has gained a marginal advantage, however, network effects and lock-in all work in its favor, eventually driving out competitors. The techniques by which firms can gain this initial market advantage are known as *tipping*. The case which has attracted most recent attention, of course, is the dispute between Microsoft and Netscape, in which Microsoft gained market share for its Internet Explorer by giving it away. However, all forms of product promotion in the form of price discounts or user education can be viewed as tipping.

Another interesting situation arises when, although there is a standard platform, there are several producers. A good example here is the relational database, for which there are numerous suppliers including IBM, Oracle, Computer Associates, Microsoft, and others. However despite their commonality there are sufficient differences between platforms to produce lock-in effects. It can be argued—though not presently substantiated—that vendors promote some degree of incompatibility in order to lock users in. Savvy vendors also exploit network effects by co-operating with third-party suppliers to produce tools and add-ons that make their platform more useful. They participate in user education for their specific platform by publishing instructional manuals, and encouraging other publishers to produce textbooks. They also engage in predatory pricing in order to sell into new markets. These incentives are possible only because the marginal costs of production are close to zero, so that almost any inducement to purchase is economically justified.

It should be noted that there is substantial theoretical and empirical research for the theory of increasing returns; however, the principles are clear and easy to apply, so that the more accessible literature is entirely suitable for the historian.[33]

---

[32] Michael A. Cusumano, Yiorgos Mylonadis, and Richard S. Rosenbloom, "Strategic Manoeuvring and Mass-Market Dynamics: The Triumph of VHS over Beta," *Business History Review*, Spring 1992.

[33] Examples of the "heavy-weight" literature include: W. Brian Arthur, "Competing Technologies, Increasing Returns, and Lock-In by Historical Events," *Economic Journal*, 99 (1989): 116-31 and Jeffrey Church and Neil Gandal, "Network Effects, Software Provision, and Standardization," *Journal of Industrial Economics*, 60 (1992): 85-103. The more accessible literature includes: W. Brian Arthur, "Positive Feedbacks in the Economy," *Scientific American*, February 1990, 92-9 and Arthur (n. 31 above).

Disruptive Technologies

The Harvard economists Rosenbloom, Christensen, and Bower have identified a phenomenon that they call a "disruptive technology."[34] Such technology is one that can replace a dominant product or platform, and cause an incumbent firm to fail. They give a number of examples: "Goodyear and Firestone entered the radial tyre market quite late. Xerox let Canon create the small copier market. Bucyrus-Erie allowed Caterpillar and Deere to take over the mechanical excavator market. Sears gave way to Wal-Mart."[35]

A classic example in the IT sector studied by the Harvard group concerned the replacement of $5\frac{1}{4}$ -inch rigid disk drives by $3\frac{1}{2}$ -inch models in the late 1980s. Initially, the $3\frac{1}{2}$ -inch drive offered no consumer benefits to users of desktop PCs, since it was more expensive, slower, and had a lower capacity. However the smaller diameter drive was adopted in portable PCs, where its lower weight and power consumption were positive benefits. The acceptance of the $3\frac{1}{2}$ -inch drive in the portable market funded further product refinement, and because the smaller drive was on a steeper technological trajectory to the $5\frac{1}{4}$-inch drive, it eventually attained a superior performance. At that point manufactures of desktop PCs switched to the new drives almost overnight, completely reversing the fortunes of the incumbent manufacturers of the larger drives, such as Seagate, while bringing enormous rewards to manufacturers of $3\frac{1}{2}$ -inch drives such as Conner and Quantum.

So far as I am aware no one has done any detailed investigation of disruptive technologies in the software area. However, the ascendancy of the relational database seems to exhibit the phenomenon. In the late 1970s a handful of database products dominated the mainframe market. These included a IBM's IMS and DL/1, Cincom's TOTAL, and Cullinane's IDMS. These used a variety of non-relational database technologies that were mutually incompatible, and all had locked-in customer bases numbering from a few hundred to several thousand installations. Although relational technology had some benefits in terms of the SQL access mechanism and superior data integrity, it was too computationally intensive for large-scale databases on mainframes. However, the new database technology found a niche in the emerging minicomputer market in the mid-1970s, where the average database requirement was much less demanding and mission critical. The market was developed by start up firms such as Oracle and Ingres. During the decade 1975-1985, relational technology matured in terms of scale and reliability, at the same time as computer speeds and memories increased by two orders of magnitude. At this point it became possible to run a large-scale relational database on mainframes, with significant user benefits over the established technologies.

IBM was the first of the incumbents to react to the new environment in 1983 by announcing its "dual database strategy," by which it offered both its traditional

---

[34] Richard S. Rosenbloom and Clayton M. Christensen, "Technological Discontinuities, Organizational Capabilities, and Strategic Commitments," *Industrial and Corporate Change*, 3 (1994): 655-85.

[35] Joseph L. Bower and Clayton M. Christensen, "Disruptive Technologies: Catching the Wave," *Harvard Business Review*, January-February 1995, 43-53.

database products and a new relational product SQL/DS (later re-branded DB2). IBM's action effectively destabilized the market, which quickly switched to relational technology. In order to introduce a relational product, Supra, Cincom made a huge R&D investment (said to be 21 percent of its turnover during 1979-1983), which enabled its long-term survival, but Cullinane came close to bankruptcy, leading to its acquisition by Computer Associates in 1989. By contrast Oracle, with its first mover advantage, went on to dominate the relational database market.

Conclusions

It would be easy to set an agenda of "What Needs to Be Done" on the economic history of software. However, it would amount to little more than a wish list, for which resources are unlikely to ever become available. Hence let me just limit myself to three modest suggestions that I think would improve the field.

I The Need for Population Studies

At present much of the history of software has focussed on the individual software entity. Thus we have histories of Fortran, Cobol, Unix, and various other proprietary operating systems and languages. Many of these studies are very good of their kind, but they are essentially biographies of a particular instance. Without wishing to disparage much early work on the history of programming (my own included), we are in danger of becoming like those railroad-buffs who are obsessed with nut-and-bolts and paint-jobs, but have no bigger vision. For historians of technology, what is interesting about railroads is that they were vast transportation systems that changed the world, and the technical details of locomotives are only a sliver of a much bigger story. We are probably not yet ready to make such a giant leap in the history of software, but we do need to move beyond the individual artifact. Even where this has been attempted—notably in the history of programming languages—the approach has looked rather like a comparative anatomy, where the technical characteristics of one individual are compared with the next. What the historian of technology and the economic historian want to know are not the technical idiosyncrasies of particular programming languages, but how they came to be created, why they succeeded or failed to become standards, why they died out, how many people used them, the size of the stock of application programs, and so on. Such studies would also make use of those early technical studies of individual programming systems—and to be used by the next generation of historians is the best compliment they could get.

II The Need for Statistical Time Series

Most business and economic historians would agree that to write satisfactorily about an industry or a firm they need numbers. Research in the history of the software industry has been handicapped by the lack of such reliable quantitative data, particularly over an extended period of time. I have noted several examples in this paper where the evidence is more anecdotal than statistical—the number of programmers, the number of software firms, the number of software products, the aggregate sales in the different sectors of the industry, and so on. As a result most writing relies on impressionistic views of the size of the industry. In fact there is a significant amount of data scattered around the literature and buried in market research reports. Anyone seriously engaged in writing a history of the software industry—whether as a research student, academic writer, or journalist—will encounter such data, and it would be a great service to include such data in their writings. Perhaps the most common failure is that of omitting quantitative data from company histories. It is usual in the better examples of the genre to include a statistical appendix of the firm's turnover, and sales of significant products. Much of this data is publicly available in company reports, but too few writers make use of them. Instead what we get is random impressionistic data culled from press cuttings. To produce a statistical time series, particularly when the data comes from inconsistent sources, is not a trivial task, but it does give a permanent value to historical writing that lives on when the author's ephemeral opinions have long been superceded.

III Better Integration with the Academic Literature

As noted in the opening paragraph of this paper, the history of software must start to develop frameworks and unifying theories to explain and deepen our understanding of the phenomena we observe. I believe the best hope for achieving this goal is to make use of the academic literature of economics, business, and innovation. Much writing on computers and software is still produced as if they were things apart. But in fact, computers and software, and the industries that produce them, have a great deal in common with other enterprises. Authors do sometimes instinctively understand this. For example, the analogy is often made between the standardization of railroads and software platforms. This particular analogy has great validity, but usually the author appeals to a received anecdotal history, rather than on a deep reading of modern authors such as Alfred D. Chandler.[36] Again, there is vast interest in Microsoft's current discomfort with the Department of Justice—but how much of the debate is informed by a real understanding of prior antitrust cases? Finally, I remain deeply skeptical by the killer app. thesis. What it represents is an intuitive explanation of an economic phenomenon, invented by people who are not themselves economists—mostly I think they are computer scientists. Hence I do not trust this explanation, any more than I would trust an operating system designed by economists. What a better integration with the academic literature offers us is, at the very least, a more nuanced interpretation of the development of programming; and at best, it may help us to understand and explain very general software phenomena.

---

[36] Alfred D. Chandler, *The Visible Hand: The Managerial Revolution in American Business* (Cambridge, Mass., 1977).

Commentary on Martin Campbell-Kelly, "Software as an Economic Activity"

Pierre-E. Mounier-Kuhn

CNRS et Centre Roland-Mousnier   Centre de Recherches en Histoire de l'Innovation
Paris-IV Sorbonne
1 rue Victor-Cousin
75005 Paris
France

E-mail: mournier@msh-paris.fr

Introduction

I enjoyed reading Martin Campbell-Kelly's paper. The way it reviews the historiography and criticizes the existing literature, the overviews it offers of the history and typology of software companies, the choice of economic models to orient our empirical studies (which, in turn, will help to test economic models—provided that economists pay attention to empirical, historical studies); all these components make a great programmatic paper, comprehensive and ambitious. It was written with the underlying concern to produce a durable historical tool, which will be useful for future researchers in the decades ahead. This enterprise is taking a good start here.

I will focus my brief comments on three complementary aspects: the necessity to study the economic history of software at computer manufacturers, the problem of measuring software productivity and profitability, and the problems inherent with statistical information about an emerging and rapidly evolving industrial sector.[1]

Software at Computer Manufacturers

Martin Campbell-Kelly's paper deliberately leaves aside one important aspect: Software activities within computer manufacturers.[2] This choice is certainly defendable, but it should be made explicit. I suggest the opposite choice, as follows.

---

[1] I particularly wish to thank Bill Aspray and Bruce Seely, who discussed this text with me and kindly helped debugging its style.

[2] I say "deliberately" because, in the first paper he gave on the software industry, Martin Campbell-Kelly mentioned the major role of the computer manufacturers, citing examples such as the large contract awarded to IBM by American Airlines to develop the SABRE system, or users' clubs connected with specific machines. See Martin Campbell-Kelly, "Development and Structure of the International Software Industry, 1950-1990," *Business and Economic History*

The first software producers were the computer manufacturers—apart from the academic mathematicians who programmed pioneer calculators in their labs. As far as we know, until the 1970s at least, most of the software was developed by computer manufacturers (Fortran, OS/360, etc.); and most of the rest was developed in interaction between users and computer manufacturers. IBM and the seven dwarves (later on: The BUNCH) set the stage for all programming activity to come. They shaped the conditions in which an autonomous software industry could bloom, as they created the standard "platforms" and imposed the pace through products announcements and unbundling decisions. Even in the era of the microcomputer, as Martin Campbell-Kelly puts it, in 1979 "the Apple II [the hardware and its OS] created a platform on which many software products could exist, of which VisiCalc was simply a prominent example."[3] We have all reasons to study the economic history of the computer manufacturers as software producers, and of the competitive interaction between them and the other players on the software markets.

The turning point in the measurability of the software business within manufacturers is evidently 1970, dividing history in two periods: before Big Blue unbundled (BBBU) and after Big Blue unbundled (ABBU). Other computer manufacturers generally did not wait long to announce their own unbundling. I will focus on the first period.

Even before the era of the stored-program computer, the data processing industry was marketing programming tools. Around 1950, the major programming item was the plug-board, along with the series of switches displayed on the panels of digital and analogue calculators. The plug-board (as well as the Powers connection box, its functional equivalent) was a combination of relatively cheap materials and of high added-value logical wiring. According to a Bull computer pioneer, plug-boards featured among the most profitable products marketed by punch-card machines vendors.[4] What information do we have, beyond this vague assertion? Delamarter mentions the plug-boards as an early form of "software;" yet, in spite of his wrath against IBM, his book does not mention what juicy profits Big Blue squeezed out of them.[5] The Bible of IBM technical history, *IBM's Early Computers*, briefly points that a 1957 evaluation of the WWAM project showed that the plug-board had become uncompetitive, as it "accounted for several thousand dollars of estimated product cost;" this was decisive in transforming the project into a stored-program computer, the IBM 1401.[6] Thus, it seems that the economics of wired- vs. stored-program played a central part in the evolution from traditional punch-card machines to business computers.

24/2 (1995): 73-110. The influence of such clubs, like SHARE and GUIDE, should be studied in our research program.

[3] Martin Campbell-Kelly, "Software as an Economic activity," *ICHC 2000: Mapping the History of Computing—Software Issues*, Heinz Nixdorf MuseumsForum, Paderborn, 5-7 April 2000.

[4] Bruno Leclerc, "Les premières machines électroniques Bull: du Gamma 3 au Gamma E. T.," in *Actes du 2e colloque sur l'histoire de l'informatique en France*, ed. Philippe Chatelin and Pierre-E. Mounier-Kuhn (Paris, 1990), 180.

[5] Richard T. Delamarter, *Big Blue – IBM's Use and Abuse of Power* (London, 1986), 18-19.

[6] Charles J. Bashe et al., *IBM's Early Computers* (Cambridge, Mass., 1986), 468.

Meanwhile, programming (in the modern sense) was modestly mushrooming in the shadow of the "giant electronic brains" of the time. In *IBM's Early Computers,* again, we read that "in August 1952, some thirty customer representatives and the same number of IBM engineers and programmers participated in a one-week meeting in Poughkeepsie," demonstrating "two assembly programs and perhaps three dozen shorter programs, collectively known as 'utilities' [...]. The programs had been contributed by [IBM's] Applied Science [Department] and by Rochester's planning group." This provides us with a glimpse of the variety of programs written, the number of programmers involved, and their positions within the corporate structure. This account offers us a more precise description: "The size of programming and operating staffs [still for the 701s, in Aug. 1953] were surprising. With thirty people, Mason [manager of IBM's Scientific Computing Service] was low on the scale; two users reported 45-person staffs. At $15,000 per month, 701 rental was roughly equivalent to the pay of thirty employees, and so computer cost was doubled or more when staff cost was added. Backus heard, moreover, that about 40% of useful machine time was used for preparing and debugging new programs. All told, nearly 3/4 of the expense of operation involved programming and debugging. Backus first expected Speedcoding and similar systems, as they came into use, to moderate this figure. But it soon became clear that the situation would instead deteriorate.[...]."[7]

These figures suggest that the global software expenditures were far above the usually accepted proportion of 20%, at this early period of computer history. While they concern mostly users, they also imply that IBM initially underestimated the investment demanded by software development—as did most computer companies at this stage.[8] Things improved, as in 1954 a new department was created, Programming Research, which was in fact devoted to program development for the 700 family (60 programmers in mid-1955). In 1957, an Applied Programming department was established, while the IBM Service Bureau became a separate corporation. In 1961, the new position of Director of Programming appeared at corporate staff level. These institutional developments helped recognize the new profession, acknowledging that it required: "[...] a corporate-wide career ladder and recognition and reward system for programmers [...]."[9]

The expansion of programming personnel was also due to the proliferation of incompatible computers at IBM, and meant a "substantial loss of productivity." It is well known that this concern was a primary cause for recommending, as early as 1959, a unified product line that would make "a single community of all our customers."[10] A programming crisis was being felt at IBM, a decade before the famous "software crisis." In both cases, the solution was found in standardization.

---

[7] Bashe et al., 339.
[8] In France, initial underestimation of the software effort was a major cause, around 1960, for the delivery delays of the Bull Gamma 60 and of the STRIDA air defense system designed by IBM France. See Pierre-E. Mounier-Kuhn, "Calculateurs électroniques et nouveaux systèmes d'armes: Interactions Armées/Recherche/Industrie (1946-1959)," in *Colloque: La IVe République et les problèmes d'armement,* ed. Maurice Vaïsse, Centre d'études d'histoire de la Défense—ADDIM, 1998, 376-405. A comparable underestimation was observed in Germany: Hartmut Petzold, *Rechnende Maschinen* (Düsseldorf, 1985), 504.
[9] Bashe et al., 369.
[10] Ibid., 579.

IBM nevertheless had to hire hundreds of new programmers to develop OS/360; that effort involved over 1,000 programmers, i.e., a 5,000 programmer-year effort.[11]

In other computer companies, things followed more or less the same pattern, at another scale. At ICL, in the mid-1960s, the Programming Division was part of the Marketing Group, "since software was seen largely as an aid to sales [...]."[12] The development of software for the new, compatible 1900 series faced huge problems, similar to IBM OS/360's: ICT "was unprepared for the escalation in user demand for software on third-generation systems, and the lack of reliable tools for estimating costs and production time-scales. Another problem was the shortage of programmers in Britain."[13] It took a full year to hire a hundred additional programmers. By 1966, the ICT Programming Division employed some 600 people. "Software costs escalated to £1.7 million during 1965, which was about 50% more than budgeted." However, "The ICT GEORGE 3 operating system involved no more than about 75 programmer-years of effort, and was generally considered to be a much better system."[14] By 1970, ICL's programming staff was the largest in Europe, with 2,000 employees. The response to IBM's unbundling decision of May 1968 was fast. ICL created two independent subsidiaries in 1968-1970: a software house, Dataskil; and a service business, International Computing Services Ltd., which merged with a similar branch of Barclays Bank to form BARIC.[15] These creations exemplify the intimate links that may exist in history between the computer manufacturers and the nascent software industry.[16]

This does not mean that, considered nationally, the success of the software industry was mechanically proportional to the prosperity of the local computer manufacturers. It was rather a direct function of the number of computer installations, including the machines marketed by foreign manufacturers. In Europe, the triumph of the IBM 1401, then of the IBM 360 systems put the national computer companies in difficult situations, while it offered decisive opportunities to local software entrepreneurs who based their growth on selling programs for these American machines. One could even consider that the development of software companies was a counterpart of the problems suffered by local computer manufacturers. In France, each time Bull or CII had a crisis, frustrated engineers quit and started up a software business. This was the origin of Société d'Informatique Ap-

[11] See Franklin M. Fisher, James W. McKie, and Richard B. Mancke, *IBM and the US Data Processing Industry: An Economic History* (New York, 1983), 151. See also Frederick P. Brooks, *The Mythical Man-Month: Essays on Software Engineering* (Reading, Mass., 1975). Delamarter's book (n. 5 above) contains descriptions of the "lock-in" strategy based on IBM software, but it does not support them with financial data from the IBM corporate records.

[12] Martin Campbell-Kelly, *ICL: A Business and Technical History* (Oxford, 1989), 237.

[13] Ibid., 238.

[14] Ibid., 239.

[15] Ibid., 268.

[16] In France, spin-offs took place earlier and were due to the problems of the local computer manufacturers. The Société d'Informatique Appliquée, a subsidiary of SEMA for which the word "Informatique" was coined in June 1962, was created by Philippe Dreyfus and other escapees of the then staggering Bull Cy; most of them soon left again for CAP. In 1967, the heads of the Bull-GE sales offices in Grenoble and Lyon, fed up with the "colonial" manners of General Electric, quit and created a fast growing software house, which eventually merged with the latter to form CAP-Gemini. There are other examples of this spin-off process.

pliquée (SEMA Group) in 1962, of the French CAP (Centre d'Analyse et de Programmation), of STERIA later on.[17] ... In 1967, after General Electric managers had retired the GE 600 line and killed the Bull-GE 140 series, a few mutineers from the Grenoble sales office left Bull and embarked on creating a new company, which they developed as CAP-Gemini-Sogeti.[18]

After 1970, the computer manufacturers were in direct competition with the young software industry, but only on some limited segment of the software market. Operating systems and other "basic" types of software remained the computer manufacturers' lot, until IBM subcontracted the development of MS-DOS. In this last event, again, it was a decision made, and the platform offered, by the leading computer manufacturer which boosted—unwillingly—Microsoft to the leading position in the industry.

On the more open market of application software, we need to know more about the strategies followed by interacting computer manufacturers, software houses, and the users; and on their economic rationales.

Productivity and Profitability of Software

Manufacturers' archives can also provide us with their own reflections on the economics of software. For example, they attempted to measure productivity and profitability of this particular good.

In addition to software products that are sold independently, other software exists whose profitability cannot be considered independently of another hardware or services. These last software products may be billed separately (unbundled), but it is not possible to analyze their profitability *per se*. Their unbundled price is not determined in order to produce a profit for the development team, but only to make it difficult for competitors to enter the market. Thus, the margin may be high in a monopoly situation (IBM MVS or Microsoft Windows), but it may be zero or negative in the case of a producer of mobile telephones or mini-computers.

As far as I know from the history of GE, Honeywell and Bull, attempts to design a satisfactory model of ROI (return on investment) on software appeared to be unfruitful. The main obstacle was the accounting method. Software was accounted as R&D expenses on the fiscal year. In "conservatively" managed firms, software was not recorded as an investment. It did not appear in gross margin calculation, since its "manufacturing" cost was negligible. The market diffusion of a software product depends on its price level, among other factors. This price was determined according to the level of competition. It does not seem that any complete cost analysis model existed within firms doing combined hard-

---

[17] Jean Carteron, *STERIA—30 ans de création continue*, Le Cherche-Midi éd. (Paris, 1999). Various papers were given during a session on software companies (STERIA, SEMA, SARI) in Pierre-E. Mounier-Kuhn and Philippe Chatelin, eds., *Actes du 2e colloque sur l'histoire de l'informatique en France* (Paris, 1990). The SEMA paper was translated and published in Jacques Lesourne and Richard Armand, "A Brief History of the First Decade of SEMA," *Annals of the History of Computing* 13 (1991), 341-9 along with other articles on the history of computing in France.

[18] Tristan Gaston-Breton, *De SOGETI à CAP-Gemini—1967-1997—30 ans d'histoire*, CAP-Gemini (Paris, 1997).

ware/associated software systems, although I do not know how IBM or Microsoft operated. Practically, internal reorganizations, including restructuring by product line, "crafts" or markets, allowed executives to demonstrate anything they wanted, by arguing on the profitability or non-profitability of such and such business segment. Two measures were used in the industry:

- The man/month,
- The KLOC (kilo lines of code source).

Productivity in KLOC per month has grown dramatically, along with the decrease of memory price! and also thanks to the improvements of the programming tools. Productivity was reduced by the inclusion of the analysis and evaluation phase in the cost of software. Productivity rates as low as 100 LOC/month existed in operating systems or in embedded systems. It could be augmented through the creation of a distinct "corps" of analyst and programmers. It was improved by measuring (in KLOC) a product development's productivity in its final version; or by reusing code. In the case of the transfer of a code on a different platform, the productivity rate becomes evidently very high (up to 20 KLOC/month).

The Problem with Statistics

Martin Campbell-Kelly's insistence on the need for population studies, and for (re-)constructing coherent series of data, provides us rightly with a research program for the years to come (and the sooner the better, as data and records disappear every year in this fast-evolving economy); I would perhaps also suggest that we study, in parallel, the demography of software companies: birth and death rates, age pyramids, etc. The bright success of the leading software houses has tended to hide, since the beginning, the fact that many firms have failed and disappeared.

Yet, as the very word "software" implies, we are studying a multi-dimensional object which has no precise limits—no precise limits with various sciences, with engineering practices (as Martin Campbell-Kelly noted in the case of minis used in process control), with management and services, and, arguably, even with computer hardware. So (and this is a major difference between historians and most economists) we have to be very cautious about how and in what context the statistics we find were created. I can only offer a set of remarks and examples. For instance, there is an appallingly huge gap between the OECD statistics on computers, in the 1960s, and the real installations that we may count in companies' records).[19] How exactly did OECD compute that the world's software stock was US$500 billion in 1982?

As heterogeneous as it is, the "software and services" sector seems to exist and be taken for granted, in most countries, in the statistics and in professional organizations. One could object that putting, for example, Microsoft and CAP-Gemini together in the same trade does not make more sense than, say, a "fuel and taxis" sector. How was it built as an economic category? It obviously came directly from

---

[19] OECD, *Ecarts Technologiques – Calculateurs Electroniques* (Paris, 1969): 169-83.

the manufacturers' early practice, where programming was part of marketing, maintenance and after-sales services to the clients, and of service bureau operations. What were the debates behind the "boundary work," the development of new departments or subsidiaries, the construction of professional identities and institutions, for activities which seem to stretch between engineering, consulting and publishing?

Can we observe trends of evolution? For instance, in the 1960s, consulting and accounting firms acquired expensive computing capacities that made them enter the "software and services" sector; yet, in many firms, the main know-how concerned applications for a specific clientele, like accounting, insurance policy management or bank cards operations (First Data in the US, Sligos in France, etc.). Today, as computers have become a common, ordinary commodity, these firms' competitive advantage lies much more in their knowledge of their specific clientele's needs. In fact, there is no longer reason to consider them as parts of the computing and software industry, any more than any computer user.

A useful source is to be found in bank archives, which are often more carefully kept than market research firms. In the late 1960s (certainly earlier in the US), banks started to write studies, for internal use, on the software industry as a possible target for investment. Even if the data provided by software firms tended sometimes to be overoptimistic, these records offer precious information on the relationship between the growing software companies and the world of finance which would eventually support their growth.

Once we have gathered statistics on manufacturers' software investment (number of programmers, financial data), how do we interpret them? A large number of programmers could mean, either an early understanding of the importance of software, or great difficulties in the development of a system, or else a costly multiplication of parallel developments for incompatible machines (in the case of GE-Bull-Olivetti, or of the French national champion CII, which was entangled in three lines of computers).[20]

An anecdote is of interest for those of us who work on financial records as well as on oral history. In 1961, the French Navy created a Programming Center, which designed the software of the missile guidance computers and of on-board early warning systems (the NDTS-derived SENIT/B2 system which was later shared with the West German Navy). When I consulted the archives, I was surprised to find accounting records which showed that this Programming Center purchased an impressive amount of concrete, of steel goods, of various spare parts. Then I interviewed the admiral who had created and directed this Navy Programming Center. He was an old fox who had been in the Navy since the 1930s, and he explained: "Of course we never really bought concrete or steel, but if we had asked the Treasury to grant us 10 million FF for something called 'software', we'd never have obtained a penny!"[21]

---

[20] Pierre-E. Mounier-Kuhn, "French Computer Manufacturers and the Component Industry, 1952-1972," *History and Technology* 11 (1994): 195-216. Idem, "Le Plan Calcul, Bull et l'industrie des composants: les contradictions d'une stratégie," *Revue historique* CCXCI/1 (1995): 123-53.

[21] Oral interview with Ingénieur Général de l'Artillerie Navale Maurice Brunet, 2 and 19 September 1997.

This anecdote is, of course, a warning about the way we use financial data; in this case, as in many others, the number of programmers gives more reliable information on the software endeavour than accounting records (which, in this case, revealed no software development at all). It also tells us about the emergence of 'software' as an economic category in mentalities. To many managers, until the early 1960s, 'software' was a strange concept, and the mere idea of buying it made no more sense than buying wind. This intellectual barrier made it difficult for any company to attempt to sell 'software.' From this respect, the fact that software was initially offered for free by manufacturers, along with other services, helped it to get a toe-hold on the market. Thereafter, it became possible to consider selling such a commodity.

Commentary on Martin Campbell-Kelly, "Software as an Economic Activity"

David C. Mowery

University of California at Berkeley
Haas School of Business
Milton W. Terrill Professor of Business Administration
545 Student Services #1900
Berkeley, CA 94720-1900
USA

E-mail: Mowery@haas.berkeley.edu

Introduction

Campbell-Kelly provides a valuable overview of the (limited) literature on the history of the computer software industry and an especially useful agenda for further research. He correctly criticizes the rapidly growing literature on this industry for its lack of rigor, minimal use of the (admittedly modest) quantitative data, and its focus on narratives of the histories of individual firms or software products. His call for better analysis and data on populations of software firms, for the collection of better longitudinal data, much of which necessarily will rely on employment data, rather than measures of output, and his advocacy of closer integration with the academic literature on innovation all are valuable guidelines for future research.

Nonetheless, Campbell-Kelly's discussion of alternative "frameworks" or "unifying theories" overlooks some key aspects of the economic history of computer software. For example, he sketches out a taxonomy of firm capabilities to explain the performance of software firms in various product segments and at various points in the industry's evolution. But (especially at this early stage in scholarly research) the firm may not be the most appropriate or illuminating unit of analysis for understanding the software industry, as Campbell-Kelly acknowledges elsewhere. After all, computer software is a "general-purpose technology," with very broad applications across multiple sectors, and software complements the much broader class of information technology products. It is difficult to understand the evolution of the software industry without devoting a good deal of attention to the development of computing technology. Indeed, the powerful influence of domestic government policies on the contrasting paths of development of the software industries of Japan, the United States, and Western Europe reflects the historic links between the development of the computer software industry and the computer hardware industry. Because of its importance for national security, the computer hardware industry was an important target of government promotional policies throughout the Cold War era.

Campbell-Kelly also does not discuss one of the signal characteristics of the software industry, the tendency for international competitive advantage to be located among a shifting collection of firms from the United States. Indeed, one useful analytic framework for studying the economic history of the international computer software industry is the "national innovation system" approach pioneered by Christopher Freeman, Richard Nelson, and Bengt-Ake Lundvall.[1] The computer software industry's development is a product of the interaction of individual firms and entrepreneurs with an institutional environment that displays remarkably sharp contrasts among the industrial economies. Another advantage of employing the national, as opposed to the firm-level, perspective on the economic history of the software industry is the greater availability of data on software-related employment, output, and international trade for this unit of analysis.

In the remainder of my commentary, I summarize some earlier work on some of the possible reasons for the contrasting development of the software industries of Japan, Western Europe, and the United States.[2] Although the details of this summary are not fully fleshed out as yet, this overview is intended to provoke further work on the comparative economic history of the computer software industry.

National and Sectoral Innovation Systems in Software

The development of the U.S. and Japanese software industries exhibits some of the same contrasts associated with other postwar high-technology industries in these economies—new firms are very prominent in the U.S. software industry, and established producers (especially mainframe computer manufacturers) remain far more important in Japan. Differences in national financial systems and intellectual property rights regimes clearly underlie much of the U.S.-Japanese contrast. The Western European traded software industry, however, occupies something of a middle ground between the extremes represented by the U.S. and Japanese industries. New entrants have been somewhat less prominent in the Western European software industry than that of the United States, although some, such as SAP, have been very successful. But the weakness of European computer manufacturers has prevented their software subsidiaries from developing strength in domestic markets comparable to that of the Japanese computer vendors' software subsidiaries.

A number of factors underlie the contrasting patterns of development and competitive strength of the U.S., Japanese, and Western European software industries. These include the structure and role of central government policies toward the industry; the relationship between competitive strength in computer hardware and

---

[1] Christopher Freeman, *Technology and Economic Performance* (London, 1987). Richard R. Nelson, *National Innovation Systems: A Comparative Analysis* (New York, 1993). Bengt-Ake Lundvall, *National Systems of Innovation—Towards a Theory of Innovation and Interactive Learning* (London, 1992).

[2] David C. Mowery, ed., *The International Computer Software Industry* (New York, 1996); David C. Mowery, "The Computer Software Industry," in *Sources of Industrial Leadership*, eds. David C. Mowery and Richard R. Nelson (Cambridge, Mass., 1999), 133-68.

software in the evolution of the software industry; and the importance and characteristics of user-producer relationships in software. Many of these themes are
rooted in the contrasting structure of the national innovation systems of the competing economies, while others are more specific to the software industry. The
collective influence of these factors seems likely to maintain significant differences in the structure and the likely future path of development among the software industries of these three regions. And these factors have affected the validity
and influence of some of the analytic constructs proposed by Campbell-Kelly to
interpret the economic history of software.

Defense-Related Technology Policies and Software

One important similarity between the software industry and other electronics-
based postwar "new industries" is the pervasive role of government in its development. The close links between the computer hardware industry, seen by many
postwar governments as an important component of their defense industrial base,
and software meant that from its inception, the software industry benefited from
defense-related R&D funding and procurement. As in other postwar high-
technology industries, the scale and structure of the U.S. Department of Defense's
policies differed from those of other industrial governments, and seem to have had
stronger positive effects on the competitiveness of the U.S. commercial industry.
The effects of defense-related R&D and procurement spending in the U.S. software industry were influenced by two characteristics of these expenditures: (1)
military demand for software, which accounted for a substantial share of industry
revenues, required very different product characteristics than those of commercial
software; and (2) defense-related R&D funding supported an extensive academic
research enterprise.

These two factors meant that the direct spin-offs associated with defense-
related expenditures in software differed from those in other U.S. postwar high-
technology industries. There are few examples of commercially successful civilian
software products that were derived directly from military development or procurement programs, in contrast to the U.S. semiconductor or commercial aircraft
industries of the 1950s. Rather than "embodied" spin-offs, however, the U.S.
software industry benefited from defense funding for a large domestic R&D infrastructure and technological advances that could be applied in modified form to
civilian products.

Other postwar governments, including Great Britain and the Soviet Union,
were also concerned with the development of a strong computer industry for national security reasons (often in connection with nuclear weapons programs), but
their policies failed to create a national research infrastructure that could support
innovation in civilian software products. Surprisingly, the defense-oriented "industrial policy" of the postwar U.S. government was more successful in establishing a strong domestic industry than the civilian "strategic technology" programs of
a number of other governments. But rather than creating a large flow of defense-
civilian technological spin-offs, defense spending aided the growth of the U.S.
computer software industry by supporting the establishment and growth of computer science in U.S. universities. In addition, the rapid growth of defense-related

markets for software created substantial opportunities for the employment of software engineers and developers, many of whom went on to establish firms or develop products for civilian markets.

Intellectual Property Rights

Another important arena for government policy in the software industry is intellectual property rights.[3] The software industry is characterized by high fixed costs and relatively "nonrivalrous" output (i.e., the information-intensive nature of software means that its exploitation by a number of parties does not degrade its quality, in contrast to a piece of grazing land), and strong intellectual property rights may create significant monopoly power.[4] On the other hand, the history of the Japanese software industry suggests that weak intellectual property protection can limit the growth of a domestic packaged software industry.

The importance of intellectual property rights in software has increased since 1980, because the growth of mass markets for software has increased the value of property rights in such products.[5] But the effort to define intellectual property rights in software in Japan, the United States, and Western Europe has also begun to press against the limits of existing structures of patent and copyright statute and interpretation. Technological advance in software often has a cumulative character; one generation of product technologies relies on the previous generation, and strong technological complementarities link different software programs. Tight protection of prior generations of art therefore may slow technological advance on a broad front.[6] This concern motivated the European Union's recent efforts to define acceptable forms of "reverse engineering" of protected software programs, which produced a policy that is more lenient in its treatment of this practice than is U.S. policy.[7]

The software intellectual property rights regimes that have emerged from legislative debates and court battles in Japan, the U.S., and Western Europe are partly endogenous. Industry political action and legislator perceptions of national economic interest have produced intellectual property regimes that serve the dominant economic interests within the software industries of each of these areas—in some cases, these dominant interests are independent software vendors, and in others, they are subsidiaries of computer manufacturers or even users of software. The evolution of intellectual property protection thus is affected by the path of industry

---

[3] See Robert P. Merges, "A Comparative Look at Intellectual Property Rights and the Software Industry," in *The International Computer Software Industry: A Comparative Study of Industry Evolution and Structure*, ed. David C. Mowery (New York, 1996), 272-303.

[4] Paul M. Romer, "Implementing a National Technology Strategy with Self-Organizing Industry Investment Boards," *Brookings Papers on Economic Activity* 2 (1993): 345-90.

[5] Stuart J. Graham and David C. Mowery, "Intellectual Property Protection in the Computer Software Industry," presented at the National Academy of Sciences conference on "Intellectual Property Rights," Washington D.C., 2-3 February 2000.

[6] See Robert P. Merges and Richard R. Nelson, "On the Complex Economics of Patent Scope," *Columbia Law Review* 90 (1990): 839-916.

[7] Merges (n. 3 above).

development, rather than operating as a strictly exogenous influence on development.

Competition Policy

Another area of policy that has affected the economic history of the software industry is competition policy. Postwar U.S. antitrust policy was more stringent that those of Japan or most Western European economies, and contributed to the importance of new, small firms in the postwar U.S. semiconductor and computer industries.[8] Among other important developments, the "unbundling" by IBM of its software and hardware product pricing in the late 1960s was influenced by the impending U.S. antitrust suit against the firm. During the 1980s, U.S. antitrust policy was relaxed significantly, especially in sectors characterized by high R&D intensity and strong foreign competition, and owners of intellectual property rights benefited from a more benign judicial attitude. But Justice Department antitrust scrutiny of the U.S. industry, especially the dominant supplier of packaged software, has increased dramatically since 1993, as has private antitrust litigation. The federal antitrust suit against Microsoft that was filed in 1998 could constrain this firm's behavior and affect the course of technological advance in the software industry, although the effects of antitrust action on the long-term innovative performance of this industry are controversial.[9]

Simultaneously, the emergent EU policies toward market power and intellectual property rights seem to be moving somewhat closer to the policies of the U.S. government. Indeed, one of the most novel aspects of the 1994 Microsoft antitrust investigation and settlement was the close coordination between EU and U.S. Justice Department antitrust authorities, in a tacit acknowledgment of the growing similarities in their enforcement philosophies. And the EU competition policy authorities expressed concerns in 1997 and 1998 over Microsoft's market power that echoed those of the U.S. Justice Department.

The Role of Universities

Government policy has affected the role of universities in the software industry. The legitimation of computer science as an academic discipline in U.S. universities, for example, received a substantial boost from the funding commitments of the Advanced Research Projects Agency and the National Science Foundation during the 1960s. The organizational and disciplinary flexibility of U.S. universities in computer science has been less significant in the national university sys-

[8] David C. Mowery, "The Boundaries of the U.S. Firm in R&D," in *Coordination and Information*, eds. Naomi R. Lamoreaux and Daniel M. G. Raff (Chicago, 1995), 147-76.
[9] See, for contrasting views on these issues, David J. Teece, "The Meaning of Monopoly: Antitrust Analysis in High Technology Industries," presented at the Institutional Analysis Workshop, Haas School of Business, University of California at Berkeley, 30 April 1998; Michael L. Katz and Carl Shapiro, "Antitrust in Software Markets," presented at the Institutional Analysis workshop, Haas School of Business, University of California at Berkeley, 23 April 1998.

tems of other industrial economies during the postwar period, reflecting the unusual scale and structure of the U.S. higher education system and its research funding infrastructure. This difference is important, because university-based computer science research activities have been important sources of the innovations that have spawned new products and firms in the U.S. In addition, university-based research has played an important indirect role in the software industry's growth, by training skilled personnel whose movement into industrial employment transfers university research findings to industry. Throughout Western Europe and Japan, shortages of skilled personnel have impeded the development of domestic software industries.

Does a Strong Domestic Software Industry Require a Strong Domestic Hardware Industry?

The interaction between the development of national hardware and software industries is an issue whose full complexity can be appreciated only through a comparative analysis. U.S. dominance of the Western European software industry, for example, has been facilitated by the European computer hardware industry's weakness, especially in desktop computers. A comparison of the U.S. and Western European computer software industries suggests that (especially in standard software) a strong domestic hardware industry is necessary to support the growth of a strong domestic software industry.

Comparing the U.S. and Japanese software industries, however, requires that this conclusion be qualified. Historically, Japan's computer hardware industry has been stronger than that of Western Europe. But Japanese strength in computer hardware has not been translated into strength in traded software. Competition among Japanese computer manufacturers resulted in the development of competing architectures in mainframes, minicomputers, and microcomputers, retarding the growth of its packaged software industry.[10] As in Western Europe, Japan's domestic software industry is strongest in the development of custom software solutions (by hardware manufacturers or independent firms) that require extensive familiarity with user needs.

The interaction between domestic hardware and software producers that has influenced the contrasting paths of development of the U.S., Japanese, and Western European computer software industries thus appears to vary among segments of both the hardware and software industries. The importance of strong links between hardware and software developers also has changed over time. In the early years of the industry's development, U.S. software producers derived competitive advantages from their links with the dominant global producers of computer hardware in the early development of mainframe, minicomputer, and desktop systems. But the importance of these linkages appears to have declined. Nevertheless, the central position of the U.S. market as a "testbed" for developing new applications in such areas as networking and the Internet reflects the enduring importance of

---

[10] Thomas Cottrell, "Standards and the Arrested Development of Japan's Microcomputer Software Industry," in *The International Computer Software Industry: A Comparative Study of Industry Evolution and Structure*, ed. David C. Mowery (New York, 1996), 131-64.

user-producer interactions in the software industry. Regardless of the national origin of the hardware on which new software operates, U.S.-located software firms will have advantages over firms without a presence in this market.

The Economic Theory of Innovation, National Innovation Systems, and the Economic History of Software

The comparative national approach to the economic history of computer software highlights some important qualifications to the various elements of "conventional wisdom" concerning the development of this industry and technology. As Campbell-Kelly points out in his paper, the emphasis in journalistic accounts on the "killer app" overlooks the importance of rapid and widespread adoption of a very few "dominant designs" in desktop computer architectures in creating an environment within which a "killer app" could penetrate a mass market quickly and profitably. In this connection, the appearance of VisiCalc in the United States requires less explanation than the rapid rise to dominance within the U.S. desktop computer market of the PC and Apple architectures and the much slower rates of adoption of a few "dominant architectures" in Western European and Japanese desktop computer markets.

The popular concept of "disruptive technologies," innovations introduced by entrant firms that result in the displacement of incumbents, also requires some qualification in a comparative framework. One of the characteristics of such "disruptive technologies" as new form factors in computer disk drives or integrated circuits, for example, is the tendency for these technologies to be associated with the entry of new firms and the displacement of established firms only in the United States.[11] The software industry may also be characterized by a similar tendency for disruptive technologies to exert a more disruptive effect on incumbents and market structure in the United States than in other industrial economies. But this issue merits further research within the historiography of the software industry, as do the conditions that give rise to this apparent difference in the effects of disruptive technological change on market structure in the United States and other industrial economies.

Conclusion

The search for a single paradigm or unifying analytic framework for studying the economic history of computer software is likely to be frustrated by the sheer pervasiveness of computer software. The development of user-driven innovation in this technology, for example, is likely to trace a different path than the development of packaged software sold in mass consumer markets. As Campbell-Kelly points out, "embedded software" is another segment of the software that has been scarcely studied, yet is likely to play a more and more important role in the future

---

[11] See Henry W. Chesbrough, "The Organizational Impact of Technological Change: A Comparative Theory of National Institutional Factors," *Industrial & Corporate Change* 8 (1999): 447-85; David C. Mowery and Nathan Rosenberg, *Paths of Innovation* (New York, 1998).

of many complex manufactured products (e.g., aircraft and automobiles). In my commentary on Campbell-Kelly's paper, I have tried to briefly summarize some elements of a comparative framework for the analysis of the economic history of the software industry. This comparative approach has significant weaknesses. Many of the historical outcomes are overdetermined—e.g., the important role of new firms in the U.S. software industry reflects the operation of a large number of factors, and the contributions of individual variables is nearly impossible to isolate. Nonetheless, the comparative approach highlights some key issues and influences on the development of the software industry, and thereby provides a framework that can be combined with many of the concepts outlined by Campbell-Kelly to develop a richer economic history of the computer software industry.

A Note on Martin Campbell-Kelly's "Software as an Economic Activity" and David Mowery's "Commentary"

David A. Hounshell

Carnegie Mellon University
Henry R. Luce Professor of Technology and Social Change
Pittsburgh, PA 15213
USA

E-mail: Hounshell@cmu.edu

As with the history of any technology, business, or industry, the history of software raises the question for the historian of what unit of analysis should be used. Reading Martin Campbell-Kelly's paper, "Software as an Economic Activity," and David C. Mowery's commentary suggests the clear need for greater methodological rigor and consistency, vis-à-vis analytical units, in studying the history of software.

Although certainly illuminating, Campbell-Kelly's analysis is quite inconsistent in its unit of analysis. Sometimes the unit is the period of time; sometimes it is the type of software product. More frequently Campbell-Kelly uses the firm that produces the software as the unit of analysis, but certainly his treatment is, on the one hand, sometimes aggregated, and on the other, often episodic or anecdotal. Ultimately, he suggests that historians of "software as economic activity" resort to taxonomies of software firms and packages.

Mowery characterizes Campbell-Kelly's central unit of analysis as the firm but then dismisses its utility by suggesting that more interesting questions and powerful analyses can be gained by employing the analytical framework of national innovation systems that Richard Nelson and other economists have used in the last decade. In this framework, analysts examine technological and economic change through the lens of such factors as scientific and technical education, defense technology policies, intellectual property regimes, competition policies, and university-industry relationships to explain the competitive advantages (or disadvantages) of nations. Mowery's comment constitutes a brief application of this framework to software—something that he has done with distinction in other venues.

I suggest that Campbell-Kelly's paper and Mowery's comment are quite orthogonal to each other and that the root of the problem lies in their respective choices for an optimal unit of analysis. I would further suggest that both the problems with the history of software that Campbell-Kelly bemoans and the questions that obviously drive Mowery can be addressed if the historian were to commit to a rigorous study of software using the firm as the principal unit of analysis. Such an approach will allow two things to occur. First, it will ensure that the history of software is interpreted through the lens of Chandlerian business history, in which the firm has traditionally been the basic unit of analysis.[1] Here, the historian opens the black box of the firm for analysis of management practices, culture, strategy, and structure; research and development; product manufacture; market development; and the like. Through systematic study of a large number of firms, one can begin to understand with some degree of confidence the nature of the software industry, how business segments evolved, and the competitive forces that drove both firms and the entire industry over time.

Second, if carried out methodically, a study whose basic unit of analysis is the firm will yield an understanding of industry evolution and the determinants and dynamics of change in the industry far superior to what we have gained to date. Specifically, I advocate the emulation of research approaches that have been employed at Carnegie Mellon University over the last decade to understanding technological change and industry evolution.[2] Like the approach employed by population ecologists, Carnegie Mellon University researchers have sought to gather comprehensive data on the number of firms in an industry over time as a way of understanding patterns in industry change over time. But going well beyond population ecologists, Steven Klepper et al. have sought to look intensely inside both the firms and the technologies being studied. For example, most recently, in jointly conducted work with Sally Sleeper, Klepper has been examining the entry, evolution, and exit of firms in the laser industry. With a complete census of firms in the industry, he and Sleeper have studied the conditions of entry of each firm in the industry. They have assembled systematic data on the founders of laser firms and their respective prior experience in either the laser industry, in closely related industries (such as semiconductors), or in fields distant from lasers. Also, they have sought to understand the product through which a new firm entered the market and the relationship of that product to the products of incumbent firms. Finally, they have sought to understand the interplay of technological change in the industry and related industries to changes in firms, products, and the laser industry. Gaining such extensive data over time has yielded a deep understanding of both industry and technological evolution in lasers. The software industry should be studied in a similar way.

---

[1] For a discussion of the firm as the unit of analysis in business history, see David Hounshell, "Hughesian History of Technology and Chandlerian Business History: Parallels, Departures, and Critics," *History and Technology* 12 (1995): 205-24.

[2] See, for example, Steven Klepper, "Entry, Exit, Growth, and Innovation over the Product Life Cycle," *American Economic Review* 86 (1996): 562-83; Kenneth L. Simons, "Technological Change and Firm Survival in New Manufacturing Industries," Ph.D. diss., Carnegie Mellon University, 1995; Sally Sleeper, "The Role of Firm Capabilities in the Evolution of the Laser Industry: the Making of a High-Tech Market," Ph.D. diss., Carnegie Mellon University, 1998; Daniel Holbrook, "Technical Diversity and Technological Change in the American Semiconductor Industry, 1952-65," Ph.D. diss., Carnegie Mellon University, 1999; Daniel Holbrook et al., "The Nature, Sources, and Consequences of Firm Differences in the Early History of the Semiconductor Industry," *Strategic Management Journal* (Chichester, forthcoming); Steven Klepper and Kenneth Simons, "Dominance by Birthright: Entry of Prior Radio Producers and Competitive Ramifications in the US Television Receiver Industry, " Paper Delivered at the Eighth International Meeting of the Joseph A. Schumpeter Society, Manchester, U.K., 1 July 2000; Steven Klepper and Sally Sleeper, "Entry by Spinoffs," *Mimeo*, June 2000.

Such a project will require the work of scholars dedicated to more than counting the number of firms in the industry, the number of employees, or total sales over time, to more than treating its leading firms, to more than writing a history of software languages, to more than considering the industry's principal heroes and heroines, and to more than studying such interesting questions as whether software is science, engineering, or something else. Campbell-Kelly's call for taxonomic work will have to be heeded. At the same time, no firm or no software product can be treated as a black box, for only by grasping a firm's history and only by understanding a software product internally can one understand what is taking place over time. Finally, both changes in computer hardware and in the larger scientific, technological, economic, and social environment over time will have to be factored in before software can be understood fully as a business and as economic activity.

Obviously this is an agenda and a set of requirements that are beyond the capabilities of any individual. Some of the basic data are already available—what might be termed the low hanging fruit. But a large amount of data I am calling for have not been systematically gathered and organized. To do this will require collective action led by institutions such as the Charles Babbage Institute and the Heinz Nixdorf Museums Forum working together cooperatively and using Web-based collaboratory software that can leverage both the expertise of trained historians and the insider knowledge of industry participants. Although, obviously, data can be sliced and diced in many ways, I would urge that one basic unit for organizing these data, which in turn will both call for and drive the organization of other data, be the firm. From this basic unit of analysis can spring a far richer history of software as business and economic activity than either Campbell-Kelly or Mowery has been able to realize to date.

Discussion following
"Software as an Economic Activity"

Thomas Haigh

University of Pennsylvania
Department of the History and Sociology of Science
303 Logan Hall
Philadelphia, PA 19104-6304
USA

There was much discussion following the paper and commentaries on "Software as an Economic Activity." The two main topics were regional issues in the software industry and embedded software but other interesting subjects were also considered.

Some participants raised the question of an intermediate level of analysis between population of individual firms favored by Campbell-Kelly and the handful of national innovation systems advocated by Mowery. Historians have paid considerable attention recently to regional networks of small and medium sized producers as a viable alternative to giant corporations. This framework has been applied to the hardware industries of Silicon Valley and Route 128. Mowery suggested that regional location is much less important in software than in hardware because its infrastructure is different. While firms cluster around universities or large companies, the networks between them are much less important—clustering is an historical accident rather than a system of production.

A follow-up question raised the existence of regional labor markets for software developers. Firms are in general reluctant to invest in training because widespread shortages make the trained employees more attractive to competitors. They therefore worry about nearby competitors, but seek a source of trained workers for themselves. The optimum location would therefore be close to a supply of workers, such as near a university, but far away from competing firms. Mowery acknowledged this kind of regionalism, and suggested that extreme shortages of web developers were forcing firms to locate in the Bay area and New York City, in the midst of a sea of competitors. This led to some speculation as to the location of Microsoft in an area formerly devoid of software producers.

Another discussant asked Mowery the inverse question: can we still talk of national innovation systems in this era of global markets? More specifically how could we deal with the case of multinational companies within the software industry context? Mowery replied that national advantages seem to be more compelling for certain kinds of software than others. One interesting question was where do US software companies do well and where not? US firms dominate markets for generic, general purpose software but hold a much smaller share of the market for niche and custom software. Why? Another question was what gave rise to multinational software companies? One needs to look at the origins and initial growth of multinationals. A further interesting question would be what kind of software do multinationals do best?

It was pointed out that the papers had all focused on packaged software, making no attempt to consider the economics and costs of embedded software. Because such software is not sold separately to consumers, its worth consists of the value it can add to an overall product. Campbell-Kelly admitted that this was a tricky area. Firms performed some of this work internally and outsourced some to specialists. The result was to bring programmers into new roles. Another discussant suggested that this had broad implications in established industries, such as automobile production. Ford now expects most of its engineers to have at least a Masters degree due to the increased complexities of computer usage. Meanwhile, General Motors is fast becoming one of the world's largest computer oriented firms, and is spinning off much of its more traditional work on mechanical parts to focus on this area. This illustrated a point salient to all the sessions: the difficulty of thinking about software in isolation from the broader systems in which it plays a part.

Campbell-Kelly's suggestion that the overall proportion of computing expenditure devoted to software had remained constant and quite low was debated. While Campbell-Kelly asserted that one might not expect to spend $4,000 on software for one's $1,000 personal computer, others pointed out that one might easily spend that much on specialist software to configure a database server or an engineering workstation. In addition, the cost to develop and maintain custom corporate software can dramatically exceed the purchase price of the commodity hardware on which it is run. This seems to be another area in which experience of mass-market packaged software can be dangerous when extrapolated across other kinds of software. It also shows the impossibility of breaking out all corporate software expenses from other budget categories such as staff and the proportion of hardware capacity used for development and testing purposes.

When asked about possible a "non-economy of software" emerging through free, open source products such as Linux, both Campbell-Kelly and Mowery found the prospect intriguing, but suggested that we were currently too close some of these events to comment historically. Issues concerning the history of software in France, Italy, and Eastern Europe were brought to the attention of the meeting.

The final area of discussion was the applicability of ideas from economics and economic history to the study of software. Campbell-Kelly was interested by the idea of "path-dependence" and believed that this was a chance to build bridges between historians and economists. By giving some theoretical meat to history, and some historical richness to economics, this could enrich both camps. Others were more sceptical, pointing out that path-dependence and other forms of "institutionalism" are highly controversial and somewhat marginal within economics. It was also suggested that path-dependence is just a means for economists to come to terms with something that historians have known for a long time: that historical context matters, that technological specifics matter and that historical outcomes may be contingent rather than an inevitable playing out of economic predeterminism.

Part 6
Museums and Exhibitions

Collecting Software: Preserving Information in an Object-Centred Culture[1]

Doron Swade

Science Museum
Assistant Director & Head of Collections
National Museum of Science & Industry
Exhibition Road
London SW7 2DD
UK

E-mail: d.swade@nmsi.ac.uk

Museums are part of an object-centred culture. Their essential justification is the acquisition, preservation and interpretation of physical artefacts. Physical objects, their meaning, significance and their care, dominate a curator's professional psyche. One of the first tasks, then, is to locate computer software in the artefactual landscape. Computer hardware, as a category of object, is seemingly unproblematic. It is the physical stuff of computer systems and falls painlessly into the custodial universe of conventional object-centred curatorship. Curators acquiring monitors, keyboards, systems boxes, disk drives and printers would be seen as going about their normal business in an unremarkable way. Software, a term in general use by the early 1960s, is usually defined negatively—that is to say, a component of computer systems distinct from hardware. *The Oxford Dictionary of Computing*[2] defines software as "a generic term for those components of a computer system that are intangible rather than physical". Prentice Hall's *Illustrated Dictionary of Computing*[3] irreversibly severs the material link by noting that "software is independent of the carrier used for transport". The non-material features of software have ominous implications. The Science Museum's Corporate Plan for 1992-7[4] states that one of the Museum's core objectives is to "acquire the most significant objects as physical evidence of science worldwide". Here physical objects are explicitly identified as the evidentiary medium. We have a *prima facie* conflict. If software is in some sense irreducibly abstract and what distinguishes it is something non-physical, then it falls outside the mandate of material culture and a conscientious museum curator might have qualms about his/her professional entitlement to mobilise resources to acquire and preserve it. The

[1] This paper is an edited version of a book chapter: "Preserving Software in an Object-Centred Culture," in *History and Electronic Artefacts*, ed. Edward Higgs (Oxford, 1998), 195-206. Acknowledgements: Illustrations (Pegasus computer, two simulation screens) are reproduced with the permission of the Science Museum.
[2] *The Oxford Dictionary of Computing* (Oxford, 1986), 352.
[3] Jonar C. Nader, ed., *Illustrated Dictionary of Computing* (New York, 1992), 412.
[4] National Museum of Science and Industry, *Corporate Plan 1992-1997: The Next Five Years* (London, 1992).

dilemma may seem pedantic. But there is a real issue: in whose custodial territory does software fall? Is it the responsibility of the archivist, librarian, or museum curator? Some software is already bespoke: archivists and librarians have 'owned' certain categories of electronic 'document'—digitised source material, catalogues, indexes and dictionaries, for example. But what are the responsibilities of a museum curator? Unless existing custodial protection can be extended to include software, the first step towards systematic acquisition will have faltered, and a justification for special provision will need to be articulated *ab initio*. The creation of new institutions to preserve new informational media is not without precedent: the National Sound Archive (NSA) was founded in 1955 as the British Institute of Recorded Sound (absorbed in 1983 as part of the British Library), and the National Film Archive was founded in 1935.[5]

In practical curatorial terms the abstraction of software is, in any event, something of a pseudo-problem. We do not collect prime numbers or polynomials. We collect instead mathematical instruments, physical models, seminal publications, and the written deliberations of mathematicians. In much the same way our curatorial concern for software centres on the external physical record—coding sheets, punched paper tape, punched cards, flow charts, manuals, magnetic disks, publicity literature, i.e. the distinct physical media of creation, representation, distribution, and storage. There is a looseness in our language when it comes to distinguishing between software and the medium of record. Floppy disks, for example, are often referred to as 'software'. However, if the term 'software' is reserved for the abstract relational element of programs then the floppy disk is strictly speaking not the software *per se* but the physical medium of record. Solid-state read only memory chips (ROMs) containing programs and data are often referred to as 'firmware' which at first sight seems to occupy some middle ground between hardware and software. However, the ROMs are still strictly speaking no more than a more permanent physical medium of record for software and, like floppy disks should be kept distinct from the relational element of the information they contain.

Software represents a substantial human endeavour, and the intellectual, economic and material resources involved in its production and distribution represent a major technological movement. Its importance is not in dispute. So one way of by-passing philosophical misgivings about the materiality of software is to appeal to the broader mandate of science museums to maintain a material record of technological change, and to offer curatorial protection to artefactual software by regarding it as part of the contextual and functional extension of hardware without which technical history would be incomplete. In this way we can perhaps bluff it out and collect software by day leaving philosophical disquiet to the troubled night.

But the lump under the carpet is still visible. Once we grant ourselves the licence to collect the physical artefacts of software, there remain, at least at first sight, respects in which artefactual software is both like, and unlike, the archetypal museum object. There is the issue of permanence, and the related issue of artefac-

[5]   See T. Day, "Sound Archives and the Development of the BIRS," *Recorded Sound, The Journal of the BIRS* 80 (July 1981); Ivan Butler, *To Encourage the Art of the Film: The Story of the British Film Institute* (London, 1971).

tual identity. Objects decay, despite our best efforts to conserve them. In the conventional acquisition model this deterioration does not apparently affect the identity of the object. The brass telescope remains a brass telescope notwithstanding inevitable degeneration. We refer to a rusted telescope as a 'rusted telescope' or more impressively, 'telescope, condition poor'. The time-scale of its degeneration does not seem to threaten its identity as a telescope, that is to say, its physical deterioration is sufficiently slow to support the illusion of permanence. That it is a telescope seems not to be at risk. Ultimately when time reduces our prized telescope to some orphaned lenses adrift in a little heap of metallic oxide we sadly shake our heads over the debris and say 'this was a telescope', or, in Pythonesque terms, 'this is an ex-telescope'.

Magnetic media, the most common means of information storage for machine-readable software and data, are notoriously impermanent. In the US in the early 1980s banks, required to retain computer records for audit purposes, were advised that no archived magnetic medium over three years old should be regarded as reliable. Posterity stretches ahead without limit. In contrast, disk and tape manufacturers, when they are prepared to commit at all, are reluctant to do so for more than a few years. Jeff Rothenberg (1995) cites two separate life-expectancy figures for various storage media—magnetic audio tape, video tape, magnetic disk, and optical disk).[6] Two figures are cited for each medium: 'time until obsolete' and 'physical lifetime'. In the case of optical disk, 'time until obsolete' is estimated at ten years and 'physical lifetime' at thirty years. So even the most durable of our current 'permanent' media offer storage durations that qualify as ephemeral when measured against the archaeological time scales of our custodial ambitions and there is a fundamental incompatibility between the life-expectancy of magnetic media and the long-term custodial needs of museums.

What are a curator's responsibilities when faced with an impermanent medium of record? At the centre of curatorial practice is an inventory procedure. This procedure formally transfers the 'title' of the object from the donor or vendor to the Museum. Each inventoried object is the direct responsibility of a named curator, the collecting officer, who signs a formal declaration of responsibility for each object when it is acquired. 'I hereby take responsibility for the objects described overleaf' is the forbidding form. An object once inventoried is subject to formidable safeguards against disposal and unqualified alteration. The physical integrity of an inventoried object is sacrosanct in museum culture and the act of inventorying marks its transition into protective custody. In what sense can a curator, the official custodian of the object's integrity, responsibly sign the acquisition declaration knowing full well that there is no guarantee that a floppy disk or tape will be readable in a few years even if pampered with executive class conservation treatment—acid-free packing, humidity- and temperature-controlled environment, and low ambient light levels? While magnetic media are in general demonstrably more robust than worst-case fears indicate, it is only worst-case life-expectancy

---

[6] Jeff Rothenberg, "Ensuring the Longevity of Digital Documents," *Scientific American* (January 1995).

figures that can responsibly be adopted in the context of systematised software archiving.[7]

The acknowledged impermanence of the medium leads to the question of artefactual identity. Is a set of floppy disks for Windows 1.0, say, like the telescope with an identity that transcends its state of repair? If the information content, represented by the magnetic configuration of the disk coating, is what makes a set of disks, Windows, then does 'Windows 1.0, condition poor' mean anything? If the magnetic configuration of a disk is the determinant of the object's identity then this identity is no less ephemeral that the magnetic information, itself impermanently stored. In more practical terms, does meaningful collection of software imply a functionally intact copy with the promise or potential of running it? If so then we have at least one clear respect in which artefactual software, acquired in accordance with the cannons of conventional museology, differs from objects acquired because of their historical significance, regardless of physical condition.[8] We do not ask 'functional intactness' of the telescope. 'Telescope, broken' does the job.

We can perhaps draw a useful analogy with pharmaceutical products. I learn from my medical sciences colleagues that the Science Museum has recently placed some proprietary drugs on inventory. Panadol, say, is now an inventoried object. There is valuable cultural information in the physical artefact: tablet form, blister-pack press-through dispenser, advertising imagery used in the logo and packaging, and printed information to decode about consumer appeal. But we can be reasonably sure that the drug company will not guarantee the potency of the sample beyond its sell-by date. We are clearly acquiring Panadol at least partly as a cultural artefact on the understanding that its chemical infrastructure and therefore its potency is ephemeral. However, in museological terms Panadol does not cease to be Panadol when it is no longer chemically potent. Similarly, the centuries-old 'poison-tipped arrow' remains so-called though the likelihood of any residual toxin is remote. Is the Windows disk like Panadol? Apart from the facetious difference that the one gives headaches which the other alleviates, there are strong similarities. 'Potency' in both cases is not visually meaningful. Function is not manifest in external form. Further, the Windows disks are no less a vehicle for contextual and technical messages than the Panadol pack: symbolism and imagery in brand logos and packaging, quality of label print, physical size, soft or hard sectored, whether or not factory write-protected, presence of reinforcing ring and so on. The disks are informative as generic objects (media) as well as conveying product-specific information about Windows. However, the richness as a cultural object of a deteriorated Windows 1.0 disk pack is cold comfort to an archivist or

---

[7] Thirty-year old magnetic tapes have been successfully read at the Science Museum, London. The 35 mm tapes were created on an *Elliott 803* discrete component germanium transistor computer dating from 1963. This computer was restored to working order and original tape stock read on the original hardware. The tapes, stored in metal canisters, were stowed in an unregulated garage environment for many years without any special conservation measures taken. In the PC context, material written to floppy disks over ten years ago is commonly still usable.

[8] Aspects of these issues are treated in "Collecting Software: A new Challenge for Archives and Museums," in *Archival Informatics Newsletter and Technical Report* 1/2, ed. David Bearman (Pittsburgh, Pa., Archives and Museum Informatics, August 1987).

historian preoccupied with preserving or regenerating the operational environment of the product. So we return to the question of functional intactness.

Software we know is 'brittle'. It degrades ungracefully. We are all familiar with the awful consequences of what in information terms may be a trivially small corruption. One bit wrong and the system crashes. There are however situations in which the value of magnetically stored information is not bit-critical. Disks used as storage media for textual data as distinct from programs provide one example. Parchment deteriorates leaving us with partial or fragmentary records. Like the parchment example a progressively corrupt magnetic record is simply a partial record but a usable record nonetheless. The residual data is not necessarily deprived of access or meaning by partial corruption. The 'all or nothing' fears do not in this case apply and we may be encouraged to re-examine whether there is some give in the apparently uncompromising need for bit-perfect records of program software.

If we look at the effects of corruption on program performance we can identify three broad categories. Non-critical corruption covers situations in which unused portions of the program are compromised—unused print drivers, irrelevant utilities or subroutines, for example. If we use a steam engine, say, as an example of a conventional museum object 'non-critical corruption' would correspond to the damage to an unused or non-critical part—a nut dropping off, a dented panel. Damage in this case does not compromise the primary function, that of producing traction. Critical corruption leading to evident malfunction is a second category— the system hangs, the cursor freezes, the operating system fails to boot, or the program produces obvious gibberish. In our steam locomotive comparison, the engine loses traction, or makes an expensive noise and stops. So far the comparison with physical machines works. The third and most worrying category is critical corruption that produces non-evident errors—a maths program that produces an incorrect numerical result, a data-base manager that cross-labels data records, for example. Comparison with the stalled steam engine is not obvious. Perhaps a closer analogy would be with a telescope that misrepresented what we were looking at. The distant unsighted object is a church steeple. But observed through our telescope (condition, good) we see the image of a mosque. There is a representational dimension to a great deal of software which renders correspondences between reference and referent vulnerable to a different class of derangement— misrepresentation. It is the possibility of non-evident critical corruption that makes it prudent to conclude that if archived program-software is to be run the need for bit-perfect records is uncompromising.

If the medium of issue is magnetic then the indefinite maintenance of bit-perfect records commits us to an active program of periodic renewal and integrity checking, or a one-off transfer to a more permanent medium.[9] Engineering instinct favours retaining the medium and format of issue to ensure compatibility with the original hardware. Transferring software to a more permanent storage medium, optical disk, for example, offers a tempting liberation from the fate of perpetual

---

[9] Gunnar Thorvaldsen, formerly with the Norwegian National Archives, reports on integrity checks on archived tapes being carried out every two years and routine transfer to new tape stock every five years. See idem, "The Preservation of Computer Readable Records in Nordic Countries," *History and Computing* 4/3 (1992).

periodic renewal. However, the interdependence of hardware and software poses formidable technical difficulties to running programs so transferred. Machine-independent software is frequently anything but. Correct operation of applications software relies more often than not on particular revisions of system software, program patches, hardware upgrades, firmware revisions and machine-dependent interfacing to peripherals. Transferring to an alternative medium requires new data formats yet to be standardised and dependence on a new generation of hardware to read or download stored information. Interfacing to these devices and executing code so stored is not straightforward. Transfer to a more permanent medium is not without penalty despite its promise of releasing Sisyphus from his fate in the copying room.

Fig. 1. The Ferranti *Pegasus*, a large vacuum-tube machine dating from 1958

The requirement for functional intactness of software not only entails the maintenance of bit-perfect records but also implies the provision at some time of operational contemporary hardware or a functional equivalent. Neither the provision of contemporary hardware or a functional equivalent is trivial. In 1989 the Science Museum, with the British Computer Society, founded the Computer Conservation Society dedicated to the restoration and preservation of historic computers and to the capture of operational know-how of computing machines. The Society has had signal success in restoring to working order a Ferranti *Pegasus*, a large vacuum-tube machine dating from 1958 (Figure 1), and an *Elliott 803*, a discrete component germanium transistor machine dating from 1963. At best such ventures can extend the operational life of obsolete systems. The life expectancy of the Pegasus, for example, has been extended by an estimated ten to fifteen years. But however successful these endeavours, we have to accept the eventual demise of such systems. The intractable fact of the matter is that in terms of archaeological time scales the operational continuity of contemporary hardware cannot be assured even when suitable specimens are available to begin with. What meaning, then, does an archive of bit-perfect program software have if the material cannot be run?

Fig. 2. The Ferranti *Pegasus* machine's console included console switches and console oscilloscope traces

One way forward presently being explored by the Computer Conservation Society is to simulate early hardware on present-generation computers using the restored original as a benchmark. Two simulations are well advanced, one for the *Pegasus*, the other for a German *Enigma* cypher machine. In the case of *Pegasus*, console switches, console oscilloscope traces, input/output peripherals (paper tape, teletype-style printers) are visually simulated in facsimile and animated on-screen (Figures 2, 3). Using this bit-level simulation the operator can write, run and debug programs by 'driving' the simulated controls and the simulator responds appropriately even to the extent of execution times. The original storage medium for *Pegasus* software is paper tape and surviving software libraries have been captured and preserved on modern hardware by interfacing to contemporary optical tape readers and storing the programs in a form that can executed by the simulator.

The museological implications of such simulations are intriguing. An implicit tenet of museum life is that the original object is the ultimate historical source. In museum culture the original physical artefact is venerated at the expense of a replica, duplicate, reconstruction, or hologram. If we wished to test a new theory about Napoleon's allergy to snuff, say, it would not make sense to examine replicas of Napoleon's clothing even contemporary look-likes. Prior to the snuff-allergy hypothesis, snuff-content would not be a consideration in the making of garment replicas. Only the original artefact with authenticated provenance would suffice for this forensic purpose. Physical replicas can only incorporate features and characteristics perceived to be significant at the time of replication and part of the justification for preserving original objects in preference to a copy is that the original can be interrogated in an open-ended way in the light of unforeseen enquiry.[10] Physical replicas are inherently limited as historical sources for practical as well as psychological reasons. However, logical replication seems to offer more. Capturing the operational persona of an early machine on a later machine promises possibilities for open-ended analysis of the kind formerly offered only by a working original. As computer languages used for the simulations become increasingly machine-independent, the simulation program, which embodies the logical and functional identity of the original machine, can be migrated from one generational platform to the next. The technique seems to offer a form of logical immortality that is museologically new and a view of hardware in which the physical implementation of a computing machine ceases to be the sole determinant of artefactual identity.

The resource implications of a meaningful software acquisition programme are formidable. However persuasively we argue to include software in the existing fold of custodial protection, the need for the special provision of resources cannot be evaded. The maintenance of bit-perfect records requires an open-ended commitment to periodic copying and checking. This requires staff and equipment. The transfer of program-software to optical media invokes a raft of technical issues of operational compatibility that would require prohibitively large engineering and hardware design investment to solve for a museum with a conventional mandate. The restoration and maintenance of contemporary hardware on an indefinite basis demands vast financial resources and the opportunity cost is likely to be politically indefensible. The development of simulations and emulations is technically promising but the necessary skills-levels are high and the financial implications of programming, development and verification, are substantial. The progress made in this field at the Science Museum would have been unaffordable without the voluntary efforts and expertise of Computer Conservation Society's members. In custodial terms even a successful simulation exercise does no more than transfer the operational persona of an historic early machine to a currently supportable platform which will itself be duly subject to generational obsolescence. The potential of the technique lies not in the immortality of current hardware but in the prospect of machine-independent software. But the Utopia of machine-independence may not ultimately appear on the custodial atlas of the future. In the meanwhile, simulation buys time and allows us to pass the baton to the next generation which may well have to face similar problems.

---

[10] Doron Swade, "Napoleon's Waistcoat Button: Modern Artifacts and Museum Culture," *Museum Collecting Policies in Modern Science and Technology* (London, 1991); Doron Swade, "Virtual Objects: Threat or Salvation?" in *Museums of Modern Science*, ed. Svante Lindqvist (Canton MA, 2000): 139-47.

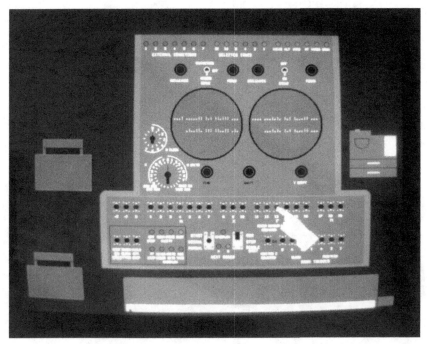

Fig. 3. Screenshot of the simulated Ferranti *Pegasus* machine's console

Despite the formidable obstacles that face a fully-fledged software preservation programme there is at least one modest but significant programme of software acquisition that is technically achievable and that has affordable resource implications, namely, software for personal computers—'shrink-wrapped' consumer software as well as custom-written special applications software. Acquiring working specimens of significant volume-production personal computers since 1977, and their variant upgrades, is still a realistic acquisition objective. The technical skills required to recommission, repair and maintain such machines are still available, and there is still time to reach back into the past and trawl relevant examples into the present. The complementary task is to identify and acquire significant examples of contemporary consumer software, from VisiCalc (an early spread sheet package for the Apple II, available in 1979) and Electric Pencil (a word processing package for the Tandy Model I, 1978), through to the last release of DOS and Windows for present day PCs. The acquisition of these products can be accomplished with existing resources. Recommissioning the hardware, copying onto fresh stock and documenting the operational quirks of the systems would require additional but affordable technical support. Once established, the 'archive' will be relatively easy to keep updated—this by purchasing off-the-shelf current software products and contemporary hardware. In the absence of an independently resourced organisation with a specific brief to preserve systems and applications software, this acquisition programme represents one practical step we can take. In overall archival terms the venture is no more than a holding operation. Perhaps the cavalry will still arrive in time.

Commentary on Doron Swade, "Collecting Software: Preserving Information in an Object-Centred Culture"

Joachim Fischer

Kulturstiftung der Länder
Kurfürstendamm 102
10711 Berlin
Germany

E-mail: ksl@kulturstiftung.de

Introduction

In this paper, Doron Swade has given an excellent overview of almost every aspect that might come up in discussions on the preservation of software. Since I basically agree with everything he says in his paper, I am inclined to say, "My lords, I rest my case," go back to the bar and wait for what the future may bring. But this is not exactly what I am expected to do in my role as commentator, so I shall try to be the devil's advocate—well, sort of.

First of all, let me briefly recapitulate on the main topics addressed in Doron Swade's paper, though not in their proper order of appearance:

- A discussion of the distinction between software (seen as a sub-species of information) and its physical medium of record
- A discussion of the volatility and/or generational obsolescence of contemporary storage media for software
- A discussion of the alternative possibilities of using either simulation and/or migration by means of machine-independent platforms
- A discussion of software compared with more or less traditional museum objects

Let me now, in turn, briefly discuss these topics.

The Distinction between Software and its Physical Medium of Record

Information in general needs a physical medium of record. This medium may be a human being, a piece of paper, a book, the Rosetta stone or—more specifically for software—a punched paper tape, punched cards, a magnetic tape, a floppy or a hard disk, a CD, or any other storage medium that might come to mind. All of the media mentioned have a limited lifetime (although there are differences of several orders of magnitude), and for all of these media we must have a means of "extracting" the information they contain or "carry." Without this means of extraction, the information will remain existent, but inaccessible. As the common saying goes, information is easily transported, copied and thus multiplied. This, however, is not quite true, for it depends on the availability of suitable extraction mechanisms: understanding what another human being says has to be learned, as has reading a notice or a book (not to speak of the language in which it is written). "Reading" paper tape, punched cards, magnetic tape, etc., also requires specific devices and, usually, a specific (non-human) recipient for the information (or "data") they contain: a magnetic tape drive transforms the information on the tape into electric pulses, but these in turn have to be "understood" or interpreted by someone or something. Thus, we almost immediately enter the field of *hardware*, which *has to be in some kind of working condition* in order to extract the information; more about this later. Information, and thus also software, can be "held" in different forms on various media. For example, the source code of a program can be printed on paper and thus better preserved, in any case more durably, than on a magnetic tape or a floppy disk, where it is usually stored in binary, executable form and thus not readable by humans. (Strictly speaking, the source code and the executable program do not really represent the same information.) But transporting information, with or without changing its form, is obviously not the desired solution of the problem we appear to face (or is it?). It is of importance, however, that we can send information from one medium to another, with or without changing its informational content; we have to be aware, though, that in doing so, we may (and usually do) lose the "direct" usability of this information. In this respect, the dictionary definition of software as being "independent of the carrier used for transport" seems admissible, though it is rather misleading in several other respects. And we should not forget that changing the medium obviously has its price, which may in some cases be very high.

The Obsolescence of Contemporary Storage Media for Software

The lifetime of the physical medium of record having been mentioned, we note in passing that in the realm of today's software we have a lot of media with rather short lifetimes, when seen against the time-scale that we are used to operating with in our capacity as custodians. Paper can be torn or burnt, but if not treated in this rather unkind manner, it preserves the information it carries very well and for reasonably long periods of time (be it in the usual form of a printed book or in the form of punched tape or card). But all of the other media mentioned, including the human being, have lifetimes that are considerably shorter than that of museums. We have some rather pessimistic estimates (but also some experience that leaves room for optimism) about the preservation of magnetically stored information; generally, it seems that the end of the physical lifetime of today's digital information carriers such as are used with computers comes later than the point at which they become technically obsolescent. According to Rothenberg,[1] this held—in 1995—for magnetic and optical disks. Extending the life expectancy by copying the information again entails the necessity of suitable *hardware*.

Simulation and/or Migration, Preferably by Using Machine-Independent Platforms

Simulation and/or migration of software *via* machine-independent platforms may be an intriguing model, but its disadvantages are equally obvious. Of course the simulation has to be more or less bit-perfect (not necessarily in the literal sense, but in that it contains exactly the features of the "original"), which is what Swade calls "logical replication." We should note, however, that this kind of simulation initially was developed in order to simulate *hardware*, not software. And, here again, we find that software may well be—in some abstract sense—independent of its carrier, but certainly not if it is to be *used*. If we wish to use software, then we must have it at our disposal on the specific carrier and in the specific form that our hardware, be it simulated or not, requires. Again, more about this later.

Traditional Museum Objects vs. Software

Let us now look at software as compared with classical museum objects. We use Swade's examples and consider the telescope first: Swade explicitly mentions four categories or states that a telescope may have. It may be simply a "telescope," which implicitly means that it still can be used as such. It may be a "telescope, condition poor," which usually means that this telescope may still be used to view distant objects, but that it may have rusty spots, some scratches on its lens(es), some loose screws perhaps—but it will still serve, though maybe with some re- strictions, its original purpose. It may also be a "telescope, broken," which at least indicates that the telescope is no longer in working order (but there might be a realistic chance of having it repaired, if so desired). Finally, we have Monty Py- thon looking at an "ex-telescope."

So where exactly does our comparison of software with a telescope go wrong or cease to be useful? If we consider only the three broad categories of software decay mentioned by Swade—and there are certainly more of these categories if only we take a closer look at software and its cooperation with hardware, we have: non-critical corruption, critical corruption leading to evident malfunctions, and critical corruption leading to misrepresentation. It is obvious that in general these three categories do not match the different states of the telescope particularly well. I observe in passing that these software corruptions may already be—and usually are, as we all know from the rather deplorable quality of most of today's pro- grams—present in the "original" software, even if every bit is correctly read and interpreted by suitable hardware. Corruption, here, obviously has a double mean- ing: on the one hand, we have corruption that is already part of the original soft-

---

[1] Jeff Rothenberg, "Ensuring the Longevity of Digital Documents," *Scientific American* (Janu- ary 1995), as quoted by Swade.

ware, and on the other, we have corruption caused either by "ungraceful decay" of the information originally stored, or by a faulty copying or transformation process. This observation alone suffices to decide the question in favour of the need for bit-perfect records; otherwise we would not be able to determine whether the original software already had bugs or whether these were produced later. Thus, if we need records or copies of software at all, the answer has to be: "Yes, we need bit-perfect records of (program) software." This being the case, I deliberately failed to mention the "telescope, lying" (which transforms churches into mosques). With this fifth "state" of the telescope, Swade himself has already stretched the comparison beyond any useful purpose, so I have no need to repeat this here. "Seeing" what a specific program does inevitably leads us back to the hardware for which the program was originally designed (or its simulation). In short: we need only consider the software problem if we wish to *run* the software—and running the software is certainly no longer independent of anything, but clearly dependent on the availability of *suitable hardware in working order*.

A similar argument would show why and in what respects comparing software to a steam engine does not ultimately yield new insights either.

Then we have the pharmaceutical product Panadol: here, the parallel to software is obviously most appropriate, and it is precisely here that I too can best draw my conclusion: Panadol is now an inventoried object—so what? Will it ever be *used* against headaches? Certainly not the Panadol tablets conserved at the Science Museum! Swade lists all the properties that make the Panadol "artefact" a carrier of valuable *cultural* information: its tablet form, press-through dispenser, advertising, printed information. But the precise chemical composition is only implicit in the artefact; this information is usually kept somewhere else (and, for patent reasons, may not even be known to the curator responsible at the Science Museum—will he or she please accept my apologies if I'm wrong here). Perhaps, sooner or later, perfect chemical analysis (without destruction) of Panadol will become possible—but, again, this is certainly not the sole or main reason why Panadol should be preserved in a museum. And, most definitely, it has not been inventoried to relieve the curator's or anyone else's headaches. The same goes for software: its carrier bears valuable *cultural* information; but after some time, and in the not-too-distant future, the most important feature of this artefact—its information—will have disappeared, as will the chemical potency of Panadol. Where's the difference? We all know that the museum's Panadol *will never be used for its original purpose*, but when talking about software, it seems that, implicitly, we wish to *use* it (forever?). As pointed out earlier, and as underlined by Swade several times, we usually do not require "functional intactness" of a museum object. When it comes to software, however, we suddenly seem to take a different view. Why should we?

Finally, the example of the "poison-tipped arrow" gives us the same clue. We all know that the likelihood of any residual toxin is remote, but we call the arrow "poison-tipped" all the same. We do so because we have a common understanding that museum objects are named according to their original purpose. But we are *not* supposed to make explicit whether the object is or is not functionally intact, because functional intactness is not the reason for collecting or displaying an object. And, because of this implicit agreement between curators and visitors, we do not consider it necessary to explicitly inform the visitor that the poison has probably lost its potency long ago.

Working Order vs. Maintenance

The problem with software, then, seems to be—a fact quite at odds with the established museum policy for "ordinary" objects—that we might want to *use* it. But if this is really what we want, then we are in deep trouble. Software comes in various forms, but ultimately it needs some kind of hardware on which it can be run or executed. This statement in turn needs further qualification: What about the kind of software that is needed for hardware to be of any use at all? Think about operating systems like MS-DOS, which in turn will not "boot" before the BIOS (which I consider to be software, too) has been loaded? What about UNIX, which comes written in "C" and thus not only needs hardware with some kind of primitive operating system already running, but also a C-compiler (which itself is software, of course) to get started? We have a *hierarchy of software*, which is determined, on the one hand, by the hardware we have chosen, and on the other hand, by the future software that we intend to install. Thus, if we are seriously considering collecting software, we should at least keep this hierarchy in mind.

Let me put it another way: I am convinced that the preservation of software is a pseudo-problem, when considered from the standpoint of a museum. As Swade correctly remarked with regard to the telescope: "We do not ask 'functional intactness' of the telescope." So why should we ask functional intactness of computer hardware? And if we do not ask for functional intactness of computer hardware, the whole question of preserving software in a bit-perfect form *in order to run it* (today, or some 10 or 100 years from now) becomes meaningless.

So is it functional intactness we should be speaking about, or, put another way: *Why* do not museums normally require functional intactness of their objects? Apart from several other obvious reasons, there is, of course, the problem of maintenance. Until the turn of twentieth century, almost everything collected and preserved in science and technology museums was purely mechanical. Except for demonstration purposes—which usually required additional features (no steam engine was under steam when demonstrated, but was driven by an electric motor instead)—none of these objects had to be in working order because, once in the museum, the object's original purpose—say, as a machine or as an instrument intended for use—no longer existed. In principle, virtually all of these objects could have been adjusted or repaired at relatively low cost and with modern materials and skills—but in practice this was done only for a negligible number of the objects preserved. Things became very different when two particular kinds of objects found their way into the museum: those containing electric or electronic components and/or those no longer manufactured by, say, mechanical workshops, but produced on a large, industrial scale. In both cases, however, "repairing" the object became a time-consuming and/or costly job—not immediately, it's true, but at least when technological change had made these objects obsolete. For a certain period of time, spare parts, special tools, etc., were still available from the manufacturer, as was the special know-how required. But even the theoretical possibility of repairing an object of these two categories (and we can think of some others, but the consequences are similar) rapidly declined in the course of the twentieth century. One example that immediately comes to mind are vacuum tubes: unless you have lots of suitable replacement tubes in your depots, you will not risk switching on a seventy-year-old receiver, let alone an early vacuum-tube computer like the Z22. However, when we are in a museum, *we do not normally use* the objects for their original purpose anymore, either for listening to the radio or for computing, so their functional intactness is not required. Anyway, we would have other serious problems with some of these objects: consider a refrigerator with toxic coolant and the danger it might cause if not properly stored or displayed, let alone operated. I had better not mention the amount of mercury in UNIVAC's delay tanks and the problem these tanks might cause. And, finally, "repairing" a chip is out of the question—either we replace it, as long as we have an identical chip at hand, or we shrug our shoulders ("This is an ex-chip"). We all know this, but we do not normally talk about it. This matter was not given much thought even at a time when "repair" was still possible and affordable, so why bother to think about it when circumstances have become much less favourable?

Let us consider a specific example: the four pre-WW II Zuse machines, Z1–Z4. We are probably all agreed that some if not all of these four computers were of importance in the history of computing, and that it would perhaps make sense to have at least one of them in working order, for whatever reasons (but would it really?). Now, consider the current state of affairs: Z1–Z3 were destroyed during WW II, but given the importance of these machines, there are approximate replicas of the Z1 and the Z3, each of them "endorsed" or even worked on by the inventor himself (no one ever thought of making a replica of the Z2, which was originally built only to prove the possibility of combining a relay arithmetic unit with a purely mechanical storage device). After a major mechanical breakdown, the Z1 replica has not been in working order for several years now, and I doubt whether it will ever be repaired again. The Z3 replica is (or was?) in working order, but there were and will be minor breakdowns, each of them leading to wear and tear in relays, fuses and the mechanical parts of the tape reader. This will undoubtedly decrease future willingness to demonstrate a running Z3 replica, and sooner or later curators will decide to no longer keep the Z3 replica in working order. As for the only original pre-WW II machine preserved, the Z4, it is incomplete in many respects and very fragile: no one has ever thought about changing this situation, however. There are several computer simulations of the Z4. For different reasons, then, (almost) none of Zuse's earliest computers or their replicas is in working order—and I have not heard many complaints about this state of affairs. The current state of the three machines (replicas or originals) perfectly illustrates the different attitudes we have towards hardware, which—again—is a necessary prerequisite for software. And let us not forget that the Zuse machines belong to the class of objects for which repair is still feasible, at least in principle. The situation is much worse for post-WW II machines.

By now it should be obvious "where I am going today:" objects of science and technology are preserved for many reasons, but certainly not for permanent or even occasional use. Keeping an object in working order requires special consideration of why (and only as a second thought: how) this particular object should be treated differently from most other museum objects. This decision will certainly involve consideration of maintenance costs, but sooner or later maintenance itself will no longer be feasible. Looked at this way, collecting software in its original form only makes sense if it is intended to run it on original or simulated hardware equipment. This, in turn, means that the hardware equipment must be in working order, and I am sure that only very, very few computers of historical importance will or can be kept in this state.

As Swade has pointed out, the situation is slightly better when it comes to contemporary mass-produced PCs. Although museums already generally refrain from actually running early home computers and their programs (there are not too many of them still around, and the problem of *their* repair is only a question of time), computers and programs that are produced in their hundreds of thousands or even millions are widespread and inexpensive. Here, too, the original hardware for which a certain piece of software was once designed will sooner or later disappear. Things are different here, however, precisely because this kind of mass-produced hardware is and will probably remain inexpensive (but in the long run the question of its maintenance cannot be neglected either). Museums can afford to—and do— have several hardware copies of one type of machine. The succession of different storage media will continue, but each new medium is introduced while its predecessor is still around. It was never a problem to copy the information on 5 ¼ inch floppies to 3 ½ inch floppy disks—but in general it is more difficult to do this the other way round (by way of another example: consider the situation with contemporary streamer tapes and their varying densities; and many of us will remember a similar situation in mainframe days, when 7-track low-density tapes could be read, but not written, by 9-track high-density tape machines).

The problem faced in this situation is one of quantity *and* quality: it is impossible to archive all the existing software, even if it were donated free of charge. Fortunately, a substantial amount of contemporary software may well be considered worthless, and future generations of curators will not blame us for failing to preserve it. But here we encounter the same problem that our colleagues in modern art museums have had for at least a hundred years: how do *they* judge whether a certain artist will survive in the history of art? Whose works should *they* buy, when prices are still low? How, then, should *we* know which software package is important, if not in retrospect? But there is another fortunate aspect in our special field of interest: the time for retrospect is measured in months or years, not in (human) generations. Besides, if a piece of today's PC software is really important, it will usually exist in thousands or millions of copies. Even if we do not grasp its importance immediately, there will still be enough copies around for us to get hold of one or two or more. There would appear to be a need, however, for museums worldwide to cooperate in this effort, perhaps by assigning special software collectibles (operating systems, word processing programs, spreadsheet packages, etc., not to forget computer games) to specific museums, which would then be responsible for qualified collecting of *their* type of software. But, knowing my former colleagues well, I am doubtful about whether such cooperation will ever be achieved or successfully realized ... .

This may sound pessimistic, but it seems to me a fair description of the current situation. What, then, do we leave to the next generation of curators? If objects are worth it, future generations will do all they can do to reconstruct, rebuild, repair, simulate or emulate what they consider worth the effort. Babbage's Difference Engine is one contemporary example, the Z1 and Z3 replicas are others. But even these replicas will, each to a different extent—some sooner, some later—fall into the maintenance trap. The same is true of the few computers from the 1950s and 1960s that have been restored to (or kept in) working order; Swade estimates that their life expectancy has been extended for a mere ten to fifteen years. Once their maintenance has become infeasible or impossible, what is to be done with the software for these computers? Should we continue to "save" it in "bit-perfect" form? And why should we do this?

Finally, if we consider keeping some of the software at all, we should agree on a reasonable time horizon, which must be measured in terms of the availability of the respective hardware. The above discussion would seem to indicate that it makes no sense to call for the preservation of software for centuries. Instead, I would vote for at most one or two human generations, or approximately thirty–fifty years. As for PCs, this would now make the optical disk the ideal medium for preservation.

In principle, I do agree, of course, with the "holding operation" that Swade advocates. But I neither believe that "the cavalry will still arrive in time," nor do I think that this will be necessary. Science and technology museums are there to preserve the "most significant objects as physical evidence of science worldwide,"[2] or to collect "master-works of science and technology."[3] Nothing is said of functional intactness, which is simply not required. In the long run, none of the computer hardware preserved in our museums will be functionally intact, and therefore collecting software in its original, *usable*, form would appear to be merely a temporary problem.

Responsibility?

To close, let me add one final remark—concerning the custodial responsibility into which software should fall: archivists and librarians have long "suffered" from changing technologies which they have had to use and/or adapt (just think of the various video-tape formats). Their experience in this field, however, is usually unprecedented. In many cases, they have—of necessity—kept most of their old equipment running beyond the commonly accepted date of obsolescence. In addition, archives and libraries normally already have "executive-class conservation treatment" at their disposal. So I think *preserving* software is best done by either of these groups; but the decision as to *what to collect* should be made by, or with advice from, the responsible curator.

---

[2] Science Museum, London
[3] As the full title of the *Deutsches Museum*, Munich, indicates: *Deutsches Museum: von Meisterwerken der Naturwissenschaft und der Technik.*

Towards a Software Museum:
Challenges and Opportunities

Ernst Denert

sd&m AG
Thomas-Dehler-Str. 27
81737 München   &
Germany

E-mail: denert@sdm.de

Klaus-Peter Löhr

Freie Universität Berlin
Institut für Informatik
Takustr. 9
14195 Berlin
Germany

E-mail: lohr@inf.fu-berlin.de

Introduction

Although the history of automatic computation is quite young, the rapid development of electronic computers has awoken the interest of the historians, who fear important facts about early computing might get lost. The most visible result of the combined efforts of historians and computer veterans are *computer museums* which have been founded in several countries and have become quite popular.

Computer museums belong to the category of science and engineering museums. Their exhibits tend to do more than just present some fancy machinery: they try to educate visitors, i.e., convey an understanding of how technical artifacts work and how they were perfected over generations of engineers. A prominent example of this kind of museum is the *Deutsches Museum* in Munich, one of the world's most comprehensive science and engineering museums.

Presenting computers in a museum has been done very successfully in the past, but has focused on only one part of the computing business (actually a small part)—hardware. The really important part—and one of the key technologies at the turn of the century and for a long time to come—is *software*. So why are software systems not presented in computer museums? The answer seems obvious: software is immaterial and invisible, so there is nothing to be presented. Or so we think.

The authors set out to question this dogma. We are convinced that it *is* possible to make software an exciting exhibit in a museum—a *software museum*. Our opinion was confirmed when we visited the newly created *Mathematical Cabinet* in the Deutsches Museum. Here, Friedrich L. Bauer has managed to present the most elusive subject imaginable, mathematics, to the visitors, or at least to wet their mathematical appetite by allowing a playful encounter with strange objects.[1] It

---

[1] Friedrich L. Bauer, *Einladung zur Mathematik: Mathematik zum Begreifen und Erschauen, Begleitbuch zur Ausstellung Mathematisches Kabinett des Deutschen Museums München* (München, 1999).

occurred to us that software, too, could be made visible, tangible and playful, and thus reach people.

The immaterial nature of software is not the only problem a software exhibition has to solve. The sheer mass of past and existing software, the disappearance of the supporting hardware platforms and the virtually unlimited range of applications make it hard to see how a software exhibition could ever cover its subject in an adequate way. In exploring the issues, we will first develop a few principles that we consider crucial to any successful attempt to create a software exhibition. Then, to make things more concrete, we will present three case studies of "exhibits." Finally, several technical and organizational issues will be addressed.

Basic Principles for a Software Exhibition

Goals

The *raison d'être* of any museum, whatever its theme, is to save characteristic items from oblivion, to preserve masterpieces, to present them as *exhibits* and thus to contribute to an understanding of the *history* of a specific field. The *educational* efforts range from almost non-existent (as in art galleries) to rather elaborate (as in ethnological museums).

These three facets—exhibits, history, education—what do they mean for a software exhibition? While everybody knows what a painting is, few people know what a computer program is. So the educational aspect will be essential for any software exhibition. Only if people understand general software principles, concepts and techniques, will they be able to appreciate specific software exhibits and understand historical developments.

This implies that, first and foremost, there has to be a *software basics* section which explains the basic notions of algorithm, program, software, and how all this relates to hardware. Then different kinds of software have to be covered, both *systems software* (operating systems, compilers, ...) and *application software*. For each kind, it is necessary to answer three questions:

1. What are the *problems* to be solved?
2. What are the typical *approaches* to solving these problems and how have these approaches evolved over time?
3. What are the prominent historical *examples* of that kind of software and how have they solved the problems?

By way of an example, let us consider database systems: 1. (Problems) The ACID properties[2] have to be guaranteed and efficient queries must be supported for large amounts of data. 2. (Approaches) Some typical techniques are indexing, locking, logging, etc., and we have seen more refined manifestations of these techniques in the evolution from indexed-sequential files to relational to object-oriented database systems. 3. (Examples) We may want to present, say, VSAM, IMS, and Ora-

---

[2] *ACID* is the acronym for *atomicity, consistency, isolation, durability.*

cle as prominent representatives.—We will revisit database systems in section "Lufthansa's Reservation System" below.

There is one additional theme a software exhibition has to cover—*software engineering*, the very craft of building software systems. Representing the history of software engineering adequately, with its victories and defeats, may be impossible to achieve in a museum. We must admit that we have not given it much thought so far.

Arrangement

As a museum defines itself through its *exhibits*, we have to answer the question "What is a software exhibit?" The simplistic answer is:

1. A condensed, educational documentation of the system is presented on wall charts, including a requirements document, a user's manual, a design sketch and some code fragments.
2. The program is actually installed on a computer; it can be run, perhaps even be used interactively by visitors.

It is obvious that this approach would never work. The possibilities for running legacy code are very limited. Emulation is rarely supported, and exact simulation of obsolete hardware (including peripherals!) is an unrealistic task. Moreover, even if "the real system" were running, would this be helpful to the visitor who cannot check the code anyway? And even if we could check it, who would go through the documentation and try to understand what is going on? Not even the typical computer scientist.

This is not to say that exhibits should not use computers. Actually, the museum should rely heavily on computers—not for running original software masterpieces but for running special educational software, mainly for *documentation* and *visualization* purposes. Take the subject of *operating systems*, for instance. A section on operating systems would be arranged as follows:

1. An introduction to the purpose of operating systems is given (possibly drawing on the visitor's knowledge as a computer user), and the typical jobs done by an operating system are sketched using a wall chart. In addition, online access to two or three contemporary operating systems is given.
2. Typical operating-system areas, e.g., file management, are chosen for an indepth study. They are first explained, again using a wall chart, and then presented on a computer to allow an interactive, playful encounter. The installed software would simulate a simplified file management system and visualize its operation, down to the handling of file descriptors, block buffers, and disk I/O.
3. "Famous" operating systems are presented (say, THE, Multics, Unix, OS/360, ...), together with details of the people and organizations involved; prominent features of the systems are highlighted. Connections to the visualized functionalities just mentioned are established.—What kind of media support would be most helpful here remains to be seen.

We aim not only to *visualize* software, but also to make it *tangible*. This would be extremely helpful—in the software basics section mentioned earlier—for explaining to children (and others!) what software is all about.

Software Exhibits: Three Examples

In order to make the software museum concept more concrete, we will pick three examples of what might be called a *software exhibit:* the first is concerned with the very notion of software, the second is a visualization example, and the third is a real-world system. We hope that this eclectic approach will help the reader to understand our intentions better.

Coming to Grips with Software

> "I hear and I forget, I see and I remember, I do and I understand."
> Chinese proverb

"Software is immaterial: it consists of programs, which are *plans* for sequences of actions, to be executed automatically by a computer." A definition like this does not really make sense to those who have never written a program. A software museum has to reach out to ordinary people, not only to the initiated; so visitors should be led to an understanding of what these immaterial "programs" are all about.

Material Programs for Playing Music

If a program is an executable plan, then how does a programmer plan the *execution steps*, and how can a *machine* execute those steps? In our view, grasping the essentials of programming should be facilitated by allowing visitors to *physically* grasp programs as well as the executing machines and the embedding environments the machines interact with. Visitors should even be able to build and run simple programs by themselves.

A program is, of course, just a piece of *information*, independent of the physical representation that may be used for communication among humans (e.g., handwriting on paper) or machines (e.g., bits in electronic memory). Still, there are program representations—for mechanical or electromechanical devices—that are much more material than either handwriting or electronic bits. This is how we want the term *material programs* to be understood: consider, e.g., a music box that is driven by a program represented as pins on a revolving cylinder, touching the tuned teeth of a metal comb; or take the classical mechanical loom where the program is punched into a cardboard tape, or take a hand organ.

Actually, there is a "programmable" toy that resembles a music box: punched holes on different "stave lines" of a cardboard tape represent notes. The tape is fed into a mechanical device similar to a music box and "the program is executed" by turning a crank (see Fig. 1). Prepare your own tape and play your favourite tune.

Fig. 1. Primitive music box using cardboard tape

Music is, in fact, a prime example of the abstract concept of program. Admittedly, these "programs" are rather simple, as there is no memory, no parametrization and no branching (though simple repetitions do occur). But the steps to be executed have a well-defined meaning and a piece can be executed by both humans and automatic devices.

We plan to use music as the introductory analogue to computer programs. Visitors (especially children) are encouraged to punch their favourite songs (or those that are presented by the museum) into tapes and feed them into music boxes. There will be both mechanical and electromechanical boxes, and there will be traditional boxes with fixed (or removable) cylinders. Barrel organs should be on display as well.[3]

It should be emphasized that the particular designs of the different devices are less important than the fact that the differences between them do not really matter. "Greensleeves" is independent of how its notes are represented and played—and you can have an automaton play it (if this satisfies your demands). The *hands-on* experience of *different* devices is considered essential for a thorough grasp and proper understanding of the notion of program.

Grasping Graphics

Computers have memories and peripheral devices. Realistic computer programs have branches and loops, and they cause effects in memory and in their environment. To bridge the gap between computers and these simple music boxes, we suggest a simple electromechanical plotting device:

---

[3] This part of the exhibition would, of course, be organized jointly with the hardware division.

- The plotter is controlled by a program on a punched tape[4] which is almost identical in appearance (e.g., has the same number of lines) to the music tape. Each column contains one command (rather than a chord). Unlike the music tape, this tape should remain fixed; a control unit moves along the tape (in both directions).[5]
- There are a few registers, and both integer counters and Boolean switches. The values of two of these registers correspond to the coordinates of the pen.
- The content of the registers can also be observed on displays on a panel, and it is possible to modify the content from the panel. Thus the plotter can be operated both manually and by means of a program.

A fairly limited set of commands suffices for quite a variety of programs. A sample design is given in the appendix. The number of commands does not exceed the number of stave lines we used for the music box.

Understanding Programs through Visualization

"Software is invisible and unvisualizable."[6]

No matter what specific exhibits are chosen for a software museum, we will encounter all kinds of algorithms, concrete programs, fragments of systems, and complete systems. Exhibiting software items—in any representation—will only make sense if visitors are enabled to understand their important properties, both static (structural) and dynamic.

This is not possible by mere code inspection. In recent years, however, *software visualization*[7] has made significant advances in terms of program comprehension and debugging. There will be more progress in this direction, and we believe that visualization can play a pivotal role in a software museum. After all, any museum relies heavily on visual exhibits.

Program Visualization and Animation

Programs want to be executed. It is obvious that not even the most ingenious visualization of a program (as a static item) could allow us to dispense with an *animated* execution.

Program animation comes in different forms, from simple highlighting of statements to elaborate visualization of the dynamic effects on data, peripherals,

---

[4] Remember that early plotters were operated off-line in this way, controlled by a punched tape that had been produced by a computer.

[5] Instead of a punched tape, a metal rod with adjustable pins would be preferable, where each pin can be in one of the two positions Up/Down. This would make it extremely easy to build and modify a program "by hand," without the hassle of punching (or sealing) holes.

[6] Frederick P. Brooks, "No Silver Bullet—Essence and Accidents of Software Engineering," *IEEE Computer* 20/4 (April 1987): 10-19.

[7] John T. Stasko et al., eds., *Software Visualization* (Cambridge, Mass./London, 1998).

and networks.[8] We will use a mixture of different techniques as described below. Both code and data animation techniques will be applied.

In many cases, a software exhibit may lend itself to being modelled as an *abstract data object* (such as a Modula *module*). The object has a procedural interface comprising several operations. The available operations are presented in an *interface window* on the screen. Visitors can trigger operations interactively, in arbitrary sequence. Or they can construct a program in advance, using the given operations, and then step through the program. The chosen operations are composed in a *program window* in either case.

Browsing through the software behind the interface is made possible by *hypertext* functionality: a call statement can be expanded (recursively) by clicking on it, causing the code of the operation to be displayed in a separate program window. The data structures involved are visualized in a *data window*, using boxes, tables, and arrows (representing pointers). With object-oriented designs, encapsulated objects would first appear as blank boxes; clicking on them would reveal their inner structure.

Both code and data should be animated. As the user steps through the code, the current statement is highlighted. A chosen "step" can be the evaluation of a condition, an elementary statement (assignment or operation call) or a complete loop. For expanded operation calls, the system will step through the individual statements of the operations. The data structures are animated by changing box contents and arrows *and* by visualizing how data moves (i.e., is copied) from one box to the other. Depending on the specific exhibit, data flow between the program and the environment could be visualized as well.

Remember that to specify or understand the behaviour of an abstract data object we usually refer to an abstract *model* that is independent of the *representation* chosen by the implementer. Note that what is shown in the data window cannot clearly be classified as either a model or representation: it is more concrete than a model, but it may be more abstract than data declarations in program code.

Speaking of program code—which programming language should be used here? The answer depends on the nature of the exhibit. Of course, if we have a piece of original software, the language is given. But to illustrate typical techniques that occur in many systems, we should use an extremely readable (albeit formal) language, designed for the very purpose of explanation. An in-depth discussion of language issues is beyond the scope of this paper; the reader will get a glimpse of a typical language in the example in the next section.

An Example: Operating System Support for File Access

We tested our ideas using an example from the domain of operating systems: the exhibit *File Access* should convey to the visitor an understanding of an important piece of systems software. A file system can be viewed as an abstract data object exporting operations such as *open*, *read*, etc. The functionality of these operations is quite straightforward—but the implementation is not.

---

[8] Note that we talk about *program* animation here. *Algorithm* animation works on a higher level of abstraction, possibly not even showing code but only an animated model.

Hands-on experience of the exhibit File Access would start by opening a window that presents the interface shown in Fig. 2. A kind of mixfix syntax is used here. For example, READ FROM RETURN is an operation name; the parameters are interspersed with parts of this name, FROM merely enhancing readability and RETURN having the obvious special meaning: it separates by-value parameters from by-result parameters. Parameter types are given below the parameter names. Possible exceptions are *not* indicated in the specification, so as to avoid information overload. They can, of course, occur at runtime (example: reading from a closed stream), aborting the execution and producing an error message.

```
INTERFACE FileAccess
        {Allows reading/writing from/to text files.
        A text file is identified using a file name.
        Opening a file creates a stream through which
        characters can be read/written sequentially.}


OPEN filename RETURN streamhandle
        (Text)              (Pointer to Stream)
        {Creates stream between program and file.}


CLOSE streamhandle
        (Pointer to Stream)
        {Discards a stream.}


READ howmany FROM streamhandle RETURN data
        (Number)      (Pointer to Stream) (Text)
        {Reads specified number of characters from stream
        to data.}


WRITE howmany data TO streamhandle
        (Number) (Text) (Pointer to Stream)
        {Writes specified number of characters from data
        to stream.}


SEEK position IN streamhandle
        (Number)      (Pointer to Stream)
        {Adjust stream to continue reading/writing at
        given position in file.}
```

Fig. 2. File system specification

Clicking on an operation is done in either of two modes: interactive or non-interactive. In the former case, the operation is executed immediately. In the latter, the operation is appended to the program under construction. In both cases, the user is prompted to give the actual parameters first; the operation call is then added to the program window. Variables are introduced on the fly.[9]

---

[9] There are a few additional statements for assignments, conditionals, and loops.

The relevant data structures for File Access are *streams*, *file descriptors* and *block buffers*. They can be visualized as shown in Fig. 3; this is a screen shot from a visualization program that simulates a flat file system using conventional syntax.[10] There are five standard windows:

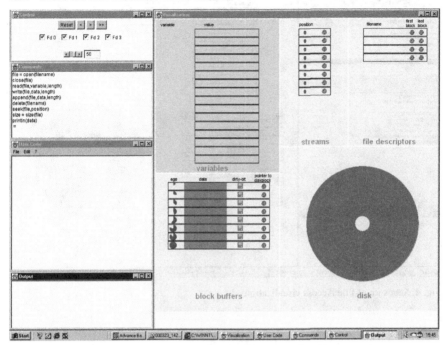

Fig. 3. Startup view of windows for File Access visualization

- *Control* allows users to step through their program (in different-sized steps, forwards and backwards, at different speeds). To avoid information overload, ticks indicate the files (up to four) whose relevant data are shown in the visualization window.
- *Commands* is the interface window; it contains the file system interface. The user can choose commands, insert actual parameters and place the resulting statements in the *user code* window.
- *User code* is the program window; it contains the program to be executed.
- *Output* displays any output produced by the *println* command.
- *Visualization* is the data window; it contains the visualized data of the file system. As the program is being executed, the data flow is animated: text and numbers fly across the screen, and arrows are drawn and redrawn.

Fig. 4 shows the screen after the program shown in the *User code* window has been executed.

---

[10] Stefan Freyer, *Visualisierung von Dateisystem-Mechanismen*. Diplomarbeit, FB Mathematik und Informatik, Freie Universität Berlin (April 2000).

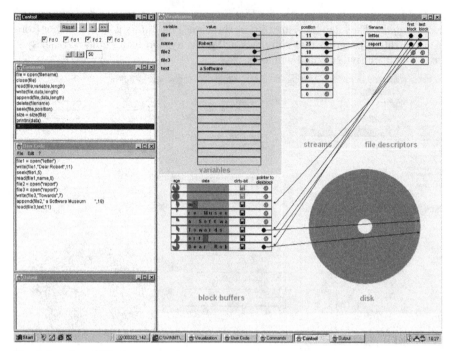

Fig. 4. Snapshot of File Access visualization

Towards a Toolkit for Program Animation

The exhibit File Access is a one-of-a-kind, hand-crafted item. Now the museum will certainly display a multitude of exhibits, from different kinds of both systems and applications software. We may want to provide insight into many of these programs, so there is an obvious need for *tools* that support the animated visualization of programs. Several such tools exist, but program animation is still an active research subject.[11] We do not know of any system that would support the animation sketched above. Existing systems tend to address the design[12] and analysis[13] of large systems; they are meant to support the expert and try to abstract from details. The level of detail we need is found, e.g., in the VCC system for C program animation.[14]

[11] John T. Stasko et al. (eds.), *Software Visualization* (Cambridge, Mass., 1998).
[12] John J. Shilling and John T. Stasko, "Using Animation to Design Object-Oriented Systems," *Object-Oriented Systems* 1 (1994): 5-19.
[13] Wim De Pauw et al., *Jinsight—Visualizing the Execution of Java Programs*, http://www.research.ibm.com/jinsight.
[14] Ricardo A. Baeza-Yates, Gastón Quezada and Gastón Valmadre, "Visual Debugging and Automatic Animation of C Programs," in *Software Visualisation. World Scientific*, eds. Peter Eades and Kang Zhang (Singapore, 1996), 46-58.

VCC also suggests the ideal solution—a tool that would automatically generate an animated exhibit, given a certain program module. While aiming at complete automation seems unrealistic, there is a fair chance of finding a semi-automatic solution. The static visualization part will not be too hard. But attractive animation will require some non-trivial manual intervention.

Semi-automatic generation of animated programs should certainly not be confined to one specific programming language. We should have a generic tool that comes in three parts: a front end that would compile the program into an intermediate-language version; a middle part that would generate a "vanilla" visualization and animation; and a back end that would allow the curator to produce a polished version interactively.

Lufthansa's Reservation System

As a third example of an exhibit, we would like to present an application that is very vivid and interesting from a user point of view and very fruitful from a technical point of view—seat reservation.

It is only for the last 30 years that Lufthansa (LH) flights have been booked using an electronic reservation system (ERS). Before that, booking was done in a huge hall at Frankfurt Airport, with boards mounted to the walls showing the individual flights, e.g., LH 400 Frankfurt-New York, with a space for each day on which they operated, for a period of several months in advance. Employees were in charge of processing all reservation requests, which they received via telephone, via telex or in writing. By attaching a pincard containing the passenger's reservation data to the board, an employee visualized the reservation and ensured that no seat was assigned twice. The hall was so big that binoculars were used for checking the boards for vacant seats on a specific flight.

In addition to this central reservation hall, there were offices in about six cities where, in a similar way, a certain contingent of flights could be booked which were assigned to these offices by the headquarters. The city offices communicated with the Frankfurt headquarters via telephone or telex.

Thus, the essential tools of this booking procedure were boards, notes, record cards and card file boxes, telephone, and telex. Most importantly, a huge number of employees were needed in spite of the relatively small volume of air traffic. Today, Lufthansa's bookings could not be handled this way: not only would the old system fail to meet passengers' demands for fast response—it would actually be infeasible. In short, Lufthansa would not be able to maintain its flight operations; scheduled air traffic would be impossible.

In order to solve this problem, Lufthansa introduced an ERS in the late 1960s and early 1970s. With the ERS, reservations are processed in a central database. This database is integrated into a worldwide network, which can now be accessed not only by Lufthansa employees but by everyone, using the Internet-based World-Wide Web. Moreover, it is connected to a network of reservation systems shared with many other airlines (the SITA network) so that their flights can be booked directly as well.

The exhibition intends to present this example of application software by contrasting the former manual procedure with today's electronic reservation system. Of course, the central hall cannot be rebuilt in its original size, but it could be presented in the form of a diorama. The main aim is to show the former tools as faithfully as possible. Visitors will then be able to see how costly, slow and error-prone the manual procedure was.

The diorama will be contrasted with the fundamental workings of an ERS. This will allow important software aspects to be demonstrated, for instance:

- What a complex application is—and the fact that an ERS is even linked to other applications, including the ticketing and the check-in systems.
- How worldwide access to a central application is made possible, i.e., how Lufthansa's employees, travel agents and, ultimately, everybody can book flights through the ERS.
- How such a system must be operated so that it works reliably around the clock.
- What a database accomplishes (being the core component of the ERS).
- How data access is synchronized so that a seat on a flight is actually given to only one passenger.

It would be a special attraction if the visitors were able to access the real Lufthansa system from within the museum. This might even be realized: taking stock of Lufthansa's old booking procedure has been the subject of a recent Master's thesis;[15] Lufthansa's archives were searched and witnesses of that period were interviewed.

Technical and Organizational Issues

As mentioned earlier, a software exhibition cannot possibly be conceived independently of a computer exhibition. Explaining what a program is will invariably be tied up with explaining the functionality of computer hardware. It remains to be explored how the "hardware" presented in the first example of software exhibits above can be related to the real hardware found in the computer exhibition.

It is obvious that extensive computer support—hardware and "meta-software"—will be indispensable for the documentation, visualization, and maintenance of software exhibits. Given the shortage of resources museums commonly face, free software and cheap hardware must be used wherever possible. A network of PCs running Linux would certainly represent an adequate infrastructure. Large-format screens and electronic whiteboards might be desirable for some exhibits (and may become less expensive in the future). As regards hardware items, we hope to find industrial sponsors who are interested in supporting an undertaking as foolhardy as a software exhibition!

The main effort will, of course, be procuring, adapting and developing the meta-software mentioned above. This would strain the resources of even the wealthiest museum. We expect, however, to find enough enthusiasts in the computer science community to help develop software and prepare specific exhibits.

---

[15] Johann A. Haidn, *Hardware und Software: Computertechnik im Einsatz in den 1960er und 70er Jahren,* Magisterarbeit, Historisches Seminar, Ludwig-Maximilians-Universität (München, 2000).

Still, a software exhibition may experience funding problems in the long run. Unlike other exhibitions of, say, cars, machines, household items, etc., maintenance does not just involve dusting (or repairing or procuring of an item once in a while). Even if the exhibits do not change, the infrastructure has to be maintained and will require permanent renewal, merely because of the fast pace of hardware development. In this respect, the museum's situation is no different from that of any other computer user.

The complexity of the task of establishing a software exhibition obviously requires a sizeable team of computer scientists, science historians, and committed custodians. Such a team does not yet exist. One object of this paper—and not the least—is to get people to help with this undertaking. Success is not guaranteed, as the subject certainly resists straightforward treatment. But this very fact makes it such an exciting endeavour.

Acknowledgements

We enjoyed our discussions with Friedrich Bauer who helped shape many of the ideas presented here. His enthusiasm for the vision of a software exhibition confirmed our hope that the idea might not be too bizarre after all. Stefan Freyer contributed to the file access example by practically exploring the required animation techniques in his Master's thesis. Thanks also to Christian Zick for providing the picture of the music machine.

Appendix: Design of a Simple Plotter

1. There are 8 registers—4 integer counters and 4 Boolean switches:

counters	C1	= x position of pen
	C2	= y position of pen
	C3	
	C4	
switches	S1	= pen up/down
	S2	= colour black/red
	S3	
	S4	

2. There are 6 elementary commands:

inc	increments given counter(s) by 1
dec	decrements given counter(s) by 1
clr	sets given counters to 0
init	resets given counters to their initial values
on	turns given switches on
off	turns given switches off

3. There are 8 control commands:

`if`	evaluates logical OR of given switches; if *true*, proceeds with next command, else continues after next matching `cont` or `retn` (whatever is next)

`if`   evaluates logical OR of given switches;
        if *true*, proceeds with next command,
        else continues after next matching `cont` or `retn` (whatever is next)
`ifno` evaluates logical OR of given switches;
        if *false*, proceeds with next command,
        else continues after next matching `cont` or `retn` (whatever is next)
`ifeq` checks for equality of given counters, then proceeds like `if`
`ifls` checks $C_i < C_k$ ($i<k$) for given counters, then proceeds like `if`
`if 0` checks given counters for 0, then proceeds like `if`

`cont` continues with next command (i.e., no-op)
`retn` returns to last `if` command
`exit` continues after next `retn` (or else stops program)

4. Note that the `if` command (and its variants) works both as the traditional `if` and as a `while`, depending on whether the matching command is `cont` or `retn`. Also note that the control commands are designed as nearly as possible to control *syntax*. Executing a control command requires scanning the program; the benefit is that jump instructions and the ensuing notion of "label" or "address" are avoided.[16] The nesting of control structures, however, is very limited.

5. The program tape has 18 lines, one line for each command and four lines to specify the counter or switch numbers 1-4. The possible commands could, of course, be encoded in a more compact fashion, but only at the price of worsening the look-and-feel.

6. A possible layout of the panel is shown in Fig. 5. At any point in time, the values of the counters and switches are shown in the displays. The elementary commands can be executed by hand, by pushing the appropriate buttons. Initial values for a program can be entered in this way.

7. The above design allows for many variations and may not yet be optimal for our purposes. Some experimental programming should lead to a good compromise between expressive power, complexity and ease of use—the latter certainly being the overriding concern.

---

[16] It is open to debate whether or not the machine presented here is a stored-program computer. In any case, the program store is different from the data store.

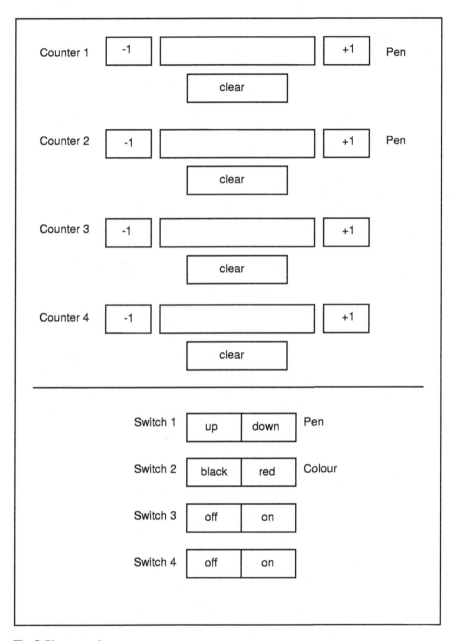

Fig. 5. Plotter panel

Towards a Software Museum: Challenges and Opportunities

Friedrich L. Bauer

Technische Universität München
Institut für Informatik
Arcisstraße 21
80209 München
Germany

Fundamentals of Software

Software, as the word indicates, lacks a fixed form and hence is the opposite of hardware. To be more precise, software is immaterial and cannot therefore be exhibited as such.

Unlike mathematics and philosophy, however, software can be regarded as a directly profitable science. Today, turnover in software products surpasses hardware turnover. Software is increasingly penetrating and influencing our daily life.

These are good reasons for devoting a room to software in a museum. There, software may occupy a central position among the more material *high technology* products.

The question is: how can software be displayed? (It is, essentially, more than its carrier.) Software is stored or coded in the forms of a language. It has its roots in the writing down on paper of a representation of the steps involved in a computational prescription, procedure or algorithm.

The *Euclidean algorithm*, as described in books, is software, too. Likewise, the computational method of multiplication in the decimal number system, still taught in schools, is software. Software is an abstract matter. This means that software can also be stored in human brains. As Joachim Fischer stated—in contrast to the established museum policy for 'ordinary' objects—software needs to be used for didactic purposes in a museum, despite the difficulties this may involve.

I believe, then, that a software exhibition in a museum should start *from the basics*. Step one could be designed like a children's game: by means of formulas—the language of software—made up of wooden pieces, and by examples ranging from numerical calculation to complex structures. Step two would be the transition to a modern medium, presenting all the possibilities of visualization on high-resolution monitors. Step three would demonstrate the possibility of manipulating software. This last step would allow us to show what is behind a formula: its usage and its meaning.

In an exhibition, all modern means of interactive representation, i.e., visualization, can be used to make software comprehensible. Software can be *touched, virtually*. (And informatics is the conceptual framework of software.)

I believe, however, that museum visitors should not be immediately confronted with sophisticated equipment. Instead, they should have the opportunity to play with objects such as pieces of wood. Below, several stages are shown at which visitors can decide when they wish to switch from concrete objects to virtual representation on a screen.

Preserving Software in History Museums: A Material Culture Approach

David K. Allison

Smithsonian Institution
National Museum of American History
Chairman, Information Technology & Society
Washington, D.C. 20560
USA

E-mail: allisond@nmah.si.edu

Introduction

The development of computer software ranks among the major historical advances of the last century. Preserving a representative historical record of this achievement is an international cultural goal. Achieving the goal, however, must be the shared responsibility of many cultural institutions working together. These institutions include archives, libraries, and museums, in both the public and private sectors. What should be the specific role of history museums?

This paper discusses examples of software preservation in the National Museum of American History at the Smithsonian, and then suggests ways that the World Wide Web might assist institutions that want to collaborate in this area in the future.

Software as Material Culture

History museums base their research, collections, exhibitions, and programs on physical objects. Software historians usually do not start by thinking of the physical forms that software takes, but this is where history museums must begin.

In dealing with software, as in dealing with any subject, museums must decide which physical objects to preserve. For software, these obviously include cards, tapes, disks, and CD-ROMS. But they are not the only materials to preserve—and often not the most important. Historical software collections should also include: manuals, reports, advertisements, film, video, and promotional paraphernalia. These supporting materials are often more valuable for historical study than code itself. They provide contextual information that is critical to evaluating the historical significance of the software products.

Besides being interested in software objects, museums are concerned with the relation of software to other historical objects. The most obvious connection, of course, is between software and computer hardware. Few museums would preserve software without keeping some computers that ran it. This means that most software is kept in computer collections. Increasingly, however, it is not limited to only these. As software becomes important in fields as wide-ranging as transportation, communications, graphic arts, medicine, and science, collections in these fields are also beginning to include software objects. Recently at the National Museum of American History, for example, we accessioned a range of desktop publishing programs for our Graphic Arts collection.

Because of their focus on material culture, history museums have a limited role in preserving the internal, intellectual history of software. Archives and libraries should have leading roles in that area, just as they do in preserving the intellectual history of art, literature, or engineering.

Likewise, history museums differ from science museums. History museums generally are interested in collections and exhibitions that show change over time; science museums, on the other hand, focus on explaining scientific principles. Some institutions, such as the Science Museum of London, the Deutsches Museum, and even the Smithsonian's Air and Space Museum, blend these functions, but conceptually they are distinct. Most science museums do not preserve permanent collections. Those that do—in their role as science museums—might be expected to preserve collections that document fundamental principles or theories about software, as compared to collections that document its historical evolution and use.

To clarify these points, compare the history of computing to the history of science. Museums, archives and libraries all play critical roles in that field as well. In simple terms, museums generally base their work on preserving and interpreting scientific instruments. Archives base their work on preserving unpublished papers and records that document individuals and their work related to development of scientific ideas. Libraries preserve published materials in the history of science. These activities compliment, rather than overlap each other. Recording the history of software is an analogous situation.

Material Manifestations

At the Smithsonian, we have numerous examples of the different forms that software has taken over time. These include diagrams, flowcharts, punched cards, paper tape, metal tape, magnetic tape, manuals, floppy disks, and CD-ROMS. Among the most interesting material culture issues related to software is why it has taken so many different physical forms. Part of the answer derives from technical systems for reading and writing code, but part also relates to cultural or economic factors.

I should note that at the Smithsonian, we do not generally aspire to operate historical software—either on the original machines on which it operated, or in simulation on current computers. Again, this is because our fundamental interest is the embodiment of the software in its original context, not in a simulated situation. On occasion we might try to operate or simulate aspects of these historical situations to learn specific points, but it is not a principal objective of our collection strategy.

In contrast, we are very interested in collecting and preserving historical evidence of software in operation, such as training films, advertisements, or marketing materials. Such historical documentation carries many important messages about the context of the operation of the software in addition to the working of the code itself. For that reason, we do aim to collect various forms of documentation that evidences the historical context of software development and use.

ENIAC

Fig. 1. Sections of the ENIAC on display at the National Museum of American History, Smithsonian Institution

ENIAC ranks among the most important objects in our collection.[1] Most of the ENIAC hardware that still exists is in the Smithsonian collection. The bulk of that is on display at the Smithsonian in Washington D.C., but other portions are shown at the Heinz Nixdorf Museum in Paderborn, Germany and at the Moore School at the University of Pennsylvania. Built near the end of World War II, ENIAC was not a programmable computer in the modern sense. To make it solve different problems, it had to be reconfigured by setting dials and changing cables.

---

[1] "The ENIAC Computer," *Bulletin of the Scientific Instrument Society* 63 (December 1999): 15-17.

Nonetheless, the men and women who worked on ENIAC developed a clear understanding of how instruction sets could be written in numerical code and entered into the machine as a program. Eventually R. F. Clippinger and his colleagues developed a rudimentary language called "Converter code" that could be used on ENIAC. In our collection of documentation supporting ENIAC, we include some materials related to this code, as well as documentation on how ENIAC was wired for program changes. We are particularly interested in using ENIAC as a baseline for showing how software would change in years to come.

UNIVAC

UNIVAC, which debuted in 1951, ushered in the era of commercial large-scale, commercial stored-program computers. It also introduced business to magnetic tape for loading and storing software. The Smithsonian Computer History Collection includes a variety of items related to UNIVAC I. These include a UNIVAC console, many components, and accessories. Among the components is a magnetic tape drive, and the accessories include a reel of metal tape, which contains a CO-BOL Compiler. Thus it documents not only the contemporary means for moving data in and out of the UNIVAC, but also the use of an important new computer language.

Also included among the UNIVAC accessories are a few items that document how UNIVAC was being used in the early days. One brochure came from Pacific Mutual Life Insurance, which prided itself on being an early entrant to the "Electronic Age" because of its use of a UNIVAC in its business. It gives a contemporary sense of the way that UNIVAC was absorbed into the prevailing business culture. The language, style, and perspective of documents such as this are useful for setting the historical context for computers and software in an exhibition format.

VYDEK

Let me jump ahead several decades to a very different era. As information technology evolved in the United States, computers and software were developed to manage a range of new functions. Among the most important for the general public was word processing. It has roots not only in the history of computing, but also in the history of typewriting, in technologies such as the IBM Magnetic Card typewriter.

Commercial word processing required specialized computer and software systems. Vydec Inc., founded in 1973, became an industry leader of this market segment. Several years ago, the Smithsonian collected a Vydec 1400 system to represent this line of technology. Vydec had two important innovations. The first was full-page display of a typewritten page in a "WYSIWYG," or "What You See is What You Get" format. The second was the use of 8" floppy disks for storing information. Each disk could store 80 to 100 pages of information. Generally the disks were used for storing data, but they could also be used for specialized programs. This was a step in putting software into the hands of users as well as computer professionals. The Smithsonian collection includes around 1 cubic foot of storage disks, manuals, and training materials related to our Vydec artifact.

Altair

The Altair introduced personal computing to the public. Announced in the January 1975 issue of *Popular Electronics*, the Altair was based on Intel's 8080 microprocessor and was a fully functional computer that sold for less than $400. Hobbyists quickly ordered Altairs by the hundreds. Although the Intel microprocessor gave the computer much latent capability, it couldn't do much without running software. As is well known, Bill Gates and Paul Allen saw the Altair advertised and decided to write a BASIC interpreter for it. The program worked, was widely adopted by Altair users, and became the foundation of the new start-up company, Microsoft.

Some copies of the BASIC operating system were stored on paper tape, such as one copy from the Smithsonian Collection. Our copy is reputedly version 1.1. Bill Gates once remarked, "If anyone is using BASIC version 1.1, you have a copy of a tape that was stolen. ... No customers were ever shipped 1.1, as it was experimental and is full of bugs!" From the early days of the company, Gates was very concerned with combating software piracy. The Smithsonian copy thus documents a variety of interesting aspects of the early history of Microsoft.

Radio Shack TRS 80

For personal computers to reach a broad market, they needed a keyboard, monitor, and inexpensive storage. The Radio Shack TRS-80, which was introduced to the market in the summer of 1977, had them all, and became a big seller. Equally important for customers was software that would allow them to write their own programs or run those written by others. BASIC was generally the language of choice, and many BASIC interpreters became available. When the Smithsonian collected its TRS-80, it also collected samples of many software programs of this era, languages, manuals, and assorted publications. They are actually more voluminous than the object itself. From a material culture perspective, the form and design of these materials are as significant as the coding they contain.

Software Paraphernalia

For museums, interest in software extends beyond just the languages and programs. It includes cultural paraphernalia: tee shirts, buttons, ashtrays, posters, banners, publications, and the like. Many of these are exhibited in a display in the *Information Age* exhibition at the National Museum of American History. The display includes eight early personal computers. Stacked underneath them are piles of books, magazines, and boxes of packaged computer software. On the wall behind them are the paraphernalia, including such gems as the announcement of the first West Coast Computer Faire, the first newsletter of the "People's Computer Company," the first Apple Macintosh Tee Shirt and a PC Jr. ashtray. The point of the display is to show that personal computers brought not just a technical change to our lives, but also a social change that included a wide range of peripheral products that began to become integral parts of homes and offices.

Fig. 2. Radio Shack TRS-80 computer

Video History: Bill Gates

Museums cannot collect people, so they often try the next best thing: collect oral and video histories. In 1993, I had the opportunity to conduct several hours of interview with Bill Gates on the history of Microsoft. My goal was to interview him reflecting about many of the objects that were important parts of his career. In one sample of the interview, Gates talks about developing the first BASIC interpreter for the Altair computer.[2]

> Well, I had no doubt that I could write a BASIC Interpreter. I thought through in my head all the things that I hadn't done before on those mini-computers. Doing things really small, fascinated me. These machines, you could actually buy it with no memory card. After we got there a lot of people were calling up asking, "What do they do with it?" Well, if you don't buy a memory card you can't do anything. But, the memory cards were 1K. So, if you bought four of those you could have a 4K machine. 4K bytes. And I thought I could do a pretty decent BASIC. Fitting the BASIC in, allowing you to have both your program and your data storage in 4K bytes. That was going to be hard. But, it was a fun challenge.
>
> People had done 8K BASICs on the PDP-8. But this was a much better instruction set. I had some ideas on how to do things a little bit in a new way. There was no doubt in my mind we could write a BASIC. I was fairly self-confident in those days. We didn't know how long it would take us. And it was kind of funny because we were sort of acting like we had it already. We went to work day and night. Paul first worked on the simulation software. He took the Macro 10 Assembler and defined macros, so we could just type in sort of a form of 8080 code. Then he modified the DDT-10, the symbolic debugger that was on the 10, to understand these instructions. He then wrote a simulator to simulate these instructions.
>
> It was a reasonably simple instruction set. Paul was very good with the PDP-10 Assembler. I, in the meantime, laid out the design and charged off coding the BASIC. Paul later came in and helped out with that. A third person, Monte Davidoff, sat down for lunch with us and said he knew floating-point packages. So, we had him write some of the math routines. And then we just kept squeezing it. So, we wrote without ever seeing this machine [pats the Altair], except in this picture, and the simulator and got the BASIC running. And then we called them back and said, "By the way, what's the sub-routines for reading a character from the Teletype and writing to the Teletype—how do you do that?" And we got Bill Yates on the phone, who was the co-author of this article. And he said, "Well, that is pretty interesting. All these other guys call us up and say they are going to do things. But nobody ever asked us how you get data in and out of the machine. You guys sound pretty serious. You ought to come out and show it to us." And, because we'd never had the chip, just the book from Intel, if we had made any mistake in terms of how the instructions worked, the thing never would have run.
>
> And so Paul was scheduled to fly out to Albuquerque. He decided to go get some sleep. I stayed up all night reading the book to see if we'd miscoded some of the instructions. And finally, I decided it was all okay, punched out the paper tape, and made sure Paul got that before he went off on his plane. He wrote the bootstrap loader, that is the thing you have to key in to make this computer smart enough to know to go get data off the Teletype to read it into memory. He wrote that on the plane on the way out. It was actually 46 bytes, the first one. I eventually wrote it in 17 bytes.
>
> He took the BASIC to MITS. They had a machine they had run with 6K of memory, which for them was a big, big thing. And loaded up the paper tape. The first time, for some reason it didn't work. The second time they loaded it in and it worked. Of course, the simulator is very slow because you go through lots of instructions to a single instruction. So, actually, the real machine [pats the Altair], even though it is such a simple little microprocessor, was faster than our PDP-10 simulator. About five times faster. And so to Paul, when it finally came up and said, OK. ... Actually that first version said

[2] Transcript of a Video History Interview of William "Bill" Gates, conducted by David K. Allison, 30 November–1 December 1993. Transcript available at http://americanhistory. si.edu/csr/comphist/gates.htm.

READY. Most BASICs when they are ready, say READY. Later when I was squeezing bytes out, I thought, well it is faster to print OK, and it is kind of a nice friendly word. So I shortened it to OK a little later.

Anyway, it came up, it said READY, and he typed in a program, Print 2 + 2, and it worked. He had it print out squares, sums and things like that. He and Roberts, the head of this company, sat there and they were amazed that this thing worked. Paul was amazed that our part had worked, and Ed was amazed that his hardware worked, and here it was doing something even useful. And Paul called me up and it was very, very exciting.

Video history has many advantages for museums. It provides valuable information from historical figures. Clips of interviews can be included in displays or shared over the World Wide Web. Full interviews and their transcripts are highly important to both researchers and exhibit developers. On the other hand, video histories can never substitute for in-depth and broad-ranging research. Recollections in video history form rarely provide essential information about conflicts or difficulties.

Last year, I went back to Microsoft and conducted a series of interviews with members of the team that developed Windows NT. In addition to recollections, I collected a copy of the software specifications from the team leader, the computer boards that first ran NT, and copies of the first versions of compiled code on CD-ROM. NT and the successor, Windows 2000, are becoming a leading operating system on personal computers all over the world. It is interesting to compare objects related to its history with those related to Microsoft's first product.

Fig. 3. Personal computers and computer paraphernalia, National Museum of American History, Smithsonian Institution

Static Museum Displays

How can the history of software be displayed in museums? I will describe several examples of what we have done at the Smithsonian. First is a static display from our *Information Age* exhibition at the National Museum of American History. The section includes an 8-foot text rail, a shallow case, and a background display panel.

The title of the text rail is "Programming: From Plug Wires to Software." It includes images and text that puts the section in context. The case shows software objects from the 1940s through the 1970s: plug wires, manuals, cards, and disks. On the panel are images of people programming and snippets of code that showed how it appeared in different eras.

The display packs a lot of story in a small space, but unfortunately, its static nature tends not to attract much visitor attention. Also, most visitors are not immediately drawn to objects such as software cards, manuals, or disks—however important they may be historically.

Interactive Museum Displays

Most visitors are more interested in experiencing software in action. In the museum's *Information Age* exhibition, we use many interactive computer displays to supplement our cases and panels. One popular example is an interactive on "Intelligent Transportation Systems." Visitors use the computer to explore various aspects of the subject, including many software innovations that are helping to make transportation systems safer and more efficient.

Computer interactives give visitors involvement, choice, and action, all-important tools in engaging and holding their attention. In this case, we are telling a story about computer software through the story of a computer application. In general, this is an approach we favor at the National Museum of American History. Most of our exhibits treat the history of all aspects of computer development—hardware as well as software—through their use in applications of significance to society.

Live Demonstrations in Museums

Yet another way to display software is to show people using it in live presentations. Last December, we opened an installation we call "Digilab." This display combines a live digitizing laboratory and an exhibit explaining the process of digitizing and how it fits into the history of printing and graphic arts. By looking into the windows of the laboratory, visitors can see staff and volunteers digitizing images and texts, printing, creating web pages, writing java script, and doing other programming tasks. It gives them an operational look and professional use of contemporary computers and multi-media software. For those of us who use programs like Photoshop or FrontPage on a regular basis, this is not unusual, but most members of the public have never seen what it looks like. This allows them to see how digital resources and web pages are created.

Besides being open on a daily basis, the Digilab is an ideal setting for special tours and presentations on multi-media programming.

Fig. 4. Digilab exhibition, National Museum of American History, Smithsonian Institution

Software History on the Web

Effective presentation of software history requires many institutions working together to meet a common goal. The World Wide Web offers an excellent means for this collaboration. As museums, archives, libraries, and private organizations, work in the area of software history, they can share many of their efforts with each other and the public over the World Wide Web. One aspect of the web that excites us at the National Museum of American History is its ability to meld exhibit-like presentations with large bodies of background research materials. In presenting exhibits on the floor of the museum, we have often been hampered by the lack of space to share all that should be included. Virtual exhibitions on the World Wide Web do not suffer from the same limitations.

In conclusion, History Museums have an important role in preserving the history of software. Their role begins with physical collections and focuses on aspects of the "material culture" of software. These collections provide important resources for many forms of research into the history of software as well as exhibitions that touch on the place of software in modern history. Partnerships between museums and other institutions are essential to preserve a full record of software history.

Commentary on David K. Allison, "Preserving Software in History Museums"

Hartmut Petzold

Deutsches Museum München
Curator for Computer Science and Time Keeping
Museumsinsel 1
80538 München
Germany

E-mail: h.petzold@deutsches-museum.de

I agree completely with David's paper. Most important is his general statement: "The development of computer software ranks among the major historical advances of the last century. Preserving a representative historical record of this achievement is an international cultural goal."

My impression is that there are not many people in cultural and educational politics, or even in historical museums, who are familiar with this object or prepared to invest effort in its preservation. Software is a more abstract entity than, say, an old mill that counts as "industrial heritage" for whose preservation people can be mobilised. Thus, the conference as a whole and David's paper in particular help put this problem in perspective. I regret that this is not taking place at the Deutsches Museum, but that is not such a problem: our collaboration is quite good.

In Germany, we need an initiative to preserve historical software as an important (characteristic) immaterial testimony of the history of German—and European—society in the twentieth century in terms of a physical object. This said, I am sure that software is still less a part of any national culture than, say, the first car or the first computer. Of course, Carl Benz's first automobile and Konrad Zuse's Z3 are an important part of the Germany's technological heritage and, of course, WINDOWS and FORTRAN are important parts of the USA's technological heritage. But the national importance of these products is due to the international significance of the automobile and the computer over the last century. I am sure that the international significance of many software objects is greater than their national importance.

David mentioned that museums intending to collect and present software must first decide in which physical form they wish to preserve it. He underlined the difference between the view of these museums and software historians who can dispense with this question. Could it be that this argument reflects his experience with fruitless discussions on the subject? David is completely right. The consequences of the decision for the museum are far-reaching and could become expensive if the decision proved to be wrong. Unfortunately, there is not much experience in this area.

I wish to mention one more aspect. The objects in software museums are always copies. There are not any originals. The importance of a software museum is not based on its "Mona Lisas." The competition between software museums will be competition between hardware platforms. Of course, *which* software will be presented is not unimportant. But every museum that so wishes can acquire the software—the decision depends only on the museum's concept. The important thing is *how* the software is presented, i.e., on which hardware platform.

David mentioned the difference between "history museums" which are "generally interested in collections and exhibitions that show change over time" and "science museums" which "usually focus on explaining scientific principles." The London Science Museum, the Smithsonian's Air and Space and the Deutsches Museum would, he claims, blend these two functions, which were "conceptually distinct." Here, I agree only on a very abstract level in a theoretical discussion. What is pure and what is a blend? Confronted with a historical technical artefact, most visitors at the Deutsches Museum will first ask: How does this work? Only then will they ask: Why did people use this function and not the one that is used today? The first question cannot be answered by a few sentences from an engineering textbook, and the second by a few lines from a history textbook. The museum situation allows and requires different answers. Here, the museum must be creative.

I agree completely with David's statement that history museums can play only a "limited role in preserving the intellectual history of software." But within these limits, there are many possibilities.

Epilogue

Probing the Elephant:
How Do the Parts Fit Together?

Michael S. Mahoney

Princeton University
303 Dickinson Hall
Princeton, NJ 08544
USA

E-mail: mike@princeton.edu

In keeping with the themes and objectives of the conference, the authors of the five main papers attempted to approach software as a whole, each viewing it from a different perspective. The result may seem at first a bit like the proverbial report of a team of blind persons on their tactile investigation of an elephant: depending on the part they touched, it resembled a tree, a snake, a rope, and so on. At least they had an elephant to touch. Here, the authors and their commentators are grappling with a seemingly amorphous object, appropriately called *soft*ware, which is invisible and intangible, yet produces visible and tangible effects in the world. To have those effects, it must run on hardware, and at a fundamental level it must fit that hardware so precisely as to become indistinguishable from it. Yet, at higher levels of abstraction software has an existence independent of hardware, which indeed has all but disappeared from the view of a large majority of people engaged in computing. Users and producers program virtual machines defined in terms of concepts rather than circuits and reflecting human purposes rather than computer architecture. Software encompasses both the product and the means of that process. That is, one may think in terms of virtual machines because software exists to translate the virtual into the real. Software is thus multilayered, and complexity makes it hard to see through the layers. Depending on where one stands and how one tries to grab hold of it, software assumes a variety of appearances.

A looming presence in today's world, software will increasingly shape tomorrow's. That alone lends it historical significance. What makes it even more significant is that software did not exist fifty years ago, either in name or in concept. It is new in the world, and its novelty poses its own historical problem. Viewing software from a variety of perspectives, the papers and commentaries each express a sense that there is something different about it. Its science is different from other sciences, its engineering differs from engineering in other technologies, its workers are different from workers in other industries, its economics calls for different models, it poses different challenges to those who want to assure themselves of its dependability, whether as producers or consumers. But to say that is in each case simply to pose questions. In what ways is it different, and to what extent can we understand it by contrast, if not by comparison, to what went before and to the context within which it currently operates? That is, how should historians talk about it? With what should they compare it? How should they fit it into the world in which it came to be and which it then gradually changed?

One may say that it is unprecedented, *sui generis*. But that begs the question. "New" is a relative term. It can only be defined with respect to the old, else we would not recognize it as new. Moreover, nothing in human experience is unprecedented, if only because humans create precedents for the sake of understanding. They can deal with the new only in terms of the old, the unfamiliar in terms of the familiar. Inventions may have unexpected consequences but they originate in a currently perceived need or possibility, and they build on what has gone before. Discoveries may open new worlds, but they originate from questions asked in the old world. What is interesting about inventions and discoveries is what people make of them, how they incorporate the new into the old, even as they reshape it.

Intersections

Science and Engineering

If the blind persons probed the elephant long enough, their hands might touch where the parts under investigation overlap, and the encounter might cause them to combine their initial impressions into a coherent whole. That is the case with the papers at hand. Their perspectives intersect at several points, and those intersections suggest some common themes. The intersection is most explicit in Mahoney's and Tomayko's papers, since the boundary between science and engineering, hazy in any area, is particularly so in computing. As commonly viewed by practitioners themselves, engineering is in part applied science. Hence, one may ask what science of software is being applied in software engineering and how far it applies. Agreeing on its mathematical foundations, Mahoney and Tomayko also see the limits of science in the design process by which a portion of the world is translated into a computational model and the model is implemented in a program, as depicted in the top half of Mahoney's diagram. From Mahoney's point of view, it is of interest that practitioners have tried to extend the methods of formal languages to that process, so far with limited success.[1] From Tomayko's point of view, the process invites comparison with approaches to design in other fields of engineering.

Science, Engineering, Dependability

Here Mahoney's and Tomayko's papers intersect with MacKenzie's and through his with Ensmenger's and Aspray's. Historically, the perspectives of engineering and dependability are intimately related. The very notion of software engineering arose in the late 1960s in large part out of concerns about the dependability of programs produced by what seemed an undisciplined craft process.[2] "We undoubt-

---

[1] See, for example, David Gries (ed.), *Programming Methodology: A Collection of Articles by Members of IFIP WG2.3* (New York/Heidelberg/Berlin, 1978).

[2] Note that, quite independently of one another, Tomayko, MacKenzie, and Aspray/Ensmenger chose to begin with reference to NATO Conference.

edly produce software by backward techniques," said Doug McIlroy at the NATO Conference:

> We undoubtedly get the short end of the stick in confrontations with hardware people because they are the industrialists and we are the crofters. Software production today appears in the scale of industrialization somewhere below the more backward construction industries.[3]

Within software engineering, proposals to remedy the problem have ranged from formal (and ultimately automated) methods to better management of programmers.

As a form of mechanical theorem-proving, formal verification of programs was part of the agenda of formal semantics in the 1960s. Structured programming emerged from the agendas of both formal semantics and formal languages. Here MacKenzie's paper provides one of the contexts for Mahoney's discussion of those agendas. Formal methods also link Tomayko's paper with MacKenzie's on another front. Both raise the issue of failure. For Tomayko, it is a matter of incorporating into software engineering the role of failure in advancing design in other fields of engineering. There engineers learn from their mistakes: the collapse of the Tacoma Narrows Bridge led to the stiffening of similarly designed bridges. Software engineers have so far had difficulty in drawing generic lessons from specific failures. For MacKenzie it is a question of how one anticipates failure in software systems and then accommodates it. It is an old issue, going back to J. Presper Eckert's design of ENIAC and to von Neumann's paper on constructing reliable mechanisms from unreliable parts.[4] However, whereas a collapsing bridge seems deviant by any standards, MacKenzie notes that "failure" is a relative concept, dependent on context. He thus shifts our attention to the users' role in determining the failure of software systems. "Undocumented features" aside, not all bugs' bites are fatal or even annoying. The point suggests an interesting link between MacKenzie and Campbell-Kelly, namely the role of beta releases and feedback from users in both the production and the marketing of software.

Engineering, Dependability, Management

Engineering involves more than applied science and design. From the beginning, engineers have been trained as managers of large projects. Project management forms the intersection between the papers on software as engineering and software as labor process. The Systems Development Corporation prided itself as much on its management of the SAGE project as on the final product, and the books of people like Ed Yourdon, Tom De Marco, and James Martin are addressed as much to management as they are to design. Indeed, the science, engineering, and man-

---

[3] M.D. McIlroy, "Mass Produced Software Components," in P.Naur and B. Randell (eds.), *Software Engineering. Report on a Conference sponsored by the NATO Science Committee* (Brussels, January 1969), 138-50; at 138-9.

[4] John von Neumann, "Probabilistic Logics and the Synthesis of Reliable Organisms from Unreliable Components" (1952), in *The Papers of John von Neumann on Computing and Computer Theory*, ed. William Aspray and Arthur Burks (Cambridge, MA/Los Angeles, 1987).

agement of software meet at what has been called the "software paradox:" programmers have automated every productive process except their own. It is not for lack of trying. The grail of "automatic programming" has attracted the efforts of researchers from the beginning, and Tomayko, MacKenzie, and Ensmenger and Aspray all allude to it in one form or another.

In doing so, they touch on an issue that arose during discussion of Mahoney's paper and loomed as an indefinite presence through all the subsequent sessions: just what do software developers know and how do they know it? Undocumented practices in variety of contexts, especially the commercial and industrial, where proprietary concerns encourage secrecy give the question an acute historiographical edge. As Endres warns historians in his comment on Tomayko's paper,

> New engineering knowledge is valuable, so don't look for it on the streets. Companies most often try to keep new engineering knowledge to themselves. Most engineering knowledge is anyhow either local or private. The knowledge of engineers (including that of software engineers) expresses itself more in products than in papers.

Even in the absence of proprietary concerns, the failure of programmers to document their thinking has been a continuing source of concern to managers. It appears that historians may now inherit the problem. In many cases, all one has is the code. In other areas of science and technology, historians have learned to elicit what people have known from analyzing what people have done and reconstructing the cognitive structures underlying practice.[5] But without access to practices, how are historians of software to know what programmers actually do?

The problem is related to an issue raised by MacKenzie's focus on quality control and Ensmenger's and Aspray's on productivity, which lead them in common to Philip Kraft's *Programmers and Managers* and to his thesis that techniques such as structured programming were aimed at gaining control over workers by "deskilling" the work. Kraft takes the notion of "deskilling" from labor historian Harry Braverman, who in turn derives it from Marx's analysis of the mechanization of labor in the Industrial Revolution.[6] In the textile industry, for example, the spinning frame and the power loom captured the skills of the spinner and the weaver in the machinery of production and thus negated the value of those skills to the worker in negotiating the conditions of his or her employment. Ford's assembly line may be seen as a defining moment in that process, setting the stage for automation through the computer.[7] It was on McIlroy's mind when he made the statement quoted above.

---

[5] See, for example, W. Bernard Carlson and Michael E. Gorman, "Understanding Invention as a Cognitive Process: The Case of Thomas Edison and Early Motion Pictures, 1888-91", *Social Studies of Science* 20,3 (1990): 387-440, and Michael S. Mahoney, "Issues in the History of Computing", in Thomas J. Bergin and Rick G. Gibson (eds.), *History of Programming Languages II* (New York, 1996), 772-81; esp. 773-5 ("Documenting Practice").

[6] Philip Kraft, *Programmers and Managers: The Routinization of Computer Programming in the United States* (New York/Heidelberg/Berlin, 1977); Harry Braverman, *Labor and Monopoly Capital: The Degradation of Work in the Twentieth Century* (New York/London, 1974); Karl Marx, *Capital*, Volume I, Part IV, esp. Chap. 15.

[7] Ford's workers were not entirely powerless in times of a labor shortage, since they could vote with their feet. An annual turnover rate of 300% in 1913 led Ford to introduce the $5, 8-hour day, and the sensitivity of his system to interruptions from injuries prompted intense concern

As Ensmenger and Aspray show, one does not have to look far to find evidence of efforts to achieve that sort of control over programming. The idea of the "software factory" goes back to the mid-1960s, and early versions of it reflect the continuing influence of Taylorism on American managerial thinking. Whether those efforts have succeeded depends on where one looks and what one means by "success," but in general it appears that, whatever the intentions of managers, programmers still maintain considerable control over their work.[8] Hence, there is some question whether Kraft's application of the model to programmers in the 1970s was an accurate description of what was actually happening, as opposed to what was intended.

Programmers may continue to control their work precisely because it is still not clear what skill the skilled programmer possesses. Ensmenger and Aspray recount the disappointing efforts in the 1960s and 1970s to measure aptitude for programming. Replacing "programmer" with "software developer" only deepens the problem, as MacKenzie's reference to "Hoare's Paradox" illustrates. Some systems do get built more or less on time and within budget, and they work as desired. The problem seems to be that we can't explain why, or rather that we cannot distinguish the way they were produced from the way that other, less satisfactory systems have been built. MacKenzie's suggestion that in matters of dependability we might more profitably focus on systems than on software challenges the paradox by blurring the line between the software and the area of application. Good solid engineering may well underlie the success of some systems. The question is what kind of engineering or, more pointedly, which engineers? Have software engineers brought their knowledge to bear on the system, or have engineers trained in the area of application brought their knowledge to bear on the software?

Boundary Work

The four papers under discussion thus intersect on the subject of disciplines and professions, for the most part in ways that illustrate David Edge's emphasis on setting boundaries. While Mahoney's computer scientists have succeeded in establishing an autonomous place for themselves in the academic world (even if they do not entirely agree on the grounds by which they have done so), neither software engineers nor working programmers have achieved the status of professionals. After thirty years, software engineering remains engineering by self-designation only, unrecognized by the other engineering societies and, more importantly, by the state.[9] Programmers have neither unionized nor professionalized their practice.

---

with worker safety. That turnover, by the way, considerably exceeds the rates of turnover among programmers reported by Ensmenger and Aspray.

[8] For a generally positive appraisal, see Michael Cusumano, *Japans' Software Factories: A Challenge to U.S. Management* (New York/Oxford, 1991).

[9] Where one state, Texas, is now moving toward licensing software engineers, it is encountering resistance from the software engineering community itself. Foremost among the arguments against the measure is that practitioners cannot agree on how competence should be measured. An effort several years ago by the New Jersey legislature to introduce licensing of programmers met with opposition from companies such as AT&T Bell Labs on the grounds that programming of some sort is part of most their employees' work.

It is open to all, as indeed is the software industry itself. Anyone can hang out a shingle. So far it is an open, unregulated market, and the buyer must beware.

The result is an amorphous complex of activities, putting all the papers at risk of over-generalization. In a comment on Tomayko's paper, Endres admonished historians "not [to] lump all software together into a single phenomenon. Software for a space flight, a text editor, or a student's first trials in Java are quite different things." The observation reflects the distinction that emerged in the 1970s between "programming-in-the small" and "programming-in-the-large" and the often cited difficulty of teaching software engineering by means of "toy problems".[10] Intuitively, one senses the difference, but it is hard to pin down and hence to trace historically. Software engineers have had difficulty drawing the line. Is it a matter of size, of complexity, of dependability, of system? Word processors do not have to be as reliable as guidance systems for lunar orbiters, but modern word processors, which began as text editors, are arguably more complex. Certainly, they contain more lines of code by orders of magnitude. Yet, one looks for engineers behind guidance systems, but not behind word processors. Microsoft is not TRW, but precisely how does one differentiate between them? At what point do Java applets make the transition from students' first efforts to constituents of e-commerce? Where would one place Tim Berners-Lee's "first trials" with hyper-linked documents?

These questions of "boundary work" (as David Edge put it) pervade Campbell-Kelly's paper, as he tries to map the nature and scope of the software as an economic activity, especially after 1975. For the most part, the issues raised in the four other papers date from the beginnings of the industry in 1950s and 1960s and transcend the generational changes in hardware. The science of computation remains the same for microprocessor as for mainframe. Software engineering sounds the same themes of disciplinary and professional uncertainty, perhaps because embedded software has provided an underlying continuity. How does one measure the costs of software when it is embedded in a product or is written and maintained by people not classified as programmers or software engineers? As programming becomes a common skill akin to writing or driving, and as the criteria for distinguishing amateur from professional remain vague, how does one count workers and their output? Who is the producer, who the user, who the consumer?

In the 1950s the move from the laboratory to the marketplace stimulated efforts both to make the computer easier to program and to maximize the time spent in productive computation. Both goals entailed removing the programmer from direct contact with the machine. Programming languages focused attention on the problem to be solved, leaving it to the compiler and system libraries to translate the solution into a working program for the target machine. By adding layers of hierarchy, operating systems increased the distance between the programmer and the computer, replacing the latter by a virtual machine. For a time in the late 1970s, the personal computer restored direct contact, but operating systems again progressively interposed layers of software between the user and the machine,

---

[10] It has also been a problem for empirical research on programming. See Ruven E. Brooks, "Studying Programmer Behavior Experimentally: The Problems of Proper Methodology", *Communications of the ACM* 23,4 (1980): 207-13; esp. 210.

which all but disappeared behind an increasingly standardized graphical user interface. The programmer works with a notional machine: in that sense, OS/360 and the Java Virtual Machine are conceptual cousins.

Application software for the personal computer similarly continued a trend dating back to the first report generators and extensible languages. Word processors, spreadsheets, and databases enable users to compose macros that configure the application to their own needs and wishes. That programs can do that derives from the nature of the computer as a universal Turing machine: it can be programmed to program itself. In explaining perhaps the difficulties of identification and disaggregation raised by Campbell-Kelly, that property also gives software its amorphous or, better, polymorphic-quality: what it looks like depends on how one approaches it. In approaching it from five different directions, the essays aspire to have elicited some of its invariant features.